New Theology No. 1

New Theology No. 1

Edited by
Martin E. Marty
and Dean G. Peerman

The Macmillan Company, New York
Collier-Macmillan Limited, London

First Printing

Printed in the United States of America

The Macmillan Company, New York
Collier-Macmillan Canada Ltd., Toronto, Ontario

DESIGN BY R. A. KASELER

Acknowledgments

THE SPIRIT of cooperation among editors of theological journals is an evidence of the fact that the theological community *is* a community. We received evidence of this spirit when the editors of fourteen journals promptly and graciously permitted us to reprint material from their pages. Several editors made special accommodations in their policy to help us face problems in our own. We are grateful to them, and commend their journals to readers of this book.

We thank Dr. Harold Fey and Dr. Kyle Haselden of The Christian Century Foundation who lent their encouragement and who made the secretarial services of Mrs. Joanne Younggren available to us. We thank her for going beyond the call of duty to help us prepare materials.

For fifty-five years *The Christian Century* has been involved in the weekly task of translating the "new theology" of the academies for a wider reading public. We have been united in our work under its auspices, stimulated by its example, encouraged by its staff. From them we learned the kind of modesty and restraint which kept us from incorporating material from its pages in *New Theology No. 1.*

M. E. M. and D. G. P.

Contents

III: THEOLOGY IN EXTENSION

IV: A DIRECTION FOR THE FUTURE

Introducing New Theology

WILLIAM GEORGE WARD was one of nineteenth century England's most colorful individuals. A convert from Anglicanism to Roman Catholicism, he cherished the latter communion's sense of authority, tradition, and constancy. To prove his point, he averred that he would like to read a papal bull with his *Times* at breakfast every day. Such a bull would be evidence that his church and its theology were not new, had not changed. His may have been an authoritarian personality, and he may have been making an escape from freedom. Still, he honestly represented an enduring strain in theology: the legitimate desire to hear an unchanging word in a changing world.

Ward would have company in this twentieth century, for the Christian church and its theology retain certain changeless characteristics. Thus they appeal to the conservative side of man's nature. But the twentieth century has also produced heirs to the ancient Athenians who daily sought some new thing under the sun. Christians know that they live in a revolutionary world, and many of them expect the forms of church life and thought to take on revolutionary elements of change. They are dissatisfied with the theological formulas come down from other ages. Instead of an escape from freedom, this generation seeks freedom to escape from the mold of the past. There are in it a creativity, a restlessness, an impatience that bewilder the conservative and cause uneasiness in the mind of anyone questing for an eternal word from God and in the church. Christians of this restless ilk would like to read a theological journal which cites change every day along with their *Times* at breakfast.

While both those who pursue continuity for its own sake and those who pursue change for its own sake may be well-guided and sincere, neither party interests the editors of *New Theology* for that party's own sake. We are concerned rather with careful reporting, careful selection of what is representative *now*, whether it represents a sense of Christian devotion to the past or a radical reach toward the future. This little book is the first of what may become a series of periodic attempts to assess the theological climate of today. But we hope we are free from nervous interest in "spotting every trend" or being blown with every wind of doctrine.

Our reasoning goes: If change characterizes the theologians' response to today's world, change should be chronicled. The word "new" when used to designate Christian theology cannot mean that that theology is a sheer invention of men, snatched out of a cloudland of abstractions. Christian theology is at least in part a reflection upon a history, upon an event or a series of events. However philosophically abstract theologizing becomes, if it carries the adjective "Christian" it automatically carries with it the memory of Christians who existed in history. More important, it bears the burden and shares the freedom of witness to one who was titled "Christ." Had early Christians not accorded this title to Jesus of Nazareth, it would not occur to moderns to name their witness and work after the "Christian" tradition. Theology does not "start from scratch," is not wholly new at any time.

If no Christians can escape their history, restless Christians can do so least of all. Perhaps only those fail to reflect upon Christian history whose mistrust of others prompts them to impose an absolutely formal canon of orthodoxy on their fellows. Whoever is curious, whoever inquires, whoever seeks what is new in each age will find himself relating positively or negatively to something that is given to him. For that reason the word "new" could be defended minimally as referring to the fact that what is here printed has appeared recently. Of course, more than that is meant. For the contexts of the life of the church change constantly. The world changes, and with it the basic styles of living and thinking change. The teachers and masters of the past—Augustine, Aquinas, Luther, Calvin, Schleiermacher and all the rest—may have been highly conscious of their rootage in a word of God given "once for all." Yet their theology is distinctly the product of their own time and of their own magnificent alertness to the needs of their own time. "Newness" belongs in a religious tradition that was born in the experience of a new age, a new situation of man before God.

So much for the adjective. What of the noun? By theology we mean the rich diversity of analytic and synthetic undertakings by which Word of God and world of men are understood and brought into confluence. An impossible task? The best theologians of every age would hurry to say yes—and then would go about attempting the impossible. That is, none of them by their words could make God plain to men. Nor by their words could they delude themselves into believing that they were dispelling evil—which *was* plain—from history. Some, among them Augustine, spoke with the consciousness that their assertions were inadequate but necessary as the only alternative to silence and nothingness. They themselves had seen and heard something; they were impelled to witness. As theologians they may have chosen forms which differed from those of the preachers. They tried to locate and relate and translate the Word of God or words of God or words about God to and in the world of men.

In this sense, everyone who speaks a word of witness is a theologian. He may be a "good" one or a "poor" one, may be well informed or ill informed, but he is a theologian nonetheless. Even the modern godless man, in systematizing his belief in history or power, in self or sex, is some kind of theologian. But Christian theology sorts out the data of experience and testifies that one strand of history is particularly meaningful to it.

Theology, then, seems impossible but is necessary. Just as the Christian is puzzled by contemporary secular man because the Christian does not know how to define man except as a creature who fears God ("But there the secular man is; that is the problem"), so the secular man is puzzled by the Christian. For the former, God is distant or silent or dead, and man cannot be defined except as a being alone in the universe. "But there is the theologian. He exists. That is the problem." Just as some Christians say that the godless man is a fool, so the secular man may say that the Christian who sooner or later must say something or other about God—and thus becomes a theologian—is a fool. It is questionable whether such name-calling is ever fruitful. At least it does not do justice to the intelligence quotients, the reasoning and testing power, the gravity and sincerity of people who have committed themselves either to nonfaith or to faith. A number of theologians have tried to stop being theologians; the vocation, while exhilarating to some, is burdensome to others. But many have found that their questions are less unsatisfactorily answered in theological terms than in other terms, and hence have taken up the impossible necessity again.

So much for the import of our title, for the "new" and the "theology" with their hidden shadow, the adjective "Christian." As we have said, this book attempts to suggest something of the multifariousness of recent theological endeavor. "Theology" is a word which covers a number of distinct though related disciplines. All of them are related to what we may call the "traditum"—God's revelation "handed over" to the prophets and apostles, who have handed it over to the church, which has transmitted it to successive generations of believers. Central to the traditum is God's mysterious, gracious act in Jesus Christ. The biblical scholar listens to the traditum's "original sources," as it were, while the historian reflects on the career of those sources through the centuries. The systematic theologian relates to one another ideas drawn from the continuous stream that is the traditum. The practical theologian preaches and celebrates the traditum, and ministers to people on its terms. The "correlative" theologian relates it to society, ethics, the human personality, philosophy, or other religions. And the modern world presents each of these theologians with new and devastating problems.

For one thing, the modern world more and more is coming to define itself as secular. To many theologians "secular" is a neutral word, suggesting that in the affairs of men it makes no real difference whether God is or acts. On the level of life as many live it, the question of God simply does not seem to enter significantly. The universe of men and of nature is "rounded off" in itself, is an entity not open to intrusion by a "word" from outside it. To other theologians "secular" is anything but neutral. To them the word suggests that in the minds of men who have thought about God it *does* make a difference whether he exists or acts, hence the logic of modern secularism—with its philosophy and its politics—is at its root atheistic.

To the extent that the secular spirit is pervasive, Christian theologians cannot easily "hook on" to other realms of culture in order to make their systematic points. In other ages of the church's life they could do so with some ease. Crowded out of their once respectable place as custodians of the "queen of sciences" into corners of universities or segregated in seminaries, they sometimes seem to make only occasional forays into the real world where decisions are made. There they announce their relevance, encounter amused or bemused cordiality, and retreat. *New Theology* includes work both by theologians who see positive values in the secular spirit and by theologians who address this spirit in Christian terms even though to them it chiefly represents a threat.

Second, the modern theological enterprise demands a sense of newness because Christian thought is surrounded by other ideologies and religions. The *oikoumene* or "inhabited world" of the past was regarded by earlier Christians as their domain. After Christianity became the official religion of the Roman world, men who shared that world considered Christian theology to be the only theology that mattered. Men later gained awareness of other religions, but generally only as something remote, as a symbol or a foil. One could make what he wished of the Turks or, at a later date, the Chinese. Such people were near only at sword point and never in dialectic, or were merely objects of explorers' curiosity. Little interchange took place. In the twentieth century, however, Christians have become aware of their surroundings. They know theirs to be a milieu in which sophisticated non-Western religions are renascent. What does witness to Christian truth do to the many and varied truths by which men live?

Third, Christian theologians are perhaps more aware than are laymen of the gravity of division within Christendom. Orthodox, Roman Catholic, and the many kinds of Protestant theologies have for long gone their separate ways. What does the competitiveness between communions and confessions do to theology? What does the conflict between various schools of theology do to the regard with which Christian truth is held by the generality of mankind?

We may also cite the problems of specialization in a technical world. Theology, once viewed as a unifying discipline, today is viewed as one among other disciplines. Frequently it seems to be off to the edge of the concerns of academies (where most professional theologians are working). There is a gulf between these theologians and their "secular" colleagues, between them and Christian laymen interested in practical church life. Some Christian thinkers spend a good deal of time commiserating with each other about this plight. Others, equally conscious of the problem but knowing that everyone must begin his work somewhere, set themselves to their tasks, however modest these may be.

In this setting the theologians represented on our pages make their entrance. All of them show that they are conscious of the problems of contemporary theology, though few of them would claim they are breaking wholly new ground. *New Theology No. 1* is not a gathering of obscure materials about "new finds" so much as a sharing of representative concerns. In some instances—as in the essay by Karl Barth—we encounter a thinker in an informal and "unbuttoned" mood. We are proceeding on the theory that our readers will prefer general theology by professionals to specialized theology by amateurs. People who reject theological claims can learn from these pages something of the diversity of what they are rejecting. Christian readers who are disinterested in theology may possibly find their interest awakened in regard to one or more of its branches. Theologians who are specialists may use the book to converse with exponents of fields outside their own. We would also like to think that many specialists will at least find their discipline represented in these pages. We have consistently bypassed articles which condescend or "talk down" to laymen; such a selection would hardly be indicative of what is going on in theology. While some of the essays are simply written, others demand the kind of attention (perhaps with dictionary at hand) which serious essays on science, politics, or literature demand.

Most of the writings assembled herein are taken from journals which are accessible to those who have time to browse in seminary libraries, and we hope that the experience of reading this sample will lead many to undertake such browsing. (Seminaries may appear to be self-enclosed monastic communities, but we will risk the promise that a reader will be welcomed at any of their libraries.) But not all of us have sufficient time or interest to seek out such centers of theological learning. The items we have chosen are all of quite recent vintage; with one or two exceptions all have appeared within the past fifteen months. Some of them may here and there manifest a bit of local color and denominational flavor, but we preferred to leave them intact rather than resort to arbitrary pruning.

The collection is a varied one. At least half a dozen Protestant communions are represented, and Roman Catholicism and Judaism by one essay each. A variety of theological schools and schools of thought have their spokesmen here, and the spokesmen are from a variety of countries—the United States, Canada, England, Scotland (by recent translation to America), Germany, Switzerland, Sweden, and Czechoslovakia.

We can best depict the plot of the book if we describe the current revival of theology in which its chapters participate. The Christian church has seen periods in which theology has been of primary concern and others in which it has been obscured. The creed-making era of the fourth and fifth centuries accented theology against the background of Greek philosophy; the recovery of Aristotle played a part in the development of Thomism in the twelfth and thirteenth centuries. In the sixteenth century Protestantism and the Catholic reaction produced a new high watermark in Christian thought. Nineteenth century theology focused notably on "man-centered" concerns. And the church for some years now has been engaged in a much-touted theological renewal.

Some would say that this renewal has been nurtured by the ecumenical movement. Christians, seeking unity, have had to think together—and so they have had to think more deeply. Others would turn the circle around and say that renewal nurtured ecumenism. Christians, as they thought about their past and their purpose, began to think and work together. The sources of this theological movement, like those of any significant movement, are multiple. The spiritual reaction, dating from World War I, to certain versions of the earlier doctrine of progress in its relation to the Kingdom of God was the impetus for much of the new theologizing.

If one year and one man were to be chosen to signalize the

turn, it would have to be 1917–1918 and Karl Barth, a Swiss pastor-professor who in that year produced a radical commentary on St. Paul's Letter to the Romans. For Barth, Christianity was not a man-centered religion but a God-centered faith. His name or his concerns are employed and implied on many pages of this book. Even more frequently the name of Rudolf Bultmann is cited; Bultmann remains the theologian by whom many others measure themselves. He even more than Barth has been concerned with the problem of religion in a secular age. According to Bultmann, men today do not live or think in ways that are compatible with the "mythic" framework of Biblical revelation. Still other attempts at "new theology" reflect concerns initiated by Paul Tillich, who, as a philosopher of religion, has consistently worked for positive relations between theology and other disciplines. While few names are seen on the horizon as replacements for Barth, Bultmann, Tillich, the brothers Niebuhr, we have taken pains to introduce several now coming into prominence. Still, "new theology" should not be taken to mean a pathetic quest for new names to cherish momentarily, to drop—and then really to drop.

If there has been one unifying theme to theology in the immediate past, it has been a growing concern for "the world." The first fifty years of the ecumenical period (after 1910) seemed to find theologians turning inward on ecclesiastical concerns in an effort to "let the church be the church." Today they are crowding each other at the boundaries where church meets world. There, where men experience a loss of a transcendent sense and know a new aloneness; there where the resources of the church give out and men turn their backs on churchly concerns; there where the power of God is needed but denied or neglected by men—*there* is where the alert theologians of today are busy.

The first section of the book finds systematic, Biblical, historical, and philosophical theologians at work. John Macquarrie sets the stage by defining the modest limits of the theological task in a time when men proclaim the death of God and the meaninglessness of religious propositions. His essay is followed by a profile of one of the best-regarded new theologians, Heinrich Ott. Student of both Karl Barth and

Rudolf Bultmann and heir to the former's chair at the University of Basel, he has aroused considerable curiosity in theological circles. Astute biblical scholar Eduard Schweizer provides an informal introduction to his field in its historical context with a discussion of Scripture and church tradition. James Barr, who regularly unsettles his colleagues, examines the cliché that revelation is mediated only through history.

Sidney E. Mead's genteel and gentle essay disguises the daring with which he makes his way between the historians who want history to do everything and those professional skeptics who "do" history but suggest that their discipline has nothing to say to us. Per Persson's essay looks at some past Roman Catholic propaganda pieces on the Reformation, and compares them with the more objective and irenic Catholic scholarship of recent times. Karl Barth, the "grandfather" of one form of our century's new theology, is present quietly to call for what amounts to a new Protestant reformation. This section ends with Thomas Gornall's brief note on "the imagination." Father Gornall is not to be placed on the radical end of the spectrum of Roman Catholic thought, but his efforts to relate Thomism to today's world are representative and worthy.

The three essays of the next section suggest some problems for theology. The editors quite frankly concur with none of them—nor would we know how to cope with their themes if given the assignment! The first is a strong indictment of "fideistic" theology from the viewpoint of a language analyst; the second wrestles with Christian expression in a time when "God is dead" and borrows from another religion as a way into Christian concerns; the third constitutes a Christian comment from behind the Iron Curtain, a comment interesting because it carries covert criticism of integral Marxism.

After the problematic section we have chosen to wander a bit into some theological bypaths. E. S. Brown, Jr., seeks to relate the church's liturgy to at least some of secularized man's interests. The article on Franz Kafka is representative of the relation between theology (in this case Jewish) and literature; it concerns itself with the question of personal identity and guilt, familiar themes in this genre. No ethical issue has so preoccupied the American churches in the recent past as has the civil rights issue. James Sellers calls for an extended theological justification of the issue; his piece is not so much theology as an evocation of a new theological enterprise.

Is the whole story to be wrapped up in the problem of theology for a worldly era? What about transcendence, spirituality, theological witness to a living God? Eugene R. Fairweather's study on "the supernatural" is illustrative of recent attempts by Christian scholars to move beyond false alternatives which they believe are part of the legacy of the Protestant Reformation. We are hesitant to suggest, as Fairweather does, that theology's next move will be toward restoration of a "theonomous" outlook, but it is plain that his sense of direction is shared by many theologians.

New Theology No. 1: the numeral is also part of the title. Time will tell whether there will be succeeding installments. This volume is designed as a unit in itself. We intend to continue reading, not for novelty's sake, but in quest of writing which helps men speak the things of God in a time when he seems remote and silent. Theologians cannot dangle gods as puppets or manipulate them to make them speak. They can, however, equip men to hear. Today they come with no boast that theology is the queen of sciences. But it is at least a servant and perhaps a sister. In the bewildering variety that is represented in the modern academy and the modern church, theologians go about their task. And we, for two, are curious about what is new in their achievements.

M. E. M. and D. G. P.

I

The Theologian at Work

How Is Theology Possible?

John Macquarrie

What shall be the apologetic approach of a theologian who takes seriously the fact that he lives in a world marked by a pervasive secularism, a world in which many people take for granted that "God is dead"? One thing is sure: he's not very likely to win over the "unbeliever"—or even the predisposed inquirer—with finely spun metaphysical speculations intended to "prove" the existence of God. Much more likely to "speak to the condition" of such persons is some such approach as that suggested by John Macquarrie—an approach that starts not with God but with man and his predicament, his precariousness. The despair-inducing fact that there is no human solution to the human problem points to the question: Is there a possibility of grace, of a power from beyond man which can heal his estrangement? And where do we look for grace in a world such as ours? Paradoxically, the very diffidence-before-the-facts which Dr. Macquarrie displays in grappling with fundamental questions makes his argument all the more persuasive. His article, taken from the March 1963 *Union Seminary Quarterly Review*,* originally was an inaugural address he gave in October 1962 at Union Theological Seminary, New York, where he is Professor of Systematic Theology; previously he taught the same subject at Glasgow University. Co-translator of Martin Heidegger's *Being and Time*, Dr. Macquarrie has himself written *An Existential Theology, The Scope of Demythologizing* and, more recently, the widely acclaimed survey *Twentieth-Century Religious Thought*.

SOON AFTER I first became a teacher of theology, I was invited to take part in an interesting university staff conference. Its aim was to do something toward combatting the unfortunate results of the increasing specialization of studies, whereby a theologian, let us say, is in the dark about science, while an engineer finds philosophy unintelli-

* 3041 Broadway, New York 27, New York.

gible. The plan was to get a representative from each faculty to explain as clearly as possible to members of other faculties just what was the nature of his own studies. Knowing that I would have scientists, classicists, lawyers, medical men, and indeed all sorts and conditions of scholars in my audience, I took great care to prepare a paper which, I fondly hoped, might transmit the theological theme on a wavelength that could be picked up by all present. The hope was speedily shattered in the discussion that followed the paper. A physicist said something like this: "The speaker was quite intelligible until he introduced the word 'God' into his talk. This word does not stand for anything within my range of concepts or experience, and so every sentence in which it was used was to me meaningless, and the whole paper became unintelligible. Will the speaker kindly tell us what the word 'God' signifies?"

These remarks were, of course, somewhat disconcerting to me at the time. But it soon became clear to me that my scientific colleague had rendered me a valuable service. He had taught me a first principle of hermeneutics, namely, that there must be at least some basis of common ground between an interpreter and his audience if the interpretation is to get under way. He had shown me further that in a secular age one may not assume that language about God affords a universally intelligible starting point for an interpretation of the Christian faith. And he had raised for me very acutely the question: "How is theology possible?" For if theology is the interpretation of our Christian faith in God, and if this interpretation is not merely an academic exercise within an esoteric Christian community, but has become, in the words of the founders of this Seminary, "impressed with the claims of the world" so that it must address the world, then where is a beginning to be made?

Whether we are Christians or secularists, we share our humanity. Is this then the common ground from which a theological interpretation can begin today? Christianity is a doctrine of man as well as of God. Calvin, as is well-known, having remarked that true and solid wisdom consists almost entirely of two parts, the knowledge of God and the knowledge of ourselves, went on to say that "as these are connected together by many ties, it is not easy to determine which of the two precedes and gives birth to the other."[1] Calvin began with the doctrine of God, and this is probably the logical place to begin, and was also an intelligible beginning in an age when most people took religion very seriously and could discourse in a theological idiom. But in a secular age, we have to consider the alternative.

Someone, of course, may object that Calvin began with the doctrine of God for quite another reason—namely, that man can be properly understood only in the light of God. Every Christian would agree that this is true, but it is a truth which by no means rules out the possibility of taking man as the starting point for an interpretation of the Christian faith. If man is, as Christianity asserts, a creature of God and dependent on Him, then this should show itself in a study of man. It should be possible to see man as fragmentary and incomplete in himself, so that we are pointed to God; and if we can see man in this way, then we can go on to a fuller understanding of him in his relation to God. The advantage of such a procedure is that it would help us to answer the question put by people like my scientific colleague. If we can begin from the humanity which we all share, and if we find that this humanity points beyond itself for its completion, then we have, so to speak, indicated the place of the word "God" on the map of meaningful discourse. President Van Dusen has recently written: "It is an accepted premise of Christian thought that all the major beliefs of its faith are mutually involved and interdependent. It should be possible and legitimate to make one's start from any one of them, and approach all the others through it."[2] Let us then accept his statement, and see how far it is possible to travel along the road that begins from man himself.

What Is Man?

Our question is, "What is man?" or, to put it more concretely, "Who are you?" Obviously this question admits of many answers, according to the context in which it is asked. It could be answered, "I am a British subject," or "I am a Presbyterian," or "I am a graduate," and each of these answers might be quite adequate and appropriate within a particular context. To elicit the Christian answer and to see how it makes sense, we must first understand the kind of question to which it claims to give the appropriate response. A German writer, Hans Zehrer, tells us about "the man from the hut." This man was a refugee from the east, now living in an overcrowded hut in what once had been a military camp. Once he had had a wife and two children as well as numerous friends, once he had had a home and a well-stocked farm, once he had had what we call the comforts of life and a secure place in society. Now all these have been stripped from him and he is thrown back on himself. For the first time the question "Who are you?" has thrust itself on this man in a radical way. As Zehrer formulates it: "Well, tell me, who am I, then, and what am I living for, and what is the sense of it all?"[3] We rarely ask the question about ourselves in this radical way. It may even be the case, as some philosophers tell us, that we shrink from the question and screen ourselves from it. Yet perhaps everyone faces it at least once in his life. To this question "Who are you *at bottom*?" the partial and superficial answers that normally suffice for the question "Who are you?" are no longer adequate.

Perhaps our secularist friend will cut in at this point with the brusque observation that this radical question just is *unanswerable*. In a sense, he would undoubtedly be correct. For if we are to answer so radical a question about ourselves, would it not be necessary for us, so to speak, to detach ourselves from ourselves and to stand back so as to view all time and all existence and thus learn where we fit into the scheme of things? Manifestly it is impossible to do this. If the question "Who are you?" has disturbed us, would we not do well to put it out of our minds as an insoluble enigma? We might gladly do this, and perhaps for a large part of our time we might succeed in doing it. But we are deceiving ourselves if we believe that we can get rid of the question altogether. If it is true in one sense that *we cannot answer the question*, it is paradoxically true in another sense that *we cannot help answering it*. For this is no speculative question such that we could take it up or lay it aside at pleasure. It is the question of ourselves, and because we have to live and make ourselves, it is demanding an answer all the time. In every policy that we adopt and in every unrepeatable action that we perform, we are giving an answer. Always and already, we have decided to understand ourselves in one way or another, though such self-understanding may not be explicit.

These reflections introduce us to the basic polarity of our human existence. We are on the one hand *limited*. We find ourselves thrown into an existence, and we cannot by any means step out of this existence in order to get a detached objective view of it. We can never know with certitude its why and wherefore. On the other hand, we are *responsible* for this existence. Every day we have to take the risk of deciding to understand our existence in one way or another. It is little wonder if to some this polarity seems an insoluble contradiction, so that human existence is essentially an absurdity and foredoomed to failure. "Man," Sartre tells us, "is a useless passion. To get drunk by yourself in a bar or to be a leader of the nations is equally pointless."[4] But before yielding to such pessimistic conclusions, let us ask if it is possible to understand our existence in a more hopeful way. With this question, we are ready to consider what Christianity tells us concerning ourselves.

The Christian answer to the question "Who are you?" frankly acknowledges that polarity or tension that lies at the core of all human existence. The finitude and precariousness of man's life is a familiar theme in the Bible—his origin from the dust, the limitation of his power and knowledge, the brevity of his life and the inevitability of his death. At the same time, there is the theme of man's freedom and distinctive place in the world—he has dominion, he aspires after ideals and realizes values, he is accountable for what he makes of his life and his world. There is here no flight from the human condition, no comforting concealment of its dilemma. Man has to walk the razor-edge between his finitude and his responsibility.

Sin and the Need for Grace

A further element in the Christian understanding of man seems to heighten the difficulty of making sense of human existence, and to carry us just as far as Sartre in the direction of hopelessness. This further element is the doctrine of sin. There is a pathological disorder in human life, a radical alienation deep within our existence, whereby we fall down on one side or the other from that razor-edge along which we have to walk. Sometimes, perhaps, in protest against an optimistic humanism, theologians have exaggerated the doctrine of sin, especially in some of their formulations of the ideas of "original sin" and "total depravity," but all would follow the New Testament in maintaining the universality of sin, and its gravity.

Some theologians, such as Reinhold Niebuhr, have seen the essence of sin in pride, so that sin is interpreted as man's attempt to be rid of the finite pole of his existence and to exercise an unlimited freedom. Niebuhr, however, has been criticized for his alleged neglect of the sins of indulgence, which would seem to arise rather from an attempt to be rid of freedom and responsibility in seeking to descend to the level of a merely animal existence. But in either case, man becomes untrue to the being that is his. He refuses to accept himself as *at once* free and finite. Of course, although he may not accept his destiny, he cannot escape it either, and hence comes the language of "alienation" in regard to sin. Sinful man is estranged from himself by his refusal to take upon himself *both* his finitude *and* his freedom.

This Christian understanding of man, as so far expounded, is just as desperate and radical as Sartre's. But of course Christian theology does not remain at the point of despair. It must bring us to that point, to make clear its conviction that *there is no human solution to the human problem*. If man is abandoned to his own resources in the world, then Sartre seems to be right; our life is a useless passion for which failure is ineluctable. But must we halt here? Already the analysis of the situation suggests another possibility, though only as a possibility. This is the possibility of *grace*—a power from beyond man which can heal his estrangement and enable him to live as the being which he is, the being in whom are conjoined the polarities of finitude and responsibility. This possibility of grace seems to be the only alternative to despair if we are to take as honest a view of the human condition as Sartre does, and not conceal from ourselves how insoluble is the enigma of man in human terms.

But where are we to look for grace? Clearly we cannot look to the world of things. That world knows nothing of our predicament. Sartre indeed feels nausea for its senseless plenitude of being, which throws into relief the isolated lot of man as the fragile existence that is "condemned to be free."[5] We may not share Sartre's disgust, but clearly a lower order of being cannot *of itself* provide grace, even though it might be a vehicle of grace. Are we then to look to other persons? Sartre is inclined to see other persons chiefly as obstacles to one's own existence. We would hope that we did not share such an egocentric understanding of life, and would acknowledge that a man can be helped and strengthened by his fellows. But is this the kind of grace we are looking for? Clearly it is not, for without depreciating the help that one may receive from another, we must not lose sight of the fact that all men are in the human situation together and that sin and its divisiveness are universal.

If grace is to be found anywhere, it must come from beyond the world of things and the society of human beings, though it may indeed come through these. We are directed toward a transcendent source of grace. This is neither a senseless nor a speculative idea, but rather a question of life and death that arises directly out of the structure of our own existence. It is the question of God, for "God" is the word which the religious man uses for the transcendent source of grace. When people like my sophisticated colleague ask what the word "God" signifies, we can only invite them to ask themselves in a radical way, "Who are you?" for this question of man already implies the question of God, or is even, as Bultmann says, identical with it.[6] The word "God" finds its place on the map of meaningful discourse, and so do other theological words—"finitude" may be equivalent to "creatureliness" and "sin" may acquire its full signification as "separation from God."

So far this is a meager result. We have raised only the *question* of God. Nothing has been said about His reality, and the word "God" remains as a formal expression with a bare minimum of content. It is, of course, important that we have found the question to be one that is raised by the very structure of our existence, for this provides the orientation that enables us to see the possibility of theology as a meaningful area of discourse. But can we now go further?

The Question of God

In asking the question of God, man must already have some idea of God, for every question has its direction, and it is impossible to seek anything without having some understanding of what is sought, however vague and minimal that understanding may be. The next step toward grappling with our problem is simply a phenomenological exploration of the question of God itself. What is the structure of this question? How should it properly be formulated? What is already implicit in the question? What conditions would have to be fulfilled for it to receive an affirmative answer?

We must remember that our question is the *religious* question of God, and that it has an *existential* structure. That is to say, it is not a theoretical or speculative question, raised by the intellect alone, but a practical question posed by the whole being of man who has to exist in the world and decide about his existence. Perhaps the question of God can be raised in a purely theoretical way, but this would not be a question of any interest to theology, and perhaps it would not even be a meaningful question. We could think, for instance, of the question of God as a *cosmological* question, in which "God" would stand for an explanatory hypothesis, put forward to account either for the world as a whole or for certain events in the world. For a long time men did try to account for many happenings in terms of supernatural agencies. With the rise of science, however, we have learned to look for our explanations in terms of factors immanent in the natural process itself. The famous remark of Laplace to Napoleon, "I have no need of that hypothesis," simply expresses our modern attitude to the world as a self-regulating entity. Science, of course, stops short of the ultimate question of why there is a world at all, but this is simply an acknowledgement that for the finite human intellect which is within the world, such a question is unanswerable. The religious question of God, as existentially structured, is different from any theoretical question about an explanatory hypothesis. We are not looking for some invisible intangible entity the existence of which we might infer. Perhaps we are not looking for an entity at all, or for anything that could be conceived as a possible object among others.

These remarks at once suggest that we must be highly suspicious of the traditional formulation of the question of God —a formulation which runs, "Does God exist?" For this question already contains implicitly the idea of God as a possible existent entity. The question is parallel to such a question as, "Does there exist another planet beyond Pluto?" This is not at all like the religious, existentially structured question of God. This latter question would need to be formulated in some such way as: "Can we regard Being as gracious?" It is a question about the character of Being. Either Being may have the character of indifference toward man, in which case he is thrown back on himself and must understand himself in a secular way; or else Being has the character of grace, so that human life can be lived in the strength of a power from beyond man himself, and ceases to be the tragic contradiction which it would be in the absence of grace.

"God" is the religious word for Being, understood as gracious. The words "God" and "Being" are not synonyms, for Being may have the character of indifference, and in that case it could not be called "God." "Being" can be equated with "God" only if Being has the character of grace and is responsive to man's existential predicament. Now Being itself cannot be regarded as an entity, for it is manifestly absurd to say "Being exists." Being does not itself belong to the class of particular beings—or "entities," as they may be called to avoid confusion—of which one can say that they either exist or do not exist. In Heidegger's language,[7] Being stands to entities as the wholly other, the *transcendens*, the non-entity which is nevertheless "more beingful" (*"seiender"*) than any possible entity. But if God is equated with Being as gracious, then the question "Does God exist?" involves what British analytical philosophers have taught us to call a "category mistake." The question is not whether some entity or other exists, but whether Being has such a character as would fulfill man's quest for grace.

Can we see more clearly what conditions must be fulfilled if Being can be recognized as God? The question of God arises from man's estrangement from himself, and his inability to bring into unity the polarities of finitude and freedom which constitute his being. These two poles must remain in perpetual and frustrating conflict if there is no relation between the Being out of which man has emerged as a finite center of existence, and the values and ideals toward which in his freedom he aspires as the end of his being. If Being has the character of grace and can be identified with God, the condition to be satisfied is that the Being out of which man arises coincides with the end of his freedom, thus bringing into unity the polarities of his existence and healing his estrangement. Among modern theologians, this idea comes out most clearly in Tillich, who has two typical ways of talking about God, as "ground of being" and as "ultimate concern." But precisely the same structure is discernible in the more traditional ideas of God. For instance, Oliver Quick writes: "God is the alpha and omega of all things, the source from which they proceed, the end towards which they move, the unity in which they cohere."[8] The language here is cosmological rather than existential, but this description of God has precisely the same structure as the one at which we arrived by an existential and ontological route.

This must suffice for the phenomenological description of the question of God. The question has been clarified and we see its meaning and its requirements. But the matter cannot be left here—otherwise I might be accused of showing that theology is a possible study of the possible, rather than that it is possible as a study of the most concrete reality. But what kind of evidence can we now seek, to bring content into the formal structures of the analysis?

The Possibility of Theology

It is clear that I have already cut myself off from the rationalistic natural theology by which so many theologians of the past sought to ground their subject and establish the reality of its matter. Apart from the fact that their arguments have been largely discredited by modern criticism, I have tried to show that their speculative approach was a mistaken one and that their leading question about the existence of God involved a logical defect in its formulation. In any case, all those who tried to prove the existence of God already believed in Him, and must have had a more primordial source for their conviction than their own arguments. Where then are we to look?

At the risk of lapsing into theological incomprehensibility, I must now boldly introduce the word "revelation." Yet this is not a word that need frighten us. Clearly, nothing whatever can be known unless in some way it reveals or manifests itself. The character of Being can be known only if Being reveals itself. Of course, something more than this obvious commonplace is implied in the theological idea of revelation. When it is said that the knowledge of God is revealed, the word points to a kind of knowledge distinct from that which we attain through our own effort of thought. The knowledge of God comes to us as a gift, and to indicate its distinctiveness by the word "revelation" is simply to remain true to the phenomenological analysis of belief in God, for such belief testifies that God makes Himself known to us rather than that we attain to the knowledge of Him. The Bible never suggests that man has to strain his mind to figure out a shadowy Something behind the phenomena. There is indeed recognition of man's innate quest for God, but God Himself meets and satisfies the quest. Man does not search out God, but rather the reverse is true. One of the greatest of the Psalms begins: "O Lord, thou hast searched me and known me!"[9] and goes on to describe the ubiquity and inevitability of the encounter with God.

What kind of language is this? Of what kind is this knowledge of God where that which is known towers above us, as it were, and it is as if we ourselves were known and brought into subjection? Perhaps we glimpse an answer to these questions if we consider three possible ways in which we may be related to that which stands over against us. The first case is our everyday relation to things, as objects of which we make use or have knowledge. They are at our disposal, and even by knowing them we acquire a certain mastery over them. The second case is our relation to other persons. This "I-thou" relation, as Buber has taught us to call it, is of a different order, for the other person is not my object and is not at my disposal. The relation is one between subjects. It is a mutual relation, founded on the same kind of being—personality—on both sides. Now it is also possible to envisage a third kind of relation in which we stand over against Being itself. In this kind of relation, we do not have the other term of the relation at our disposal, nor do we stand to it in a relation of equality, but rather we are grasped by it and brought into subjection to it, but in such a way that something of its character is disclosed to us.

Correspondingly there are three modes of thinking. We think of things in objective terms, the commonest type of thinking. We think of our friends differently, as those with whom all kinds of relations are possible that are impossible with things. And it is possible to think too of Being which, though it towers above us and subjects us, does not annihilate us but rather communicates itself and gives itself in the experience of grace. To talk of revelation means not an abrogation of thinking, but only that not all our thinking is of the same pattern. Tillich talks of the ecstatic reason which still does not cease to be reason.[10] Heidegger speaks more soberly of the thinking that is submissive (*hörig*) to Being.[11] Whatever expression we may prefer, it is this kind of thinking that makes theology possible, as the task of sifting and explicating and interpreting God's encounter with man, as it is recollected in tranquillity.

If someone is still asking, "What does all this prove?" then the answer must be in line with what has already been said—it *proves* precisely nothing. Perhaps what we take to be the encounter with God is an illusion; perhaps it is all explicable in terms of a naturalistic psychology; perhaps all our talk of sin and grace and existence and Being is only mystification. These are possibilities that cannot be entirely excluded even when the experience of grace has begun to produce its fruits of wholeness and serenity in place of estrangement and anxiety. The impossibility of demonstration in these matters is simply a consequence of what we have learned from the analysis of man himself—that he is finite, that his is not the godlike but rather the worm's-eye view, that so long as he is *homo viator* he lacks the unclouded clarity of vision, and must go forward in the attitude of faith and in the risk of faith. But on the other hand, if nothing has been proved, at least something has been described. The way has been described that leads from man's confrontation with himself to his confrontation with God, and, with the aid of the concepts of contemporary philosophy and theology, that way has been shown to possess a coherent pattern, an intelligible structure, and an inner logic. When challenged to produce the credentials of his subject, the theologian cannot in the nature of the case offer a proof, but he can describe this area of experience in which his discourse about God is meaningful, he can ask his questioner whether he recognizes his own existence in the Christian doctrine of man as finite, responsible and sinful; whether he finds hidden in himself the question of God. He can show that faith is not just an arbitrary matter, and he can make clear what is the alternative to faith. Beyond this, perhaps, he cannot go, but is not this sufficient? For it brings us to the point where we see that this discourse about God has to do with the most radical matter in life, the point where, exercising our freedom in finitude, we decide to take either the risk of faith or the risk of unfaith.

NOTES

1. *Institutes of the Christian Religion*, Vol. I, p. 37.
2. *Spirit, Son and Father*, p. 3.
3. *Man in This World*, p. 13.
4. *L'Être et le Néant*, pp. 708, 721.
5. *Op. cit.*, p. 515.
6. *Jesus Christ and Mythology*, p. 63.
7. *Was ist Metaphysik?*, Nachwort.
8. *Doctrines of the Creed*, p. 18.
9. Psalm 139, 1.
10. *Systematic Theology*, Vol. I, p. 124.
11. *Was ist Metaphysik?*, Einleitung.

Who Is Heinrich Ott?

A LETTER FROM BASEL

Robert C. Johnston

But first, who is Robert C. Johnston? As the newly elected
Dean of Yale University Divinity School, he is sure to become
better known fast. Said the faculty advisory committee responsible for selecting him as dean of the Yale seminary: "He has
displayed balance between critical reflection on the Church
and its ministry and sustained scholarly theological inquiry."
Dr. Johnston comes to the Yale faculty from Pittsburgh Theological Seminary (Presbyterian), where he was a professor of
systematic theology. His writings include *Authority in Protestant Theology* (based on his Vanderbilt Ph.D. thesis), *The
Meaning of Christ* (in the "Layman's Theological Library"
series) and a study document for his denomination, *The
Church and Its Changing Ministry*. Dr. Johnston spent the
1961–1962 academic year in Basel, Switzerland; while there
he got to know Heinrich Ott, who in that same year succeeded the renowned Karl Barth as Professor of Systematic
Theology at the University of Basel. Johnston also became
familiar with Professor Ott's mediating position in the Barth-
Bultmann battle; thus he is well suited to introduce this
"young Turk" to American and British audiences. Johnston's
"letter from Basel" is taken from the June 1963 issue of the
Scottish periodical *The Expository Times*.* Those who desire
firsthand acquaintance with Ott's thought are encouraged to
read his contribution to the symposium *The Later Heidegger
and Theology*, edited by James M. Robinson and John B.
Cobb, Jr.

THE MORNING mail brought the fifth letter this
month in which the correspondent asks—not facetiously, but
quite seriously: "Who is Heinrich Ott?" It obviously would

* Published by T. & T. Clark, 38 George Street, Edinburgh 2,
Scotland.

34

be poor stewardship of time to ignore an opportunity to reply to five letters with one. Therefore, Who *is* Heinrich Ott?

1. The one bit of common knowledge is that he is the just-elected successor to Professor Karl Barth in the renowned University of Basel Chair of Dogmatics. The wave of shock which followed the announcement of his appointment traces almost entirely to his age, thirty-three. Apparently it has been forgotten, even in Basel, that Calvin wrote the *Institutes* at the age of twenty-seven and Barth his *Römerbrief* at the age of thirty-two. Ott's appearance may also have contributed. From the shoulders down, he is natty, almost ivy-leaguish. From the shoulders up, he rather resembles a playful, lovable teddy bear in need of a haircut—with a distinct twinkle in his eye, which will preserve a cherished tradition! Long accustomed to the shuffling, august, authoritative figure of his predecessor, it is perhaps understandable that Baslers are finding it difficult to visualize the boyish Ott filling the enormous vacancy created by Barth's retirement.

Even so, the shock has been somewhat milder in Basel than north of the border. This is in large part because the appointment was much less unexpected than has been supposed in Germany and elsewhere. Ott is a Swiss, recently a Basler, who has served the University of Basel for several years as a *Privatdozent*, lecturing without salary in addition to his duties as one of the pastors of a large local congregation. He has many friends of long standing in Basel. Those familiar from within with the Canton-centered pride of the Swiss were much less surprised when he, one of their own, was chosen.

What may we anticipate of Ott, theologically speaking? Only the future can say, of course. But there are a few clues that tempt one to conjecture. These clues are much more formal than material, or they primarily suggest a line of development, what Ott calls "a programme of theological work," with the promise that the basic orientation and theological substance will emerge in the course of the development. This is the express theme, and the subtitle, of two of his four major writings to the moment. The others, although excellent, are of little help in answering this question. They are almost purely interpretative discussions of contemporary thought. This is because the European Professor writes as he teaches, teaching (reading) what he writes, and until now it has been Barth's assignment, not Ott's, to develop a dogmatic.

The pieces of the puzzle that must fit together, if we are to venture a guess, are curious at first glance. In fact, they become even more curious at second glance. But they are curiously fascinating.

Ott has declared flatly in print that he wishes and intends to stand in the succession of Barth. And there appears to be nothing in his published works to create serious doubt about the firmness of this intention. But it is not unimportant that he both studied with, and acknowledges a deep indebtedness to, Rudolf Bultmann. Nor is it without significance that the bulk of his writing to the present, the two interpretative works, are studies of Bultmann and Martin Heidegger. If for no other reason, his dissertation would snap one to attention because it seems to be the only book in existence, and it is very likely the only one that will exist, with a dedication that reads: "To my revered teachers, Karl Barth and Rudolf Bultmann, with gratitude and respect."

The curiosity that this arouses, needless to say, traces to the relationship between Barth and Bultmann (or Bultmann and Barth, if one happens to be in Germany), which even in retirement is approximately as cordial as that between former Presidents Truman and Eisenhower. To now it has been assumed, not without substantial grounds, that ne'er the twain can meet, that one simply must make a choice. Bultmann's name invariably creeps into the discussion of Barth's seminars, and in this hearer's presence a kind word has yet to be spoken —by either Barth or his students. It is inevitable that we should wonder at first glance if Ott has braced himself to defy this prevalent custom, if he seriously believes that he can avoid the decision which all young theologians in central Europe today face, the partisan decision between Bultmann and Barth.

2. There is sufficient evidence to suggest that this would be, at best, only a partially accurate reading of the matter. With regard to Ott's future theological relationship to Barth, two clues may be mentioned. Ott recalls with some glee the spontaneous but apparently deeply felt remarks that Barth made to his students at a demonstration in honor of his seventieth

birthday. Barth seized this occasion as an opportunity to shudder publicly at the threatening prospects of the development of a "Barthian scholasticism," a school that would enlist "followers" who would stand within his system for a generation or two and devote their lives to discussing and disputing the questions and problems that it provokes. He asked his students to understand clearly that one can "follow" him in one way only, by beginning at the beginning (as he did) and reworking the whole of theology. Ott assumes that Barth was wholly serious in these remarks. And he has stated for publication his intention to take them seriously.

The other clue is a pointed citation from Barth's so-called "retraction," *The Humanity of God.* Ott regards this little work as the *locus classicus* where Barth himself has indicated the direction for the future development of theological thought. The decisive phrase which Ott seizes upon, and proceeds to employ as a thesis, is *eine Wendung zum Menschen.* "Theology must move on," he says flatly, and then remarks that Barth himself has seen and pointed in the direction which this movement should take: "a turning to man."

Whatever Barth may have intended, Ott's understanding of this phrase will undoubtedly evoke a response. Before the applause breaks out, however, it should be clearly understood that Ott has no intention whatever of forsaking the plot of ground which Barth labored for years to clear, and upon which he built his system. He is as convinced as was Barth of the necessity for an open break with the anthropocentrism of nineteenth century theology; this we shall have occasion to note again when we glance at his relationship to Bultmann. He is likewise committed to the correlate of this break, the need for a consistent theocentrism. Even more, to all appearances to the moment he is thoroughly convinced of the necessity of Barth's kind of theocentrism—or of the necessity for a Christocentric theocentrism. Whoever views Ott's projected "programme" as a return to the man-centered orientation of the dominant nineteenth century theology will at the least misread his intention altogether.

No, when Ott insists that "a turning to man" is the theological need of the hour, he means to imply something quite different. The implication is formal and programmatic. What he intends is an abrupt reorientation of theological labor that will focus attention on the foundations of *practical theology*, and particularly *homiletics*—in the original and best sense of these terms. But he should be permitted to speak for himself.

"If I attempt to develop a programme of dogmatic work through a real coordination with the proclamation of the church," he says, "in doing so I mean to remain in the line of the work of Barth—for Barth's "dialectical theology," according to its own earlier self-understanding, a self-understanding still valid today, took its rise from the situation of the preacher. And I believe that at the same time I am taking a short step in the direction of reworking dogmatics, the direction which Barth himself has indicated, in making the focal point in an eminent sense the event of *human understanding*, by which is meant the human understanding of *God's* Word.

"Thus the 'turning to man' could be accomplished from the viewpoint of proclamation, in a way that would validly exemplify and unfold the 'humanity of God.' And this could be done without the slightest 'retreat'! For it is precisely the *verbum alienum* of the living God that is proclaimed. God speaks. But after this "first Word" has been grasped, is there not a need today to reflect on the event of the divine speaking in the *human* sphere—and where else would we find God's Word? To employ an occasional expression of Barth, there is a need to labour on a "theology of the Holy Spirit," which attempts to say once more the same thing (not something else!), but now to say it of the sphere of the human."

This is an unequivocal intention unambiguously stated. It remains to be seen if it is an ambition that can be realized standing on Barth's ground, *really* standing on Barth's ground. In advance one can only observe casually that under the best of circumstances it is a program likely to resemble the Swiss Alps that surround it—uphill all the way.

3. Turning toward Marburg: if this dialectical declaration of dependence and independence *vis-à-vis* Barth is to be taken at face value, what is left to be said of Ott's future intention in relation to his other "revered teacher"? He seems somewhat less explicit and clear here to date, but a few wide-angle observations may be ventured.

It is precisely because Bultmann has been fundamentally

concerned with the problem of communication, the problem of the "human understanding" of the *kerygma*, that Ott has been attracted to him. Undoubtedly it is to be expected that he will derive every benefit possible from Bultmann's long years of labor on this problem. It does not seem likely as of now, however, that he will venture far over this "programmatic" line. And this is the basis of the charge, quite troublesome to a theologian in Europe at the moment, that Ott is "conservative."

Ott quite correctly locates the fundamental problems of the Bultmann group not in the "demythologizing" effort as such, but rather (1) in the structure of philosophical-theological assumptions (many explicit, but others implicit) that underlies this project, and (2) in the relationship of demythologizing to preaching assumed and the noetic limits which this relationship implies. On these two fronts he has served sharp notice that he intends to fight, although it seems clear that he would prefer to do battle with the ubiquitous students of Bultmann rather than with his "revered teacher."

One of the specific points Ott has chosen to attack solicits immediate interest. Professor Ernest Fuchs is employed as the foil. Fuchs has insisted that the assault on the demythologizing project takes its rise from a confusion of the roles of theology and preaching. In reply to the charge that Bultmann "abridges" the Good News, or does not declare the "fulness" of the revelation, Fuchs replies that it should have been recognized and acknowledged from the outset that this is not Bultmann's assigned task as a Professor. "Theology is not preaching, but presupposes preaching as communication of revelation," he insists. "Theology inquires about the *possibility* of such communication as a human act. Thus theology can have no desire whatever to declare the fullness of the revelation."

This statement, with its seemingly agnostic implications for theology, obviously has a direct effect on Ott's blood pressure. He recounts in a tone of near unbelief a theological conversation with a "party line" student of Bultmann on the question of providence, whom he had asked how he would preach on the "sparrow" passage of Mt. 10. The reply was: "Yes, but preaching is somewhat different. Certainly I could preach on that. But preaching and theology are two different things."

Ott declares heatedly that we must assert precisely the opposite, that such a dichotomy would be disastrous, and that what Fuchs calls a "misunderstanding" is in reality the only defensible understanding. And in addition to his other arguments he calls in some rather impressive witnesses—Augustine, Luther, Calvin, Zwingli—and asks if they assumed this neat bifurcation of their homiletical and theological efforts. The peculiar and proper problem of theology, he replies to Fuchs in italics, is just this: *"How is the preacher to preach?"*

If this question is to be answered, and the valid contributions of Bultmann utilized in the process, Ott says there must be "another method of existential interpretation of theology." In his preliminary efforts to forge such a method two things, primarily, have been emphasized. (1) Ott feels that it is necessary to shift attention in the demythologizing effort to the "forms of expression" entailed by the times and employed by the Biblical witnesses (as, for example, the Alexandrian type of exegesis used in the letter to the Hebrews). (2) Then we must seek through these "forms of expression," not the "self-understanding" of the Biblical witnesses (as with Bultmann), but the encounter with God to which they testify, and thus at once the God who uses this Biblical testimony in encountering us.

Ott believes that this reorientation would both discard the chaff and preserve the wheat of Bultmann's contribution, and transcend the pervasive threat of theological agnosticism to which Bultmann's students seem in danger of succumbing. Following Ott's lead, it would not be merely a matter of finding in the "life movement" and "self-understanding" of the Biblical witnesses something that can create a parallel movement within us today. Rather, here a Biblical basis is afforded for explicit statements *both* in preaching *and* in theology, and *both* about the encounter of the prophets and apostles with the God of Abraham, Isaac, and Jacob, *and* about this God who encountered them. "The method may be called existential," he remarks, "except that here in distinction from Bultmann the inquiry is not primarily about the self-understanding of the Biblical witnesses, but about their encounter with God and therewith about God himself."

This is the orienting and delineating hermeneutical assumption that lies in the background when Ott focuses his attention directly upon the question of the interrelationship of theology and preaching, or of dogmatics and proclamation. This permits him to insist upon what he carefully calls the "continuity" and "reciprocity" of preaching and theology. It is not that one is assertive and the other inquisitive, or that one declares the *kerygma* while the other questions and examines the possibility of such a declaration. Each is assertive, each testifies to the God who testifies to Himself through the prophets and apostles.

Ott, therefore, contends that one both can and must "preach" if he is to teach theology correctly, that he must preach as he teaches; and likewise that one both can and must "teach theology" if he is to preach correctly, that he must teach theology as he preaches. He grants the basic difference of "style," but rushes on to affirm that the two share and must share a common substance, a common content, and that therefore we cannot, indeed we dare not, bifurcate them. The conclusion is that whatever distinction is to be made must be formal, not material. But once more he should be permitted to speak for himself.

It perhaps must be said that theology is the conscience of the sermon [he observes], and in turn that the sermon is the conscience of theology. If he is to preach correctly, the preacher must reflect theologically. And to be able to teach theology, even though he does not himself have to enter the pulpit Sunday by Sunday, the theologian must understand the intention of proclamation and keep the task of the preacher steadily in view. The preacher who does not wish to do so, and hands over the task of theological reflection to the theological 'expert,' is a poor preacher, a preacher without 'conscience.' And the theologian who does not wish to do so, and hands over concern for the proclamation of the church to the 'practitioner,' is a poor teacher of the church, and also a theologian without 'conscience.'

4. If one is to relate preaching and theology in this way, how shall—or may—they be differentiated? Has Ott left for himself a distinctive vocation as a theologian, one not fulfilled by the parson or preacher? And does he permit a recognition

of the unique vocation of the pastor or preacher, one that cannot be fulfilled by even the most effective professor of theology?

He insists that the basic difference between preaching and theological reflection, or the teaching of theology, is that the sermon is characterized formally by "one-sidedness," while theology must strive for "wholeness." On one occasion the preacher speaks primarily of the Resurrection; on another of the Crucifixion. Here he speaks more of grace; there of judgment. One Sunday justification is his concern; another Sunday sanctification. (Ott is thinking, of course, of European preaching.) The grounding of a sermon in the Biblical text, together with a pastoral sensitivity to the needs of a congregation, requires this *ad hoc*, "one-sided" approach. This is, Ott says, as it should be. "An essential distinction between proclamation and dogmatics lies in the mode of explication of their common, given oneness. Dogmatics is designed to show the whole together. Proclamation, on the contrary, unfolds the whole of the gospel *ad hoc*, in a one-sided way, with regard for the particularity of the text and the pastoral situation."

This rings a bell. A sermon that attempts "wholeness" is a burlesque of preaching. In its furtive effort to communicate everything, it rarely communicates anything. Likewise, a theology that suffers from lack of "wholeness" is an immediate threat to the health of the Church.

Is there not, nevertheless, a missing ingredient: the clear, unambiguous recognition that on the one hand preaching is the communication of the gospel of Jesus Christ, while on the other theological education is the academic preparation for this communication? Preaching may "accidentally" aid in the process of preparation for preaching (let us hope that it does!). But we must remember that this is at no time its essential role. Similarly, the rigorous process of preparation may "accidentally" communicate the gospel in an "existential" as well as academic way (let us hope that it does!). But this is not its assigned and essential role. These "accidental" occurrences in no way annul or alter the necessity for the working distinction crucial to the order and mission of the Church. The professor of a theological faculty presumably is within the *sanctorum communio*. This being so, undoubtedly everyone would agree that the Professor who had no concern for the "care of souls," the "spiritual health," or the "existential encounter" of his students would be a questionable teacher of the Church and a poor risk for a theological faculty. This should be granted with deep conviction. But when it has been granted, an unanswered question remains—and it is one that should not be permitted to remain unanswered.

In terms of order and primacy of responsibility, to whom is the work of proclamation and "care of souls" committed, and to whom is the work of preparation committed? The pertinent fact is that in its best moments the Church of both past and present has seen that these are quite different functions which must be carefully distinguished, defined, and assigned.

Professor Ott's musing to the moment on this difficult but crucial question is both provocative and instructive. It is, in fact, an earnest (and a needed one) which suggests, that one day the entire world Church may be indebted to him.

The Relation of Scripture, Church Tradition and Modern Interpretation

Eduard Schweizer

How should the Christian interpret the Scriptures and traditions of the church? What authority do they have? "Where is truth, and where is untruth?" What is the Bible's attitude toward itself? What is the significance of Easter? Of the Holy Spirit? Eduard Schweizer poses such basic questions as these —and in addressing himself to them he passionately upholds both Scripture and tradition but just as passionately scorns "killing legalism" and "petrified" orthodoxies. His position is reflected pointedly, for instance, in what he says of the sermon: "A sermon without burning love towards modern man, a sermon in an outlived language, no longer understandable in a modern world, is probably no sermon of the Holy Spirit." Schweizer affirms the power and reliability of the Scriptures while declaring that they, like faith and love, do not give us guarantees. Dr. Schweizer, a noted New Testament scholar, teaches at the University of Zürich, in Switzerland. He is author of such books as *Lordship and Discipleship* and *Church Order in the New Testament.* The academic year 1963–1964 brought him to the United States, where he joined the faculty of San Francisco Theological Seminary as a visiting professor. His article, from the Summer 1963 *Theology and Life,** is also included in the symposium *Essays on the Heidelberg Catechism.*

IF I understand the situation in modern New Testament research correctly, it seems that it is no longer possible to consider the Bible as a kind of quarry out of which the Church orders the foundation stones for its dogmatic buildings, the proof texts for its doctrinal statements. Even if we went back in history to the first credal statements of the early Church or to the genuine words of Jesus, it is impossible to find a pure expression of the truth like some kind of dis-

* Lancaster Theological Seminary, Lancaster, Pennsylvania.

tilled water cleansed from all foreign substances. Luckily enough this is so. For, as we know, distilled water, deprived of its minerals and salts, no longer quenches our thirst. A "distilled" truth, not affected by the way of thinking, the insights and errors, needs and hopes of its respective time, would be but an ineffable mystery available for god-like beings only, and of no help for us. *The* truth encounters us in the body of the truth for the hearers of Jesus, for the Palestinian churches in 30 AD, for the Hellenistic communities of the fifties, for the church in Rome in 400, for the Reformation time, for the church of 1963 in U. S. A., etc. All these truths are undoubtedly different, and yet only different bodies of one truth. What enables us to preach confidently the truth for our time and our country, without going astray? Where is truth, and where is untruth?

A. History and Tradition

1. THE ORIGIN OF THE TRADITION IN EASTER AND PENTECOST

The basis of the New Testament writings is the Easter event. Even the gospels are written in the light of Easter so that the earthly Jesus and the post-Easter Christ become one.

What does Easter mean? According to John 20:21-23 Easter is also Pentecost. On Easter the risen Lord breathes the Holy Spirit on His disciples and sends them into the world. But also for Matthew the Easter event is the beginning of the mission of the disciples, and the promise of the heavenly Lord to be with them to the close of the age is actually the gift of the Spirit. For Paul, seeing the risen Lord and becoming His apostle was the same event (1 Cor. 9:1; Gal. 1:16). Luke is the only one who distinguishes between Easter and Pentecost, but even he sees the two events very closely connected; for it is the risen Lord who, on Easter day, gives the commandment of the proclamation of the gospel to all nations and the promise of the Spirit. Even if we had the best sound film of a Jerusalem newsreel of the year 30 AD (or whatever it was), it would not help us much, since it could not show what really happened on that day. Only Easter, the revelation of the Spirit, shows what really happened.

It is therefore absolutely appropriate when the author of Revelation introduces his letters to the seven churches as the words of Christ, just because they are the words of the Spirit. Hence the introductory formula always refers to the heavenly Christ, the closing formula to the Holy Spirit as the real author of these letters. Revelation only explicitly states what, in the Synoptic or Johannine tradition of the deeds and words of Jesus, went on for decades. In new situations, the heavenly Lord, through His Spirit, explained His former words and reinterpreted them in a new situation. The authority of the heavenly Lord could certainly not be less than that of the earthly Jesus. Why, therefore, should the New Testament hesitate to formulate His words so that they meant in the very situation of the Church of that time what they were to mean from the beginning? Probably nobody purposely and consciously altered the words of Jesus; they only heard them in such a way that they spoke directly into their own problems and their own time.

We may formulate our point 1: *The New Testament never severs the earthly Jesus from the risen Lord. It is the risen Lord only who, speaking through the Spirit, gives meaning to the words or deeds of the earthly Jesus.*

2. THE RELATION OF A FACT TO ITS UNDERSTANDING

Modern physicists know about the problems which we touch, even in the area of physical facts. The questions which we ask alter the result of an experiment. This is certainly even more true in the area of history. There is evidently some difference, at least in degree, between facts in the area of history and human encounter, and facts in the area of physics. The role that our understanding plays is greater in the former area than in the latter. A cancer, for instance, has its effects whether we know about it or not; it can be removed by surgery, and it does not affect the healing if we do not know that it was cancer. Quite differently, a deed of love usually has its effect on us only if we know about and interpret it as was meant. It is possible that someone loves us for years without our knowing. In this case such a love would not affect us or change our situation. It is equally possible that someone does something for us out of mere love, but we misunderstand his motive and are driven into inferiority complexes or even hate. Therefore a historical positivism which puts historical facts on exactly the same level as physical facts is impossible. It forgets that, in the area of human encounter, the interpretation and understanding of a fact is sometimes even more important than the fact itself. This may be true, for instance, for the history of the conquest of the West and its interpretation in movies and television.

This, I think, may help us to find our way towards a solution of the problem of "scripture and tradition." Let us choose a very simple example. Let us assume that a girl pays all the debts of her boy friend, because she loves him and wants to give him a new start. Let us assume that they marry. The problem of their matrimony will be how he copes with what his wife has done for him. His feelings of inferiority towards her may grow more and more. Even doubts may arise whether she really did it out of love or, perhaps, out of sheer calculation. Hence, the task of this girl will be to accompany her husband in a continuing love in order to interpret her initial deed to him and to "bring it home" to him. This leads to our point 2: *A deed of love and the continuing interpretation by love belong closely together.*

3. THE ONENESS OF GOD THE SON AND GOD THE HOLY SPIRIT

Our first step is a comparatively easy one. As it is, in our example, the same person who does the deed of love for her friend and who makes him understand this deed, so it is one God who, as the Son, speaks to us in His incarnate Word, and, as the Spirit, interprets this Word to us, so that it becomes meaningful for us. This is the truth of the Trinitarian concept of the Church. The saving events in the life, death and resurrection of Jesus Christ, and the proclamation of these events which brings the Church into being, are both the acts of the One God and cannot be separated from one another. "God was in Christ reconciling the world to Himself, and entrusting to us the message of reconciliation" (2 Cor. 5:19). "The Spirit of truth will not speak on His own authority . . . He will take what is mine and declare it to you" (John 16:13f.). According to all four evangelists the Baptist announced Jesus as the one who will baptize with the Holy Spirit. Paul once even identifies the Lord and the Spirit (2 Cor. 3:17), and, according to the seven letters of Revelation, the words of the Spirit are the words of the risen Lord.

However, this first easy step is like the step from the safe soil down to the frozen pond. It is very easy, since it goes down to the pond, but after this first step we are skating on ice, possibly on very thin ice. For, as soon as we grant what we have said, two main problems arise: first, how do we distinguish the Spirit of God from so many other, rather ungodly spirits? and second, if we succeed in doing so, is the authority of this Spirit higher when speaking in the first century within the New Testament than when speaking in the 16th century or in 1963? We shall deal with the first problem by warning, in sections B and C, against two opposite dangers, both very much alive in modern theology, and with the second problem in a following section D, before drawing the practical conclusions. However, before doing so, we conclude point 3: *The interpretation of the saving events in the tradition of the Church, from the first preaching of the apostles to the preaching of the Church today, is the act of the same God who acted in Jesus Christ.*

B. The Danger of Not Being Modern Enough

1. THE FIRST MARK OF THE SPIRIT: HIS AFFECTION FOR MODERN MEN

What is the standard by which to test the utterances of the Spirit and to separate right and wrong tradition? In the pre-Pauline church, the Spirit was naively identified with an extraordinary power for healings, prophecies, etc. This led, in Hellenistic congregations, to an extreme preference for ecstatic phenomena. The only alternative to this was an ecclesiastical institutionalism, as it was probably to be found in Jerusalem under James, after the persecution in 44, and the departure of Peter. Paul was the first to reflect carefully about the nature of the Spirit of God. He points to the fact that the Spirit speaks "for the common good" (1 Cor. 12:7). He speaks so that He "edifies the Church" (14:4). He speaks in such a way that every member of the Church understands Him (14:2, 6-12). This means: the Spirit of God is always directed towards contemporaries. He is always speaking in modern language. If this were not the case, it would be best to put the sermons of Paul and Peter on a tape recording and to play them in our services, instead of training ministers who are, in spite of their expensive training, not always on the level of Paul and Peter. A sermon without burning love towards modern men, a sermon in an outlived language, no longer understandable in a modern world, is probably no sermon of the Holy Spirit. Thus let us keep in mind point 1: *It is the sign of the Holy Spirit that He does not speak into the air, but in modern language to modern men, knowing their needs, their hopes and their dangers.*

2. HIS CRITICISM OF A PETRIFIED TRADITION

"The Scripture kills, but the Spirit gives life," says Paul (2 Cor. 3:6). "We do not serve under the old Scripture, but in the new life of the Spirit" (Rom. 7:6). There is no doubt that Paul reads his Bible very carefully, and that he finds the new life of the Spirit in this very Bible. Long passages of his letters are interpretations of the Scripture. But when the Scripture is used, as it is used in a fundamentalist theology, in a legalistic way, it becomes the "written code" against which Paul fights so vehemently. Against some groups of Jewish Christians, Paul fights vigorously for his thesis that, in his mission to the Gentiles, the history of salvation goes on, although it seems to be in contradiction to some words of Jesus if literally understood. Whatever the roots of the Johannine

tradition be, it is certain that it is a totally new interpretation
of Jesus' words and deeds by the post-Easter Spirit which has
not much to do with a literal repetition of the sayings of
Jesus. Even Matthew, who is rather close to the conception
of a new law, and for whom Jesus is, first of all, the teacher
of a new righteousness, in many respects offers a new interpretation for new needs. Besides, it is exactly Matthew who
emphasizes that the Church has the power of binding and
loosing (18:18), i.e., of creating new law or invalidating old
law, and of forgiving or keeping sins. Luke distinguishes different periods of a continuing history of God, in which the
Spirit leads the Church to new insights. A petrified tradition
which can no longer be developed by the living Spirit into
new insights is legalism which kills instead of bringing into
life, even if it were the tradition of the genuine sayings of
Jesus.

Hence our point 2: *An orthodoxy which replaces the life
in the Spirit by an acceptance of the historicity of Biblical
facts and a legal authority of Biblical words or of credal formulas would be a killing legalism.*

3. THE NEW QUEST OF THE HISTORICAL JESUS

The new quest of the historical Jesus is certainly not such
an orthodoxy. It seems to be, on the contrary, a very modern
and unorthodox approach. However, everything depends on
the place which we give to such a quest within our theological
thinking. In the creed of the post-Easter Church "Jesus
Christ," the title "Christ" says who Jesus is. He is the one in
whom God finally and once for all encountered the world and
saved it. But equally well, the word "Jesus" determines the
word "Christ." It is a crucified man, rejected by Israel, who is
this Christ, not the national king subjecting all Gentiles to his
nation. It is therefore necessary that Jesus does not remain a
mere name without concrete content. If we understand the
new quest in this way, it is indeed a most necessary reaction
against a theology in which Christianity was in danger of
developing into a mere doctrine without any historical roots.
However, this new quest of the historical Jesus seems to

have a quite different goal with most of its representatives. It seems to assume that modern men when confronted with a historical pre-Easter Jesus not yet presented in the light of the Easter event by believers who see in Him already the Christ, would be led to detect in Him the Christ of the New Testament. Jesus then becomes the first of the believers, the one who enables us to believe, who takes us into his own relation to God. If the quest of the historical Jesus is meant in this way, I think that it is a new and very modern way of petrifying a tradition. The only difference would be that it is not the tradition of a developed ecclesiastical orthodoxy, but the tradition of the genuine sayings of the historical Jesus.

This would lead us into a new legalism by which Jesus would become a mere ethical example and teacher. I cannot see why we then should go exclusively to Jesus and not to Socrates whose example and farewell discourses still move us, or to Epictetus who not only ate and drank with the socially low classes, but was a slave himself and helped thousands of slaves to bear their destiny. Who would deny that Jesus was an outstanding teacher and example? He really helped men to believe and led them to God, and all this is important and helpful. But all this does not distinguish Him basically from other helpers, teachers and examples. The one fact which distinguishes Him from all others is, according to all books of our New Testament, Easter. "His disciples did not understand this at first, but when Jesus was glorified, then they remembered" (John 12: 16). When the New Testament creates the new phrase "believing *in* Jesus Christ," when it speaks so often about "believing *that* Jesus Christ was crucified and raised from the dead," it means much more than believing because He helped us to believe. This faith can only be experienced, lived, witnessed to, but it cannot be deduced from a no longer possible historical reconstruction of a pre-Easter Jesus. Historical facts never create faith, only faith creates faith. We therefore close section B by point 3: *The starting point for all Christian proclamation is the faith that Jesus is the Christ, crucified for us, raised by God, not simply teacher and ethical example. The quest of the historical Jesus is a second step only, which prevents this belief from becoming a mere idea without a basis in real facts within history.*

C. *The Danger of a Christianity
Losing its Roots in History*

1. THE SECOND MARK OF THE SPIRIT: HIS TESTIMONY TO JESUS

The other standard for judging the utterances of the Spirit which Paul mentions is the testimony to Jesus the Lord. Whoever witnesses to Jesus as the Lord is moved by the Spirit, and whoever denies this is far from the Spirit of God (1 Cor. 12:3). Christianity, unlike all other religions, is shaped by the fact that the preached Word of God is but the vehicle by which the incarnate Word of God meets us. If we lose this basis in history, we shall have lost the content of the gospel. God is not to be restricted to His actual speaking in the preaching of our time. His Word to the world is a man of flesh and blood, so real that he was hanged. A spiritualized preaching, severed from the history of Palestine in the first three decades of our era, would be like a tree whose roots were pulled out of the soil which gave it life. Our point 1 therefore understands *the gospel not as a doctrine about eternally unchangeable ideas, but as the praising proclamation of God's deed which in Jesus Christ, once for all, changed the situation of the world.*

2. THE AFFINITY OF THE SPIRIT TO HISTORY AND TRADITION

For Paul himself, the fact of the crucifixion of Jesus was so scandalous that he was never in danger of forgetting that Jesus was a real, historic person. This was different for Greek congregations which were living far away from the historical facts of about 30 AD in Jerusalem. They were in a real danger of developing into a gnosticism as we know it from groups of the second century AD. Gnosticism presents a comprehensive doctrine of salvation, containing even a myth which tells about the descent from and the ascent to heaven of a man-like saviour, but here only the kerygma matters. The myth is but an illustration of the eternally unchangeable truth. Therefore it does not matter at all whether uneducated people believe that all this really happened in distant primitive times, or more educated people take this myth as a mere image for the truth. Against such tendencies John formulates what Paul had written in a simpler form in 1 Cor. 12:3: "Every spirit which confesses that Jesus Christ has come in the flesh is of God, and every spirit which does not confess Jesus is not of God." (1 John 4:2f.). Even more important is the fact that, when some time had elapsed and the real historical figure of Jesus of Nazareth was in danger of fading away, four Gospels were written in order to defend the gospel against being converted into gnosticism. The historical facts are nothing without their interpretation by the post-Easter Spirit—therefore all the Gospels present the earthly Jesus in the light of the risen Christ. However, this interpretation, in and of itself, is equally meaningless if not understood as the interpretation of these facts.

To sum up point 2: *The New Testament writers are not concerned with a distinction between the so-called historical Jesus and the risen Lord speaking through the Spirit, but they are certainly concerned with the distinction between a mere doctrine or a mere myth and a history interpreted by the Spirit.*

3. THE KERYGMATIC THEOLOGY

Is it not enough to say that it is only the kerygma that matters whatever the historical facts may be? In this extreme formulation, this thesis is at least open to severe misunderstandings. For the very content of this proclamation of the first Church was the fact that God's saving act happened in the life, death and resurrection of Jesus, that it was not a new doctrine, but an event within a definite period of time and a definite geographical area, that God's redeeming Word consisted of flesh and bones, and not only of syllables. Hence, this event must, for the believer, mean more than a mere name. It is not important whether or not all the stories told us in the gospels happened. But it is important that Jesus is, for us, not a mere ghost, but a man with specific features.

There is quite a difference between an image on which many details are uncertain, and a vague idea which is not much more than a mere name.

Let me give you an illustration. Let us assume that we had to write the history of the Christianization of some heathen country. We could describe one outstanding conversion. Everything else would be historically accurate. And yet, the book would be absolutely deceptive. There would be nothing about all the defeats, the mistakes, the sins, the hypocrisy and apostasy which also took place. We could do it in another way. Granted that we knew about all the highlights and the deep shadows of this history, that we really had investigated everything, we could choose one average family of that country and describe what happened. We could invent their names, we could describe in the example of this one family what happened in thousands of different families. It would be fiction, and yet, this would be the truth, not the first book. Not the historical accuracy alone decides, but the deep understanding of what happened. And yet, it is important that, even in this fictitious family, we recognize the real events, the main features of the history which passed there.

Point 3 states that *a theology in which the kerygma of the first church is the center must be corrected by the insight that this very kerygma proclaims that a man of flesh and blood in his concrete life and death and resurrection is the mystery in which God encounters the world.*

D. The Relation between Jesus Christ, the New Testament, the Tradition and the Proclamation of the Church Today

1. THE THIRD MARK OF THE SPIRIT: A GIFT TO THE WHOLE CHURCH

According to Paul, it is extremely important that the whole congregation understands the message of the Spirit and is able to agree with its "Amen" (1 Cor. 14:16). Therefore the prophet speaking in the Spirit must be judged by the congregation (v. 29). The Spirit is given to all believers. "Any one who does not have the Spirit of Christ does not belong to Him" (Rom. 8:9). "You shall receive the gift of the Holy Spirit; for the promise is to . . . every one whom the Lord our God calls to Him" (Acts 2:38f.). In the New Testament, the Spirit is always the gift to the whole Church. This means that the preaching of the Spirit is always subject to control by the members of the Church. I, therefore, always prepare my sermons together with a group of church members, listening for an hour and a half to their discussion of the text. Thus our point 1 will be that *the Spirit is given to the Church and is therefore controlled by all the brethren.*

2. THE ROLE OF THE TRADITION

God cannot contradict Himself. Therefore we must listen carefully to all our brethren and, if we disagree, ask ourselves whether we are not hard of hearing for the voice of the Spirit. But the Church did not start in 1963, and the Spirit did not begin to speak in 1963. There are brethren throughout all the centuries of church history. Some of these brethren are in an outstanding position. They have suffered and died for the truth that they proclaimed, and/or they have proclaimed that truth not as individuals but as Church, in common agreement. This is the case, for instance, with the declaration of Barmen in the Confessing Church of Germany in 1934, or with the Heidelberg Catechism, in 1563.

This is one reason for listening to the tradition, but there is another one. Past centuries had their own way of thinking. On the one hand, being men of another century we are usually quite aware of the errors which were involved in their thinking. In the discussion of the Lord's Supper, for instance, Lutherans and Calvinists thought in categories totally foreign to the New Testament, because they had a conception of matter or substance conceived in the Middle Ages, but unknown in New Testament times. Hence it goes without saying that we must read the tradition with a critical mind, avoiding their inappropriate categories of thinking as far as possible. On the other hand, being men of our century, we are usually blind to the inappropriate categories of our own century. And here, the tradition renders us the most necessary service of helping us to see the limits of our own thinking. It may, for instance, be impossible for us to repeat literally the clause in the first answer of the Heidelberg Catechism that Jesus Christ paid with his dear blood completely for my sin and redeemed me from all power of the devil. And yet, it reminds us that there is dimension in the New Testament message which is not yet covered, if we consider Jesus mainly as a teacher or ethical example or even the messenger of justification by faith. We may therefore formulate point 2: *It is the advantage of tradition that we, while better aware of its limits and errors than of those of our contemporary thinking, may see in its light the deficiencies of our own theology.*

3. THE ROLE OF THE SCRIPTURE

What is the particular position of the New Testament within this tradition? A first answer would be that what is true for the Heidelberg Catechism or the declaration of Barmen is even truer for the New Testament. It is surrounded by a cloud of martyrs who died witnessing to its truth. It is a team work in an excellent way, and its acceptance by the whole Church is without parallel. However, all this is only a difference in degree.

A second answer starts from the fact that the New Testament distinguishes the first encounter of the risen Lord with the apostles clearly and definitely from later visions by which the heavenly Lord gives some guidance to the believer. Paul's encounter with the risen Lord near Damascus is the basis of all his preaching and is referred to in Gal. 1:16 and 1 Cor. 9:1, also in Rom. 1:1 and similar places. The vision of 2 Cor. 12 with its extraordinary ascent to heaven should not be mentioned at all, since it is a more personal experience without any importance for the Church as a whole. Luke draws a strict line between the appearance of the risen Lord within the first forty days and heavenly visions like the one before Peter in Joppa.

Easter is the event which always reminds us that it is God Himself who gave us this understanding, once for all, unchangeable in its essence. The New Testament is certainly not identical with this understanding that God Himself gave to men. It is written in Greek, and every human language involves necessarily quite a lot of categories of thinking which are partly appropriate, partly inappropriate for expressing the divine truth. It is written by men who understand and misunderstood what God wanted them to understand. And yet, the New Testament is, first, historically the closest to the event of the incarnate Word of God. Second, it has been tested by time, and again by the whole Church. Third, it stood the test in the sufferings of the Church before and after its acceptance as the canon of the Church. Fundamentally it does not lie on another level than all teaching of the Spirit throughout the history of the Church. Therefore, the canon is still open. However, this would be a merely theoretical thesis. Theoretically also a gentle stroke on the hand of a child is the same as a whipping which leaves a cripple, since both are fundamentally corporal punishment; but actually there is all the difference in the world between the two. And yet, it is impossible to draw a mathematically clear line. Therefore we may close point 3: *The New Testament is part of the tradition, therefore necessarily expressed in human language, limited by contemporaneous possibilities of understanding, imperfect, and yet standing in a unique position as the beginning of the tradition, historically close to the incarnate Word of God and sign for its "once-for-all-ness."*

Conclusions

Faith, not unlike love, lives without having guarantees. If a husband hires a private detective and gets his written reports which prove the faithfulness of his wife, it is not the beginning, but the end of his love. Faith that requires guarantees is no longer faith. There are witnesses, there are signs, there are experiences, but there are no guarantees which would relieve us of believing. It is most illuminating that the first canon was created by Judaism, as soon as it had parted definitely from Christianity. The canon becomes a petrified tradition no longer able to create any life, as soon as it is considered as the guarantee of the orthodox truth. But if it is not a new law, a guarantee which could be taken over literally in a new legalism, it is the outstanding testimony of the contemporaries of the incarnate Word, tested and accepted by the whole Church. The canon is a fact, an event which gives us no guarantee, but which has proved its power and reliability. Except for a few short sayings attributed to Jesus and handed down outside of the New Testament—"whoever is close to me, is close to the fire," etc.—there is nothing which could earnestly be considered as worth adding to our New Testament. It might be that we could do without, for instance, the letter of Jude; but no church would dare to exclude a book from the canon, and I think we are glad that Luther did not exclude James and Revelation, as he first would have liked to do.

A sermon which earnestly tries to interpret its Biblical text gives, of course, no guarantee that this message is really understood and that it offers us that bread which God wants to give us today, but it is at least an earnest attempt to listen to those witnesses to whom God spoke before He spoke to us. It is, at least, a help that can free us from our own favorite thoughts that are not always identical with the thoughts of God. In a similar way it is wise for the Church to listen carefully to its tradition, as it is handed down, for instance, in the Heidelberg Catechism. Again, a repetition of its formulas does not guarantee that we mean the same as they meant in their time, let alone that this meaning is the unsurpassable truth. But again, it is, at least, a remedy against an individualism which sees nothing beyond the limits of its own personality or its own time. We shall certainly read the Scriptures and read the Catechism as men of our century. We shall translate the message of the New Testament into the needs of our time. We shall not forget that the ecumenical movement is God's gift and challenge to our time. Hence we shall not consider the Heidelberg Catechism as an exclusive possession of our denomination. We shall interpret it in such a way that other denominations are also able to understand its intention, and we shall also listen carefully to similar documents of other denominations. But we shall listen to the Scriptures and to our tradition; we shall listen humbly and intensely ten times before speaking once.

On the one hand, whoever possesses guarantee, has got salvation in his own possession. No longer is he forced to ask questions and to pray for an answer. No longer is he entirely thrown on God alone. No longer is he a poor beggar expecting everything from his Lord. On the other hand, whoever believes in nothing but his own spirituality has equally well got salvation in his own possession. No longer is he forced to listen except to himself. No longer does he know a God outside of his own soul, an incarnate Word of God, and a Word given to a Church which is greater than he. No longer is he a poor beggar expecting everything from his Lord.

Let me close by a reference to Luther and a last reference to the Heidelberg Catechism. Luther distinguishes "certitude" from "security." Faith knows no security, because security means a guarantee of which we could dispose, a guarantee in our own hands. Security needs no God. But faith knows certitude, that last peace which knows that God is absolutely trustworthy and that He will give us every morning anew what we do not possess. The Heidelberg Catechism closes in an extraordinary way with a section on prayer. According to question 116, prayer is the main part of our gratitude, the best that can be said of man and his work. Whoever prays needs no other security and guarantees, but is not restricted to his own spiritual wisdom either. We could not close our lecture better than with the last answer of the Heidelberg Catechism: "Amen means: this is true and certain; for it is much more certain that God heard my prayer than that I feel by the testimony of my heart that I am praying to Him."

Revelation Through History in the Old Testament and in Modern Theology

James Barr

James Barr is proving to be something of an iconoclast in the field of biblical studies. Not that his purposes are entirely negative; there are times when faulty foundations must be demolished before new, solid ones can be built. His 1961 book *The Semantics of Biblical Language* dealt a devastating blow to the "word study" approach to biblical exegesis—a method which has played a notable part in the revival of biblical theology. In that book he accuses a number of prominent scholars of hypostatizing lexical items and disregarding their syntactical setting and "plain meaning." His more recent book, *Biblical Words for Time,* constitutes a specific application of the thesis of the earlier work. In the article below, Dr. Barr launches still another assault—this time on a formula of almost sacrosanct status in modern theology, that of "revelation through history." It is his contention that this formula, while not without considerable value, does not do justice to certain aspects of biblical thought, nor will it yield an apologetic adequate for our times. Dr. Barr is Professor of Old Testament Literature at Princeton Theological Seminary. His article, from the April 1963 issue of *Interpretation: A Journal of Bible and Theology,** originally was an inaugural address delivered at Princeton Seminary in December 1962.

I WANT in this lecture to ask one question only, and it is a question which may have very far-reaching importance. Its basis and its source of validation lie to some considerable extent within the Old Testament, and that is why I feel able to take it up on this occasion. But its implications

* Published by Union Theological Seminary in Virginia, 3401 Brook Road, Richmond 2, Virginia.

run, I believe, through the whole range of theological thinking, and have practical relevance for the ecumenical movement and for the missionary strategy of the church among other religions. The question is this: is it true that the biblical evidence, and the evidence of the Old Testament in particular, fits with and supports the assertion that "history" is the absolutely supreme milieu of God's revelation?

In putting this problem in the form of a question, and not as a plain assertion, it may be that I am approaching the archheresy of modern times. No single principle is more powerful in the handling of the Bible today than the belief that history is the channel of divine revelation. Thus the formula "revelation through history" is taken to represent the center of biblical thinking, and interpretation of any biblical passage must be related to this historical revelation. The characteristic of extra-biblical religion, it is held, is its timeless or non-historical emphasis, while the centrality of revelation through history marks the biblical religion off clearly from such other religion. These ideas today are not only common, but they enjoy almost unqualified acceptance.

The emphasis on some such formula as "revelation through history" is, one might say, a unifying factor in modern theology. The concentration upon it is enormous, and no other formula has enjoyed such uncontradicted prestige. No important school of theology really challenges it. Amid the bitter feuds of modern theology it is common to hear voices which accuse a rival viewpoint of failure to take revelation through history seriously enough; but there is, I think, no theology which admits this of itself. Different theological schools accuse each other of dissolving the historical basis of revelation, or of accepting myths as if they were history; but it is the assumption of all who use such arguments from either side that "history" is an absolutely regulative concept, and that any theology which does not accord it a regulative place shows itself to be unacceptable as a Christian theology. Thus, if you question the centrality of revelation in history, you will be not only heretical in the eyes of almost all schools of thought, but you will also be judged irrelevant; your voice will be heard as that of a deluded dreamer who can have nothing valid to say to the real world. Revelation through history is, to use

Galbraith's term, the conventional wisdom of modern theology. Historians of theology in a future age will look back on the mid-twentieth century and call it the revelation-in-history period.

Let us register the fact that revelation in history undoubtedly has provided something of value and importance to many different concerns within modern theology. The neo-orthodox or conservative theologian has seen in it something that could conserve and express the objective reality of God's deeds in the world, and offer protection against their dissolution into myths which express processes within man. But the existentialist's approach has also been able to latch on to the formula and to feel that from it he could work to a "historicity" which is the mode of man's authentic existence. Those primarily interested in the historical criticism of the biblical literature have also been able to gain something from the formula, for they have been able to argue that Christianity is a historical religion and that therefore it must welcome the most rigorous application of historical-critical methods to its sources. Conversely, the approach to the Bible and especially to the Old Testament through archaeological methods and the study of the cultural background has been representable as an approach through history to the revelation conveyed by it. Yet again, the emphasis on history has seemed to provide a basis for a realistic social-political ethic. And even aspects of the older liberal theology have been able, one may feel, to find in revelation through history some shelter from the storm which has overtaken them in recent decades. Thus the idea of revelation in history has served as some sort of a component in theological approaches of many very different kinds, and all of them have made some appeal to it. It has been rather like the great tree in Nebuchadnezzar's dream, under which all the beasts of the field find shadow.

But beyond this, we may say most generally and most importantly, that revelation through history, and the constellation of our theological thinking around it, is our response to the tremendous and shocking apologetic strains of the nineteenth century imposed primarily by the rise of historical method and historical criticism. "History" was what seemed, especially in the form of materialist, sceptical, and immanentist philosophies, to threaten Christianity; but theology—bravely and rightly—chose to stand, on the whole, with history rather than to abandon it. Thus history forms the line of entrenchment along which many theological stands have been made. Where history seems to be a force threatening Christianity, empowering secular ideologies and relativizing biblical faith in a dangerous way, we answer that we affirm history just as much—no, very much more—and that if history is taken really seriously, these unpleasant consequences do not follow after all. On the contrary, we argue, nothing takes history so seriously as does true Christian faith. In many such ways does revelation in history form a basis for a kind of unity in theology today; and above all, it is the response to the apologetic needs of the nineteenth century.[1]

But if revelation in history forms a certain unity in modern theology, when we look in greater detail we can also see that it furnishes one of our greatest sources of disunity and disagreement. Nothing is more evident, within the great number of those who would affirm some kind of "revelation in history" or "historical revelation," than the violent conflicts over the nature of the "history" which is relevant in this context. Likewise, nothing is more common than to hear it said of a theologian that his concept of history is inadequate, and that his theology as a whole, in spite of his adherence to some kind of "revelation in history" formula, is thereby completely vitiated. When one considers the conceptions of history held by such representative theologians as Cullmann, Bultmann, Barth, von Rad, and Pannenberg (to stay for the moment within continental Protestantism), it is clear that for all the agreement on the central theological importance of "history" there is extreme difficulty in reaching even approximate agreement on what this history is. For this we may be able to offer some reasons a little later.

Meanwhile, however, let us turn to the biblical material. And this means principally the Old Testament material; for once again it is a matter of wide agreement that it is the Old Testament which provides the main biblical anchorage for revelation through history, that this may indeed be perhaps the greatest contribution of Israel to the church, and that it is the Old Testament scholars above all who have enforced upon the present theological generation the normativeness of the conception of revelation in history. Here, however, is one Old Testament scholar who is not so sure. Over some years I have become convinced that for certain important areas of the Old Testament the idea of the centrality of revelation through history cannot be applied without doing violence to the texts. On the one hand, I believe, there are important elements in the texts which cannot reasonably be subsumed under "revelation through history." On the other hand, even in the texts which in some degree can be so subsumed, there are important elements which equally call for attention, although they tend to be submerged when the interpretation is guided by the concept of revelation in history. The following points of difficulty may be mentioned:

Firstly, and most obviously, there is the wisdom literature. This has always been a very awkward point for those who assert that revelation in history is the center of Hebrew thought, as has been admitted by the most significant among them. Thus Wright, in his persuasive *God Who Acts*, says: "It is the wisdom literature which offers the chief difficulty because it does not fit into the type of faith exhibited in the historical and prophetic literature. In it there is no explicit reference to or development of the doctrine of history, election, or covenant."[2]

If in Proverbs "the divine work in history played no real role,"[3] the case in Ecclesiastes is even worse, and so much so that scholars have at times found themselves forced to call it "un-Hebraic" or even "un-biblical." In general, while the wisdom literature shows that it is aware God may act in human life and affairs, it gives no impression that these acts are the sole or even the central foundation for all knowledge of him. On the contrary, it talks rather as if God is knowable or known without appeal to this source of revelation. Moreover, something of the same kind can be said, though less emphatically, of a still more impressive area in the Old Testament, namely, the Psalms. To sum up our first difficulty, then: there are substantial areas of the Old Testament which do not support and do not fit in with the idea that revelation through history is the fundamental motif of Old Testament thought.

Secondly, and much more importantly, we come to those

texts which have supplied the basic examples for the idea of revelation through history, such as the Exodus story. If you treat this record as revelation through history, you commonly speak as if the basis were the doing of certain divine acts (what, exactly, they were is often difficult to determine), while the present form of the tradition in its detail and circumstantiality is "interpretation" of these acts, or "meditation" upon them, or theological reflection prompted by them. Thus one may hear the great revelatory passage of Exodus 3 described as "interpretation" of this divine act of salvation, or as an inference from the fact that God had led Israel out of Egypt.

But I cannot make this scheme fit the texts, for this is not how the texts represent the Exodus events. Far from representing the divine acts as the basis of all knowledge of God and all communication with him, they represent God as communicating freely with men, and particularly with Moses, before, during, and after these events. Far from the incident at the burning bush being an "interpretation" of the divine acts, it is a direct communication from God to Moses of his purposes and intentions. This conversation, instead of being represented as an interpretation of the divine act, is a precondition of it. If God had not told Moses what he did, the Israelites would not have demanded their escape from Egypt, and the deliverance at the Sea of Reeds would not have taken place.

We may argue, of course, from a critical viewpoint that the stories of such dialogues arose in fact as inference from a divine act already known and believed, and for this there may be good reasons. All I want to say is that if we do this we do it on critical grounds and not on biblical grounds, for this is not how the biblical narrative represents the events. We cannot attribute to history a revelatory character, in a sense having substantial priority over the particular divine, spoken communications with particular men, without doing violence to the way in which the biblical traditions in fact speak. The verbal self-declaration of Yahweh in that great passage, Exodus 3, has as much independent standing in the esteem of the traditionists as the crossing of the Red Sea had.

Such difficulties then arise even in the commonly quoted

texts like the Exodus story. Notice that I am not saying that revelation through historical divine action is not an element here; I am simply denying that it can be the principal organizing conceptual bracket with which to view the material as a whole and to identify the common and essential features within its variety.

Thirdly, the Old Testament contains a good deal of material in which a narrative deals with divine actions—so that one might talk of a revelation of God through his acts in the world—but where the circumstances are such that the term "history" can be applied only if we stretch the word far beyond any normal received usage. A good example is Noah's flood. In the flood, God certainly revealed himself through his actions just as much as is the case in the Exodus story. But one does not need to stretch the term "history" nearly so far in order to include the Exodus story as one must in order to include the flood story. But the same is true if we set the Exodus story together with yet another, the capture of Jerusalem by Nebuchadnezzar; for to use "history" of the former implies a much greater stretching of the term than is implied by its use for the latter.

In fact, experience in Old Testament exegesis has forced upon me the difficulty of applying history as a guiding category of theological status in Old Testament interpretation. Take this series of outstanding narratives: the creation, the flood, the Exodus, the destruction of Jerusalem by Nebuchadnezzar. In the Old Testament, so far as I see, all of these narratives stand on an equal plane in one respect: they are all stories of events in which God has acted and which are in this sense revelatory, if we like to call it so. As long as we say only that these are stories in which God is represented as speaking and acting, we state the position of the texts reasonably well. But as soon as we use the category "history," we destroy this position and split up the likeness of the series. For each of the four narratives mentioned stands in a different relation to anything which we would call "history." Thus we split the biblical material apart as soon as we try to insist that "history" is the aptest category to which to relate it.

Now for this situation, if we may now talk more generally and leave behind the more particular Old Testament problems, we can state a reason. The reason why we split the biblical material when we use the category of history as a normative one is, of course, that this is a non-biblical category. The Bible itself has no linguistic bracket corresponding to "history," and, as we have seen, its narrative revelatory passages are not constant but variable in their relation to what we can by any definition call "history." Thus we might say that it is all-important that history should touch the contours of biblical revelation, but that it touches them tangentially and not by coinciding with them. Just as the Bible does not use history as an organizing and classifying bracket, conversely we use the idea of history outside of the Bible and independently of the Bible. We use it to characterize certain representations of the Civil War or the career of Napoleon, and in so doing we use criteria of history which do not normally or necessarily have any connection with the Bible. Undoubtedly there is room for difference of opinion about what is the best definition or understanding of history, but my point is that this happens in the case of any definition which has any connection with normal usage. Either we split up the biblical material, or else in trying to include it all uniformly we stretch the sense of history by arbitrary redefinition so far that even its elasticity is overstrained, and it snaps off from all connection with normal usage.

In fact, both of these things are happening. The splitting up of the biblical material in the Bultmannian approach is much deplored, but it seems probable that this approach only does much more openly and deliberately something that is done much more widely but less overtly. This is inevitable, for as long as we try to use history as a central theologically-regulative category we shall, I believe, evoke and produce some protest of the Bultmannian type. History, when consulted and appealed to as a channel of divine revelation, acts rather as the Witch of En-dor acted towards Saul; and so long as we turn to her for guidance she will raise to us from the ground the familiar spirit of Rudolf Bultmann. But even more noticeable to me is the artificiality and implausibility of the distinctions which we are forced to produce in order to make history do the kind of work into which we have impressed it. Consider only the artificiality of the distinctions between

Geschichte and *Historie*, between *Heilsgeschichte* and *Welt-geschichte*, or the artificiality of *Sage* and *Urgeschichte* as used by Barth of the creation stories. And this artificiality in past discussion seems in prospect to lead to a law of diminishing returns; each new refinement on a conception of history both theologically regulative and also set on a level, biblical base seems only to make it more unlikely that a consensus will ever be reached. What chance is there really, for example, that the fairly revolutionary and deeply impressive work of Pannenberg in the last year or two will lead to a greater degree of agreement?

Now the positive function of an idea like the centrality of revelation through history has been, I believe, apologetic: it forms a front against certain hostile philosophies and procedures. As an apologetic it suffers under two peculiarities. First, like much modern Christian apologetic, it works mainly not towards persuading the non-Christian but towards providing the Christian with an assurance that the arguments of non-Christians are poor ones; and I am personally doubtful whether our advocacy of revelation through history has in fact made a very deep or effective impression upon the modern world. Second, it has been an apologetic practiced by a theology large currents of which were very insistent that apologetics was not part of their interest at all, and indeed were illegitimate for truly Christian theology.[4] In spite of these peculiarities the idea of revelation through history serves a real apologetic purpose. Meeting the thought of a period dominated by history and historical method, it shows rightly that these are true concerns of Christianity also; it restates Christianity, again rightly, in terms related to this way of thinking; and it sets forth suitable axes through the biblical material along which that material can be organized so as to fit the emphasis upon history. Thus it succeeds, and this success is the secret of its popularity, in making the Bible intelligible and accessible in a generation in which problems coming from specifically historical thinking form the chief challenge to faith.

Now if the appeal to revelation through history had been made simply in this way, there would have been less to say in criticism of it and also, I think, less serious disagreement and disunity about the nature of this all-important "history." But this appeal has been made not solely as an apologetic point of conflict and restatement. It has also, and indeed much more, been taken as a position which, entirely validated by the Bible, was also a completely reliable guide or principle for the interpretation of the Bible. This additional function, which looks at first like a strengthening of the appeal, may be its source of weakness. To begin with, it is probably not the nature of history itself, but the compulsion to find a uniform validation for it in the Bible which produces the violent disunity existing, as we have seen, among theologians in their understanding of history. In addition, the adequacy of this biblical basis is seriously shaken once biblical scholars begin to find substantial areas within the Bible itself where this basis is notably lacking. Most importantly, anyone who is anxious that all the variety of the biblical witness should find expression in our theology must feel some concern lest other axes through the biblical material, just as important as revelation through history, may be suppressed by the predominance now customarily accorded to the latter.

To say this does not mean that we are trying to get rid of the idea of revelation through history. This idea is, I believe, a fair expression of a really important element in the Bible; there really is a *Heilsgeschichte,* a series of events set within the plane of human life and in historical sequence, through which God has specially revealed himself. I would not doubt that we have been generally right in saying that this can be taken as the central theme of the Bible, that it forms the main link between Old and New Testaments, and that its presence and importance clearly marks biblical faith off from other religions. I do feel, however, that there are other axes through the biblical material which are equally pervasive and important, although they may not be so comforting apologetically. And I also feel that our apologetic situation in relation to the world outside of theology is changing, so that the value of an orientation to history may alter.

For another axis through the biblical material I shall cite only one example (though I think there are yet others which could be considered). It is a matter upon which I have already touched: the axis of direct verbal communication between God and particular men on particular occasions. Such direct communication is, I believe, an inescapable fact of the Bible and of the Old Testament in particular. God can speak specific verbal messages, when he wills, to the men of his choice. But for this, if we follow the way in which the Old Testament represents the incidents, there would have been no call of Abraham, no Exodus, no prophecy. Direct communication from God to man has fully as much claim to be called the core of the tradition as has revelation through events in history. If we persist in saying that this direct, specific communication must be subsumed under revelation through events in history and taken as subsidiary interpretation of the latter, I shall say that we are abandoning the Bible's own representation of the matter for another which is apologetically more comfortable.

And here I want, if I may use an inelegant phrase, to call a particular bluff. It has been frequently represented to us in modern times that there is a "scandal" in the idea of revelation through history, and that the acceptance of it is something seriously difficult for the modern mind, including that even of theologians. The contrary seems to me to be obviously the case. Although there is much disagreement about the nature of history, almost all theologians, as we have seen, accept the idea of revelation through history in some form. The surest way to scandalize them, indeed, is to make them think that you are going to question this idea. All our theological students accept it without much difficulty. Church education materials inculcate it. The reason why we use it so much is the very reverse: far from being a central stumbling block to our minds, it is something we use because it is a readily acceptable idea within our theological situation; thus it is one which, in our use of the Bible, enables us to mitigate the difficulty of elements which are in fact infinitely more scandalous, elements such as the direct verbal communication of which I have just been speaking, or prophetic prediction, or miracles.

One of the positive features that may follow from all this is a call to theology to explore the implications of the biblical material, theologically, along a greater variety of axes and directions. In considering this matter of direct verbal communication from God, which has much interested me recently, I have been struck by the meagerness of the help afforded by discussion from modern dogmaticians. The same is true if we try to work from the wisdom literature. But the gap seems to me to be most troublesome at the point of one of the most important of all Old Testament elements, namely, prophecy itself. On this subject traditional theology spent a lot of thought, much of it laughable as it would seem to us now, but modern theology has really failed to give us any lead along lines that come near to the biblical representation of the matter.[5] These are only some examples; but in general I would say that theology has to explore them and use them more fully—or else admit that in not doing so it is using an apologetical and theologically critical selectivity in relation to the biblical material. Which of these approaches is better for theology is one of the questions which will have to be answered.

Let us turn now to what I have called the apologetic situation, the contacts of our modern western theology with the world around us. Here I suggest there are certain elements which make the revelation through history formula, helpful as it has been, likely to be less helpful in the future, so that an awareness of our situation, as well as the influence of biblical fact, may be calling us to advance to new positions.

Historical science is no longer the chief leader and explorer in the mental environment which surrounds us and challenges us, as was the case in the nineteenth century. The modern phenomenon is the rise of sciences like the social sciences, anthropology, economics, linguistics (to mention a group from which at least one or two will increasingly influence biblical studies); their methods are only in part historical; and they show us that human life (or "historical existence" as we with our historical bias so often call it) can be and must be studied with trans-historical as well as with historical approaches. We can expect that challenges to Christian faith will arise from this newer world of thought: they will be quite different from those to which we have so far adjusted ourselves. For these challenges our present biblical and theological answers may not be relevant. There is, then, a real danger that revelation through history may furnish us with a reasonably good apologetic in relation to the questions raised in the nineteenth century, but not in relation to those which are likely to arise in the later twentieth.

There is, moreover, a question of the history of theology which is also relevant apologetically. A theology which organizes itself too exclusively around the idea of revelation through history has some difficulty in establishing its own continuity and identity, in this respect, with earlier stages of the church. For it is certain that our forefathers, emphatically as they understood that Christian faith was implanted in earthly reality, in space and time, flesh and blood, were able to do this without accepting "history" as an organizing bracket in their theology at all.[6] And the fact that they could do so, and that this memory still lives on in the popular understanding of what Christianity is, is an important reason why the insistence upon history, which to the theologian has seemed to be so attractive an apologetic, to the undecided layman and the world outside has continued to seem a somewhat irrelevant one. The maintenance of adequate relations of continuity, positive or negative, with the theology of the past is an essential aspect of apologetic. The history of theology and the consciousness of the marginal laity alike make difficult, therefore, the elevation of the category of history into a completely regulative and unchallengeable one for all future theology.

Further, an ecumenical point. This last year has seen the accession into the World Council of Churches of greatly increased numbers from the Eastern Orthodox Churches. Now nothing is more common in the West than to say that the Eastern Church is woefully deficient in a sense of history as the field of God's action. If such be the case it may well be the task of the Western churches to remind the East of the importance of history. But a great deal depends on the way in which we do this. The task has to be undertaken with a certain humility and sense of vulnerability, for we should not feel that in "history" we are in possession of a divinely-given category of unexceptionable and incomparable authority, validated by the unbroken testimony of the Bible. It may be that, much as the East has to gain from our emphasis on history, their less historically-oriented theology may represent biblical (and Hebraic!) elements which find difficulty in gaining expression in our western schemes.

Finally, a missionary point. In meeting the other religions of the East our modern theology has concentrated its apologetic argument very greatly upon the lack of a historical core, and so of an eschatological perspective, within these religions. Thus the weakness and the need within such religious situations is (it is supposed) one which will be healed or filled by the emphasis upon history as the medium of revelation within Christianity. Therefore a chief ground of commendation of Christian faith among eastern peoples comes to be the argument that it offers a sense of historical reality which eastern religions do not have. In such situations we expect that the growing Christian communities will distinguish themselves specially by their emphasis upon history and their understanding of it, by the production of a way of life of distinctively historical character.

But here again I feel that biblical evidence should make us more cautious. How do we know that this history-centered apologetic is not yet another case of cultural imperialism from the West, seeking to impose its own historical dynamism, using biblical evidence in its favor, and guiding the biblical material into its own patterns? It may be that just here a different presentation may be called for, and one which may produce a more genuine dialogue with other religions, using terms in which they may have something to say and which, on the other hand, may encourage a form of Oriental Christianity which in its degree of commitment to the centrality of history is more distinctive from, and therefore more complementary to, our own.

These are questions enough for today. Perhaps if we think them through again we shall find that modern theology has been right, and that the centrality of revelation through history should remain as a permanently valid expression of the core of Christianity. But at any rate it should be re-examined, and for two main reasons. From an apologetic point of view it may not continue to be as salutary as we have thought it would be; and the belief that the idea had total and unqualified biblical sanction may prevent us from reassessing it properly as an apologetic instrument. From a biblical viewpoint it may lead to a suppression of other important aspects of biblical thought, and the high theological value set on revelation through history may discourage us from reassessing the biblical evidence. From any direction, it is in the best interest of church and theology that the question should be kept open.

NOTES

1. One could include here certain kinds of apologetic needed and effective mainly within Christianity itself; I have in mind particularly the argument with biblical fundamentalism. The idea of revelation through history has worked with some considerable effectiveness against fundamentalism, and this is a reason for its popularity and also for reluctance towards reassessing it. It remains true, on the other hand, that fundamentalism remains immensely strong in spite of the pressure which the revelation-through-history argument appears to its proponents to bring.

2. George Ernest Wright (Chicago: Henry Regnery, 1952), p. 103.

3. *Ibid.*, p. 104.

4. The acceptance of "history" as a regulative theological category within the Barthian theology seems to be an apologetic accommodation to modern thought. In this and in certain other respects Barthianism can be seen as a compromise theology in its relation to modern thought, in this regard differing in degree and not in kind from other modern theologies. Barthianism is distinctive in laying the greatest weight on the denial or concealment of this accommodation—a circumstance which only makes it more disillusioning when one finds it to be there nevertheless.

5. The priority of revelation through history has enabled modern biblical theology to continue, in its assessment of the prophets, essentially along the psychological lines developed during the liberal theology; their words are the thoughts of the prophets, meditating on history, and not words given to them by God as the biblical tradition states them. This is one of the aspects in which modern biblical theology remains liberal in method, a point acutely established (in general) by Langdon Gilkey in his article "Cosmology, Ontology, and the Travail of Biblical Language," in *Journal of Religion*, Vol. XLI (1961), pp. 194–205.

6. That the centrality of history in theology has brought about a radically new situation in important respects is well recognized by J. McIntyre, *The Christian Doctrine of History* (Edinburgh: Oliver and Boyd, 1957), p. 3.

Church History Explained

Sidney E. Mead

Beginning with a discussion of the discipline of history *per se*, Sidney E. Mead asserts that history is concerned to answer questions about the activities, ideologies and presuppositions of individuals, groups and eras of the past, particularly as these having bearing on the present. The historian's method is twofold—(1) establishment of facts and (2) interpretation —though at times these two aspects become difficult to distinguish. His interpretation of the past will be conditioned by his own presuppositions and ideology, which furnish him a principle of selectivity. Every historian, then, has his allegiances, and in this respect the Christian historian does not differ from the non-Christian historian. The peculiarity of church history is one of content, not of method or approach. But if "the church" is the subject matter of church history, it is not a subject matter which permits of facile definition— least of all in the context of pluralist America. Dr. Mead examines the practical or empirical definition of the content of church history, finds it wanting, and moves on to construct a definition of his own. Dr. Mead, a professor of church history at the Southern California School of Theology in Claremont, is the author of the recently published book *The Lively Experiment*, a collection of essays in the area of America's religious history. His article first appeared in the March 1963 *Church History*,* the journal of the American Society of Church History, and is reprinted by permission.

HISTORY AND church history are disciplines well entrenched in the schools. This means that church historians commonly have an unquestioned place in theological school faculties. Hence there is little incentive for them to become self-conscious or troubled about the reason-for-being either of the discipline or of themselves. Probably church history is al-

---

* Subscriptions c/o Guy S. Klett, 321 Mill Road, Oreland, Pennsylvania.

ways included in the curriculum more from habit than because there is an articulated rationale for it. I dare say that many church historians if asked the question "Why have church history in the curriculums" would reply in effect that its place is obvious, and if one cannot see the obvious it is hopeless to try to explain it to him.

But, as Charles A. Beard once said, "even the historian would be a strange creature if he never asked himself why he regarded these matters as worthy of his labor and love, or why society provides a living for him during his excursions and explorations."[1] I am not *that* strange, so I have asked myself those questions and pondered possible answers. What follows is my present formulation of my view of what church history is. Perhaps its presentation will suggest an answer to the question, "why have it in the curriculum."

One's answer to the question will of course be conditioned by his opinion of (1) the nature of the history of the historians both as to content and method; (2) how the peculiar nature of "church" history is to be defined—e.g., is it a peculiarity only of content, or is there also a peculiarity of approach; (3) the purpose of a theological school which exists primarily for the education and training of parish ministers; and (4) the best possible curriculum to achieve this primary aim.

Below I shall concentrate on the nature of history of the historians, and on how the peculiar nature of church history may be conceived. My views are of course affected by the peculiarities of my professional experience. I have worked exclusively in what is called "American church history," which today is oriented more in general American history than in church history—and one is not only known but conditioned by the company he keeps. Further, I have always taught in an interdenominational situation, which makes me the servant of all, subject to the scrutiny of all. This accounts for what irritated particularists have called my expertness in chameleonship.

In our society the university is the arbiter of learning and definer of the branches of knowledge. The branches of knowledge receive recognition as *disciplines* in the university by being organized into semi-autonomous departments—often staffed by semi-autonomous prima donnas. The one-time chancellor of the University of Chicago defined the University as an "agglomeration of entities connected only by a central heating system." The president of the University of California at Berkeley has defined a university faculty as a group of "independent entrepreneurs held together by a common grievance over parking!"[2]

Be that as it may—and is—history is one of the recognized disciplines of the University with such departmental status and some such characters.

I assume that one's intellectual quest, if it is to be effective, must take place—or at least begin—within one or more of the existing disciplines, usually, but not necessarily in a University. As University organization proliferates and increasingly dominates study we more and more face the danger that we will conventionalize knowledge, and sterilize education, by organizing it in such fashion that individuals may acquire a personal vested interest in perpetuating its existing but outmoded forms. Every Professor with tenure and every administrator bears constant watching as a potential menace to the continued advancement of learning.

I also assume that whatever church history may be, if church historians are to remain in the great conversation which characterizes the historical discipline, they must remain in dialogue with those in the University's departments of history. It follows that the church historian's view of the nature of written history must be recognizable as valid by at least a significant number of general historians. Therefore I shall speak first of the nature of the historian's history in a fashion that most professional historians will grant is an acceptable view though it is not theirs.

History originates in curiosity about the past. Where there is no such curiosity there can be no historical quest, and little appreciation of the nature of historical studies and their place in a curriculum. To make a plea for history before such an audience would be an example of casting pearls before swine.

Where such curiosity exists it is manifested in questions. The type question is, "how did this present come to be out of the past?"—or, if you wish, "how did I, or we, or they, get *that* way?" The first step to understanding any written history is to ascertain what question the author intended to answer. Book reviewers who do not begin here commonly criticize an author for not writing the kind of book the reviewer thinks he would have written. Because the questions of a period grew out of that period's interests, the questions asked by historians change with changing times. The history written in one era may not interest the people of a following era because they are no longer interested in the same questions. And in history as elsewhere, nothing is as useless as the answer to an unasked question. This suggests a basic reason why histories have continually to be rewritten. It also suggests that the reason why some courses in history seem dull to the students is that they are not interested in the questions the professor is answering. Half the job in teaching history is in getting the students interested in the questions the professor deems important.

Commonly there is a practical reason for the questions. People want to know how they "got that way" in order to understand their present situation in such fashion as to suggest what they can and ought to do. As Carl Becker said, the "natural function of history" is to enable us to judge what we are doing "in light of what we have done and what we hope to do." Ralph Barton Perry stated it as the attempt "to conceive the thought of the past as truly as possible, and to connect it with the future through present analysis and appraisal." In this respect Abraham Lincoln is my ideal type of historian. He began the so-called "House divided" speech with the remark, "if we could first know where we are, and whither we are tending, we could better judge what to do, and how to do it." He then proceeded to an acute historical analysis of the immediate past in such fashion as to suggest where they then were and whither tending. And when this was persuasively presented, what they should do and how they should do it was clear. Jefferson, too, spoke in this vein when he argued that history ought to be included in the curriculum of the university because "History, by apprising . . . [the students] of the past, will enable them to judge of the future."

The corollary of what I have said is that every written history is essentially an assertion in the form of a thesis that constitutes an answer to a question about the past. The totality of such assertions constitutes the body of historical knowledge.

These assertions are made about three things.

First (only in order of mention) are assertions about the activities of people done in the past—about what people did and when and where they did it—for example, "Columbus sailed the ocean blue in fourteen-hundred-and-ninety-two."

Second are assertions about "ideology"—where the word "ideology" merely points to the content and way of thinking that characterizes an individual, or a group, or an era. These assertions about what the individual or group being studied thought he or they were doing are based upon inferences from what they said, and/or the artifacts they left. The actions of people are explained by pointing to the motives that lie back of them. The study of what people said they thought they were doing is the study of their conception of why they were doing it as they did—that is, of their motives. The ascertainment of motives is a chief goal of historical studies because our understanding of the people of the past depends upon our understanding of what motivated them. What the historian thinks motivated people is rooted in his conception of the nature of man. This consideration is very important in understanding the nature of historical interpretation.

Third are assertions about unquestioned presuppositions. A study of characteristic contents and ways of thinking leads always to presuppositions that lie behind the whole ideological structure. These are harder to get at than matters of ideology because, being assumed, they are seldom self-consciously defined and articulated. They are "obvious," and the statement of the obvious is one of the most difficult of intellectual achievements. But one never fully understands a person or a group until and unless one understands what he or they assume or presuppose and why they do so. To quote H. Richard Niebuhr,

> no movement can be understood until its presuppositions, the fundamental faith upon which it rests, have been at least provisionally adopted. The presuppositions may not be our own; we may find good reason for rejecting them in favor of others; but we cannot understand without occupy-

ing a standpoint, and there is no greater barrier to understanding than the assumption that the standpoint which we happen to occupy is a universal one, while that of the object of our criticism is relative.[3]

The historian makes assertions about these three aspects of human life—activities, ideology, presuppositions—in answer to the questions: What did they do? When and where did they do it? What did they think they were doing and why? What did they presuppose?

His context is the discipline of history which defines his method or approach. His method has two aspects.

First is the aspect of what are called "facts." The foundation of all historical work is the establishment of "facts." Granted the discipline of history, all acceptable historical knowledge consists in that which meets with the consensus of those trained to be in a position to judge when a "fact" has been established. This is to recognize the place of the specialist who has paid the price of disciplined study. A specialist will be acutely aware of the limitations of his knowledge. Hence he may appear to be at a disadvantage when confronted with the critic of his findings—as he not infrequently is—who says in effect, "I do not know much about this period, but it seems to me. . . ." A New England minister gave the specialists a ready made answer when he told such a critic, "I cannot permit your ignorance, however vast, to take precedence over my knowledge, however limited."

The historian's "facts" have their peculiar character. The assertions about activities, ideology, and presuppositions which make up the sum of historical knowledge, are to be seen on a continuum. At one end, let us say the left, are those assertions upon which there is no consensus whatsoever. At the other end are those assertions upon which there is complete consensus.

Commonly when we refer to "facts" we have in mind those assertions that lie well toward the right end of the continuum. But we must keep in mind that there are no matters forever settled and beyond question in historical knowledge. There is no finality about any of the assertions. This is to say that so far as the nature of the knowing is concerned there is no fence separating an area of settled "facts" from an area of "interpretations." So far as the way of knowing is concerned, historical knowledge is all of a piece whether one is talking about *when* Lincoln was born or *why* Booth shot him. It is all based on inferences from "remains," or, if you prefer, the interpretation of sources.

The second aspect of the historian's method is that of interpretation. An interpretation is an assertion about some aspect of the past stated in terminology meaningful to the historian's contemporary audience. Insofar as the historian's world-view differs from the world-view of the people being studied, an interpretation is a translation of a past ideology into contemporary ideology. For example we refer to dates "B.C."

Granted the desirability of maintaining a sense of continuity with the past—and this is a necessary presupposition for historical work—it is maintained by interpreting the past in such fashion that it can be sympathetically understood and appropriated by contemporary minds. Whatever in the past cannot thus be translated into contemporary ideology can be no part of contemporary historical knowledge. Hence the historian at difficult points is always tempted literally to *create* a past. This is sometimes called "conjectural interpolation."

Interpretation of course takes place in a modern mind, characterized by presuppositions and ideology largely absorbed from the dynamic community in which that mind has been nurtured. Primarily here is a conception of the final outcome or end of the story. As A. N. Whitehead said,

> The historian in his description of the past depends on his own judgment as to what constitutes the importance of human life. Even when he has vigorously confined himself to one selected aspect, political or cultural, he still depends on some decision as to what constitutes the culmination of that phase of human experience and as to what constitutes its degradation.[4]

Thus the historian's value system directly conditions his historiography—something some historians have been reluctant to admit—by giving him a selective principle. He picks from the past what will bring his story to the culmination to which he is committed.

The historian is selective in another sense. A history cannot be a description of every detail of all the past or of any small part thereof—even one hour. One of the canons of the historians is that

> every written history . . . is a selection of facts made by some person or persons and is ordered or organized under the influence of some scheme of reference, interest, or emphasis . . . in the thought of the author or authors.[5]

The historian's selection of what to emphasize in the past depends upon his conception of the end and culmination of the story he wishes to tell—which story is itself selected from a practically infinite number of possible stories. A comparison of the histories of religious or political developments in America will make this clear.

When the story being told comes down to the historian's present the culmination of his story must be an imaginative projection into the future—his conception of the shape of things to come. As has been said, "what is basic in that history involves a reference to its predicted outcome." But what is found in the present

> is not yet fully worked out. Rather, the present suggests what will eventuate in times to come. Thus we understand what is basic in a history in terms of some . . . 'present tendency' directed toward the future.

Because "the present is full of such tendencies; it suggests many different possible futures" and different tendencies appeal to different people. "The historian selects one of these possible futures . . . and uses it as a principle by which to select what is basic among the multitude of facts at his disposal."

This selection "necessarily involves a certain choice of allegiance, an act of faith in one kind of future rather than another"—a betting that this particular tendency will prove dominant tomorrow. But because the historian is himself a part of the history-that-happens, "to say that a principle of selection is [thus] 'chosen' does not mean that such choices are arbitrary. Men do not arbitrarily 'choose' their allegiances and faiths, even when they are converts." Rather "their faiths are . . . forced upon them." This is to say that "the history-that-happens itself generates the faiths and allegiances that furnish the principles for selecting what is important in understanding it."[6]

This situation is inherent in the nature of historical knowledge and written history. The historian attempts to note what people did and to explain why they did it. Insofar as he has no explanation there can be no *history* of that event. To say that a choice was "arbitrary" is just another way of saying that it is inexplicable. And what is inexplicable cannot be a part of historical knowledge.

It follows from these considerations that every written history is at least implicitly an explanation and defense of the allegiance—the faith—of the historian. It points to that to which the historian is committed. In this respect the Christian historian does not differ from the non-Christian historians. His conflict with them, if any, is a conflict of allegiances—of faiths—and should be recognized as such. This means that the basic differences between historians—or between schools of historians—are theological and/or philosophical and cannot be resolved by historical methods. This suggests at least that theology *is* "the Queen of the sciences," the final arbiter between the claims of the several disciplines and between the schools within disciplines.

It also follows from the conception of history I have adumbrated that the historical interpretation of the past by a modern mind is a pushing toward a more and more complete understanding of the forces that have shaped that mind and made it what it is. In this sense the goal of historical study is self-knowledge. I cannot conceive of self-understanding except as an understanding of how we came to be what we are, or of how I got "that way." It is this kind of self-knowledge that to my mind is of the essence of human freedom. For one is about as much the slave of the forces that have shaped him—that is, of his past—as he is ignorant of them—or of it. Only insofar as one is consciously aware of the dynamic forces within the culture in which he has been nurtured, as a fish is in water, is he freed to make intelligent choices regarding them. Indeed, once he has achieved such awareness he is forced to exercise choice. I suppose this is the reason why some have spoken of "terrible freedom." It is terrifying because to be free means to have to make decisions, and the responsibility for making decisions of significance for their own lives or for the lives of others terrifies many people.

Such freedom comes even when the awareness is of those aspects of experience which cannot be controlled or escaped —what Herbert Butterfield calls "the system of necessity" or of Providence within which we live and have our being. It used to be said that you could take the boy out of the country, but you could not take the country out of the boy. Similarly I suppose the born and bred Methodist may take himself out of the Methodist Church, but the chances are that the Methodism will never be completely taken out of the man even though his investments turn out well and he becomes a Presbyterian or Episcopalian. Thus at least one aspect of one's freedom is a self-conscious awareness of and reconciled attitude toward those aspects of his self and culture which he cannot escape. This, I take it, is what Margaret Fuller had grasped when she exclaimed, "I accept the universe." And Carlyle was probably not disagreeing with her, but only chiding her for the lateness of this insight in her life, when he snapped, "Gad, she'd better!"

So much for my conception of the nature of the history of the historians and some of the implications of this view.

In this context, how is the unique nature of *church* history to be defined?

Granted the views sketched above, it ought to be anticipated that to my mind the peculiarity of church history is one of content and not of method or approach. As the title implies, the peculiar subject-matter is "the church." This does not mean that the problem is simple because, as Professor James Hastings Nichols once put it, the basic problem for church historians today is "What and where is 'the church'?" One cannot escape this problem by conceiving of Christianity as a movement and saying he will write of the Christian movement. For "Christian" is no easier to define than "church"—and anyway the one is inextricably bound up with the other.

How then shall the peculiar subject-matter of church history be defined?

It may be defined empirically or practically. Because church history is a well established discipline the budding church historian is nurtured in the context of a generally accepted or routine definition of its content as exemplified, for example, in the text-books (in America, especially Williston Walker's). Broadly this includes all the outward, observable, and institutionalized manifestations of the Christian movement in the history-that-happens. The study presumably includes all those individuals and groups that have called themselves, or been called by others, "Christian."

The study must be serious, and begin with the realization that it may affect one's conception of "the church" and of what is "Christian." The historian cannot begin in a vacuum. He begins with *some* conception of what the church is (or is not)—probably what scholars disdainfully refer to as "a popular understanding." And as it is the business of education to violate intellectual innocence, so it is the business of disciplined history to correct the misunderstandings and distortions of popular history. It is this serious willingness to accept whatever results, or lack of results, the application of accepted methods yields which constitutes the historian's "objectivity." Objectivity is not disinterested spectatorship in the historian any more than it is in the detective or lawyer. It is acceptance only of what can be "proved" in the court.

But church historians themselves may continue to operate within the context of traditional and popular understandings of the nature of "the church." *We* have inherited the discipline of church history. Historically the discipline was shaped largely in the European situation which made it plausible to accept an institutional entity called "the church" and relatively minor entities called "sects" or "dissenters." The difference between them was that the former was considered to be the mainstream of true Christianity and the latter aberrations which if suppressed or ignored long enough would disappear. Hence the traditional categories of church history are "church," "dissenter," "sect,"—"Christian," "heretic," "schismatic."

But the proliferation of religious groups in the modern world, and especially in America under religious freedom, has made any one group's claim to be *the* only institutionalized incarnation of "the body of Christ" absurd. So today the doleful saint of many church historians is Mary Magdalene, and with her they lament, they have taken away my Lord's body and I know not where to find it. It is for this reason that the content of church history has for many become vague and indefinite, while those who tend to solve such problems by "whistling in the dark" have tended to become increasingly narrow and dogmatic in asserting what that content is. A widespread conclusion of the former is clearly stated by William Alva Gifford in his *The Story of the Faith: A Survey of Christian History for the Undogmatic:*

> I have described the twentieth century only in terms of forces and tendencies in religious life and thought; for the 'Christian Church' has strictly ceased to exist. In its place are 'churches,' very many of them, and each with a history of its own. This is especially true in the United States. The history of Christianity there is now the history of denominations, to be written in a multitude of monographs. This is not my undertaking.[7]

Mr. Gifford's conclusion is reflected in the way church history is commonly presented in the seminaries of the United States. A survey of church history carries the student down through the Reformation, or perhaps into the seventeenth century. This survey is followed by a course in the history of his particular denomination's development in America. The implication would seem to be that that denomination is the direct and/or only significant continuation of "the church" in history, so the two or three hundred other denominations may safely be ignored.

It is because of this kind of breakdown of the traditional definition of the content of church history that church historians are being prodded into asking questions about the ideal nature and content of their discipline. This means that they are being forced to consider these matters theoretically—as is always the case when routine breaks down. The practical or empirical definition of content no longer fits the actualities of the situation in which they must do their work. This pushes them into speculation about the relationship between their observed and their conceptual orders.

I suggest the following theoretical considerations.

The church historian works within the context of the whole theological tradition of Christendom. This tradition exemplifies the ways in which Christians have conceived and articulated the meaning of Christianity for Christians, and have tried to explain it to, or defend it against, non-Christians. The study of that tradition is the study of the ideology and presuppositions of the people called "Christian."

The overwhelming consensus of Christians has been and is that "the church" is one body—that it is a continuous and dynamic organic unity in history. It is, Christians have said, one in the mind and intent of God; it is one in the mystical unity of the individual believers with Christ the head; and it is one in cherishing and perpetuating the faith under the guidance of the Spirit. This is a simple descriptive, historical assertion.

In this context the appealing practical solution suggested by Mr. Gifford is theoretically inadequate and unsatisfactory.

I think the church historian may assert wherein the unity of his subject-matter consists in a way that will enable him to remain in the great conversation with general historians on the one hand, and the Christian tradition on the other. At least I have not yet been kicked out of the "secular" historians' fraternity—which is perhaps an exemplification of their Christian charity. In fairness I should add that once upon a time an eminent church-historian looked me in the eye and declared, "Strictly speaking, there is no *American* Church history, is there!"—thus consigning me-as-career to oblivion.

History is thinking about, and the study of, the *meaning* of the past to the historian's present. The historian thinks of meaning in terms of events and their consequences. Hence, for example, we say that as more and more consequences of the decision for religious freedom in the United States unfold in the history-that-happens, we more and more clearly understand the meaning of that event.

I suppose that the central event of church history—and for that matter, of the history of Western civilization—is the career of Jesus of Nazareth. Historically we understand its meaning in terms of its unfolding consequences. Hence theoretically considered, the content of church history has to do with the consequence of the career of Jesus. No self-conscious person in Western civilization can avoid taking some of these consequences into account, even in such a simple act as setting the date for the next committee meeting. Jesus Christ, as Ralph Waldo Emerson said, is "plowed" into our experience, that is, into the ground the historian cultivates.

The most tangible, ever-present manifestation of these consequences in our American society is the institutions we call denominations. Not only in profession but also in actuality, these are the outstanding observable consequences in our day of the career of Jesus.

However well or adequately these institutions manifest the real or true meaning of Jesus Christ in history is, of course, a moot question. But the only basis for adjudicating this question is itself to be found only in what these institutions have brought to us on the stream of history. The fact that the question inevitably comes, suggests that almost everyone thinks there is some guiding or normative standard carried within these institutions that can be invoked. The most common criticism of the churches is that they do not live up to their heritage and profession. But from whence did the critic learn what the profession and heritage are except from the churches?

Here is suggested a theoretical justification for the church historian beginning with a routine view of the content, form, and general structure of church history as defined for him by the discipline. In America he should begin where he is, by studying the denominations as they are.

This is to say that the beginning of the study is neither to identify nor to prove the existence of "the church" in the history-that-happens, but to assume that it is there all the time. The God of Abraham, Isaac, and Jacob—the Father of the Lord Jesus Christ—is never without His people. To identify it, or them, is a goal, not the starting point of the study. And it seems reasonable to suppose that the application of historical methods to the study of the institutions that throughout all of Christendom's history have claimed, or have been thought to be, "the church" will result in the pouring into the earthen vessel of the historian's understanding a more excellent conception of what and where the true church was, and is, and ought to be. In this sense the study of "church" history resolves itself into the study of the meaning of the actual and visible church—just as the study of the history of the United States resolved itself into the study of the meaning of the United States in history.

It is for this reason that every historian of "the church" ought ideally to be a practicing, responsible member of a denomination. It is this existing "church" *as is* that he ought to be trying to understand, and to help to a self-understanding of itself by reminding it of how it came to be what it is. And how can he know what it is in fact if he is not responsibly in it?

What he thinks the church is from his experience in it is the beginning point of his study. No one could begin the study either of the church or of the United States without some conception of their purpose to which he is committed. This is to say that the historian begins with an allegiance to one of perhaps several conceivable ends or culminations of his story of the church. It is this commitment which provides the unity to his work. Confronted empirically with all the divisions and diversities of the church (or of the United States), it is only in the projection of an ideal outcome that he can see the diversity as a unified whole. Insofar he cannot escape a consideration of "last things."

This is why it can be said that what one sees as important in the past depends upon what he wills to prevail in the future. Conversely, the surest clue to what a person really wants to prevail in the future is what he thinks is significant in his past. A historian's church, therefore, is the company of those past and present, dead and living, who have willed and do will to prevail what he does. For the Christian the church is the company of those who have willed with Jesus "Thy kingdom come, Thy will be done, on earth as it is in heaven." Christians have and do differ, not on this but on the meaning of "Thy kingdom come, Thy will be done"—that is, on what is God's will and what is His Kingdom; and on how one knows the will of God; and on how one is able, or enabled, to will that it may be done.

Within this broad context I have my own view of the peculiar nature of the church in America, and hence of the nature of American Church history.

I begin with the statement of a common working hypothesis—borrowed from no matter where—that "religion is the substance of culture and culture the form of religion." I then suppose that the religion of which our American culture (insofar as we have one) is the form, is the Judeo-Christian. This supposition is plausible because this culture as such has no pre-Christian past.

It is implied in the hypothesis that all the tangible manifestations of our culture in the flowing robe of events somehow point to their source in the Judeo-Christian religion. In it we live and move and have our being as "Americans." Therefore our American minds find no solid foundation for the intellectual quest to understand who and what we are until they are somehow oriented to that religion.

Thus beginning with the hypothesis that a culture is the form of a religion, and that the religion of which our culture is the form is the Judeo-Christian, the content of my history of that religion in America is potentially inclusive of everything that is or can be known about the origins and development of the American way of life. Theoretically everything is grist for my little mill. Actually in practice, as suggested above, I begin, and sometimes end, with those institutions and individuals commonly recognized as "Christians." But I would always leave the way open to the possibility, for example, that at one juncture of the history the religion was more truly given form in Abraham Lincoln, who claimed and was claimed by no existing denomination, than by any institution then or now commonly called "Christian." I would do this for the same reason—as I understand it—that Jesus told some of the churchmen of his day that the prostitutes and tax-collectors would enter into the Kingdom of God before them.

In the discussion of history above, I noted the place of presuppositions. In the present context, the presuppositions of our American culture have to do with a Judeo-Christian view of the existence and nature of God; the nature and structure of the universe; and the nature and destiny of man. Therefore, one of the surest clues to the presuppositions on which the ideological structure of our culture is built is to be found in the systematic theologies, the creeds and confessions of our churches. For example, all the creeds assert "I (or we) believe in God." What does this mean intellectually? I think it means, on the one hand, that we presuppose in all our thinking that God exists—that is, that we presuppose in all our thinking that there is order and purpose in the universe ascertainable in part and one way or another by man. On the other hand it means that we presuppose that the universe does not exist absolutely but is contingent—which is to say that Christians do not worship the universe, or America, or anything created, but only God the creator.

There is a sense in which we discover order through our intellectual efforts. But our intellectual quest itself was launched from the hypothesis that there is order to be discovered and used, that is, with belief in God.

Further, all the creeds assert belief in the incarnation—that is, that God assumed human form *in* history in the being who was very God and very man. Assuming that God is eternal, this means, to me, that once in history, God is always in history. Hence the study of the history-that-happens is always somehow the study of the works of God in history—and by his works we shall know Him, though now we see only through a glass darkly. The perceptive historian sees what Whitehead called "the eternal greatness incarnate in the passage of temporal fact." And in this sense church history is a continuous meditation on the meaning of the incarnation.

Because these matters may either be apprehended and accepted by faith and celebrated in worship, or presupposed as the foundation for the intellectual quest, they ideally bind faith and reason together inextricably. In an integrated Christian civilization the faithful worship of God in the churches would be a declaration of the primary presuppositions that are the foundations of its intellectual life, and the sacrament would be a constant reminder that God is eternally everpresent among those people, in history.

In summary, then, if the religion of which our American culture is the form is the Judeo-Christian, what the historian discovers to be the presuppositions on which its ideology rests ought to be the "metaphysical intuitions" that are apprehended by faith in our churches; articulated in their creeds and confessions; lifted up in worship; and remembered in the sacrament. And in this case we would expect the speculative historian's intellectual quest to lead him to greater and greater appreciation of what the churches have been all about. To my mind this expectation is somewhat borne out by what has happened to, in, and among notable so-called "secular" students of American intellectual, cultural, and social history during the past thirty years. Their work intimates that they have begun to see and to acknowledge the soil in which the presuppositions of this society are rooted. Meanwhile some scholars within the churches seem to be engaged in torpedoing the presuppositions upon which such rapprochement might begin. As the intellectual quest of those historians disdainfully labeled "secular" brings them closer and closer to the church, some men within the church seem to be advocating that the church beat a "strategic retreat," burning the intellectual bridges between them and the "secularists" behind them.

I would prefer to try to meet the advancing "secularists" half way and wish I were better equipped to do so. At present I can only say that it seems to me that Christians in their churches assert in faith and in figurative language that human history is a meaningful story with beginning, middle, and end —knowable and known in part by man but known completely and ultimately only to God (that is, human history is contingent). The assertion that human history is a meaningful story makes the intellectual quest worthwhile. The assertion that only God knows the final end of the story means that all human constructions of segments of it are limited and tentative. As Herbert Butterfield put it, all histories, even church histories, are but interim reports on the way things look to the author here and now. Hence, while there is never complete assurance of the happy or successful outcome of the story given to man, neither can there be complete despair of the outcome. Complete pessimism and complete optimism are both heresies. This in turn means that men must live by faith in the God of the living—that is, the God of those living in history.

And here is a further comment on the historian's pathway to freedom. For granted the assumption that it is the Judeo-Christian religion that has informed our culture, the end of the historian's intellectual quest to understand who and what we most profoundly are must lead him to the basic precepts of that religion which as Christians we may and do apprehend in faith and celebrate in worship. In either case we arrive at the fullest self-understanding which is our fullest freedom. On these suppositions the paths of both our intellectual and our religious quests lead us to the same point. To the Christian both paths lead to the God preeminently revealed in Jesus Christ, the author of his faith *and* the Lord of all his history. Whichever path he takes implies that he believes that at its end he shall know himself as he is now known only by his Creator. His assertion in faith is a declaration of the primary presupposition of his intellectual quest—"Now my knowledge is imperfect, but then I shall know as fully as God knows me" (I Cor. 13:12).

NOTES

1. Charles A. Beard, "Written History as an Act of Faith," *American Historical Review,* XXXIX (Jan. 1934), p. 222.

2. Clark Kerr in a letter to the editor, *Saturday Review* (Oct. 20, 1962), p. 73.

3. H. Richard Niebuhr, *The Kingdom of God in America* (Chicago: Willett, Clark & Company, 1937), pp. 12–13.

4. Alfred North Whitehead, *Adventures of Ideas* (New York: The Macmillan Company, 1933), p. 4.

5. "Theory and Practice in Historical Study: A Report of the Committee on Historiography," (New York: Social Science Research Council, Bulletin 54, 1946), p. 135.

6. John H. Randall, Jr., and George Haines, IV, "Controlling Assumptions in the Practice of American Historians" in *Ibid.*, pp. 20–21.

7. William Alva Gifford, *The Story of the Faith: A Survey of Christian History for the Undogmatic* (New York: The Macmillan Company, 1946), p. vii.

The Reformation in Recent Roman Catholic Theology

Per Erik Persson

No longer are defenders of the Roman Catholic faith inclined to claim that the Reformation came about largely as a result of Martin Luther's desire to justify his own sensuality. Today Catholic scholars, particularly in Germany and France, are busily laying such caricatures to rest and are even saying that there are elements of the Reformation which the Roman Church can and should affirm. Such is the thesis that Per Erik Persson documents in his essay, which first appeared in the Winter 1963 issue of the quarterly journal of theology called *Dialog*.* In that issue, devoted mainly to Reformation themes, an editorial writer asserts that those seeking the reunion of the separate branches of Christendom must sometimes go backward before they can go forward. "In going back to the sources of our common history and in re-examining the causes of our mutual divisions, we discover that certain myths get exploded. The debunking of menacing myths is one of the most salutary effects of historical scholarship." Touching on the current myth-debunking on the part of Catholic scholars —the subject of Persson's essay—the editor describes it as "an exciting drama of radical honesty which shames Protestants not equally zealous to part with their fondest falsifications of the other side." Dr. Persson is Professor of Systematic Theology at the University of Lund, Sweden. Parts of his article appeared in different form in the *Svensk Teologisk Kvartal Skrift*, 33, 3, 1957.

IF WE turn to Roman Catholic scholarship to find out how much it has helped to increase our knowledge of what happened at the time of the Reformation and pri-

* 315 Fifth Avenue S., Minneapolis 15, Minnesota.

marily of Luther himself, I think we could say that, ever since the disastrous events of the sixteenth century, its work has pursued a line firmly drawn by the confessional struggle. The Reformation has simply been labeled as "heresy" and as such it has been removed from the topics of discussion; on the whole it has not been regarded as a theological problem of fundamental importance to the church. Almost without exception the great surveys of church history as well as special monographs have been characterized by a one-sided and often hateful polemic.

During the last two decades, however, a striking change has taken place in this area, primarily within German and French Roman Catholic theology. This deserves our fullest attention because of its decisive significance for the current inter-confessional conversations. Since it is impossible to draw a full picture of this in an article, we will have to restrict ourselves to the language areas just mentioned, where, in any case, we find the new aspects of importance to this on-going discussion.

In starting with German theology, we must first say something about the background against which we must view the new orientation. The traditional Roman Catholic view of Luther and the Reformation received a clear and comprehensive expression in the two monumental works on the reformer which appeared at the beginning of this century and caused much heated discussion during the next decades. In spite of its limitations the most important one was written by Heinrich Denifle, a Dominican, and given the title *Luther und Luthertum in der ersten Entwicklung quellenmässig dargestellt* (Luther and Lutheranism in its Early Development as Shown by Original Sources). The first volume of 860 pages was published in 1904, and in 1909 it was followed by a second volume, completed after Denifle's death by Albert Maria Weiss, who belonged to his same order. Denifle had previously established himself as a prominent medieval scholar. With his indisputable knowledge of medieval tradition and by mobilizing an enormous number of texts, he wanted primarily to trace clearly the development of the young Luther into the reformer. Let us add parenthetically that this provided a great impetus for Luther scholarship to turn to the young Luther.

It must be said, however, that the objectivity and impartiality exhibited by Denifle on medieval material is completely absent here. By a tendentious selection of sources and often remarkable misinterpretation he set forth the following conclusions: 1) The so-called Reformation was partly founded on Luther's lack of knowledge of classical medieval theology, especially of Thomism. 2) The development of the Reformation is mainly to be seen as a result of Luther's unbridled sensuality (thus Luther's doctrine is characterized as being "more sarcology than theology," and the work is filled with rude attacks against Luther's carnal passion and drunkenness. 3) To make his atrocious way of living seem righteous Luther invented his doctrine of justification which made it possible for him to give free rein to his unbridled behavior. This work was received with enthusiasm in the Roman Catholic world, and there is an echo of Denifle's theses in the papal encyclical "Editae saepe" of 1910, in which the reformers are described as "presumptious and rebellious people . . . who were enemies of Christ's cross and had their stomachs as their god."

While Denifle's work was mostly concerned with the history of doctrine, which explains why it is still possible to find important observations in it, especially on the relationship between Luther and the Middle Ages, Jesuit Hartmann Grisar's three volumes of more than 2500 pages, published in 1911–1912 under the title *Luther*, are more of a psychological or rather psycho-pathological study. The work of the Reformation as well as Luther's doctrine are here explained from an analysis of the reformer's abnormal mentality, and in lengthy sections the necessary historical judgment with regard to the temporal situation is lacking. The tone here is different from that of Denifle; instead of his high-tempered attacks we are met by clear and cold repudiation. Luther stands forth as a man altogether deplorable and sick, governed by a pathological megalomania. The polemical tendency runs through the whole work, and this is true also of the comprehensive work published by Grisar in 1926, *Martin Luthers Leben und sein Werk* (Martin Luther's Life and Work).

From these late and wide offshoots of the bitter polemics through the centuries, where historical sources have been chosen in a prejudiced way according to their usefulness as weapons against what is being described, it is like entering another world when we come to the change visible during the last decades. Here church historian Joseph Lortz is epoch-making. In 1939–1940 he published his two-volume work *Die Reformation in Deutschland* (The Reformation in Germany), printed in a third edition in 1949. Lortz, then a church historian at Münster, has been since 1947 a professor of the history of Western religions on the philosophical faculty of the University of Mainz. He has carried forward his views through several series of lectures and his continuous preoccupation with the problems has also led to a series of smaller works. Among these we can mention *Die Reformation: Thesen als Handreichung bei ökumenischen Gesprächen* (The Reformation: Theses as a Help in Ecumenical Talks), *Die Reformation als religiöses Anliegen heute* (The Reformation as a Religious Concern of Today), and *Wie kam es zur Reformation* (How the Reformation Came About). In his main work as in the others Lortz speaks quite frankly of "reformation," whereas previous Roman Catholic accounts had used concepts like "schism," "apostasy," "heresy," or at least said "the so-called Reformation." The irenic tone in this work was also new. It marked a definite departure from the earlier use of only black and white paints and tried to apportion shades and light in a more correct way. Thus the state of the church at the end of the Middle Ages is depicted with a surprising openness. This is true with regard to the secularized papacy, the numerous and open abuses and the decadence of theology. From this Lortz concludes that the Reformation was historically necessary and he even speaks of the Catholic share of the guilt.

At the center of Lortz's history of the Reformation there stands, of course, Luther himself. The new evaluation and interpretation of the reformer that he gives is of decisive importance to the whole exposition. He firmly rejects Denifle's as well as Grisar's calumnies, and instead paints a picture of Luther as a *homo religiosus* whose reaction against the expressions of late medieval theology and piety was justified on the whole. Luther's theology of the cross, his trust in God, and his dependence on Scripture are also positively evaluated. Lortz also admits the fact that Luther did not actually aim to divide the church, and notices how Luther defended the objective character of the Word and the Sacraments against the "enthusiasts." According to Lortz, however, this objectivity was ultimately an inconsistency and self-deception, and here we reach his main critical objection against Luther. The real cause of the Reformation lies in the fact that Luther was subjectivistic to the core.

According to Lortz it is possible to maintain a real and true objectivity only if you accept the final and ultimate authority that rests in the teaching office of the church. Luther's fundamental subjectivism, contends Lortz, prevented him from a full hearing of the Bible, while, guided by his own experience, he allowed a fundamental Pauline thought to overshadow everything else. Seen from the perspective of evangelical theology, this is perhaps the most serious objection raised by Lortz. It has also caused a new discussion to occur on this point. At the same time we are inclined to ask whether a full hearing of the Bible does not finally coincide in Lortz's mind with a full hearing of the church and thus mean something else than it does to a Protestant theologian. Another important idea in Lortz's exposition is that the Reformation is regarded as a result of a mutual misunderstanding. On the one hand this consisted in the fact that Luther, by his one-sided schooling, was led to equate Catholicism as a whole with Occamist Scholasticism. The latter is regarded by Lortz as a rather insignificant but deplorable phenomenon of corruption. The Occamist theology was rightly criticized by Luther, but this criticism did not hit genuine and true Catholicism. But here we should like to raise the objection that it was because of this criticism of contemporary theology that Luther was driven out of the church. Also this was the form in which he met the theology of his church—he was never given the privilege of experiencing either the Counter-Reformation or neo-Thomism. On the other side, the fatal misunderstanding consisted in the fact that the church itself misunderstood Luther. Thus Lortz can speak of the papal bull of excommunication against Luther as a document that, although containing statements correct in themselves, unfortunately did not sufficiently understand Luther's deeply religious intentions. In this connection Lortz says of Luther's theological adversaries, especially Eck, that they were not equal to their important task but carried it through in a theologically unsatisfactory way. According to Lortz this also results in making the church an accessory in the guilt of the Reformation tragedy. To quote Lortz himself: "The Catholic side was particularly guilty in the fact that from the very beginning of the Reformation the genuinely religious concerns of the evangelicals were not taken seriously enough." (J. Lortz, *Die Reformation: Thesen als Handreichung bei ökumenischen Gesprächen*, p. 2).

Still more obvious is the positive evaluation of Luther in a work published in 1947 entitled *Luther in katholischer Sicht* (The Catholic View of Luther), whose author is Johannes Hessen, a philosopher of religion at Cologne. Among other things he repudiates Lortz's main thesis concerning Luther's subjectivism. Luther's basic experience was subjective only in form, while its content was as objective as possible—the reality of God. Hessen maintains that Luther is to be understood in the same manner as the prophets of the Old Testament. Luther fought his fight not against dogma or good works but against what Hessen summarizes by the terms Intellectualism, Moralism, Sacramentalism and Institutionalism. Hessen often reminds us of Adolf von Harnack in the way he evaluates Luther, and he often quotes Harnack. While admitting that Luther went too far in his struggle—and even to Hessen everything is finally focused in the question of the teaching office of the church—still he thinks that Luther's message is of guiding importance for contemporary Catholicism.

A number of other witnesses of this change in the view and evaluation of the Reformation could be mentioned. Let us cite only two or three examples. In his book *One and Holy* dogmatician Karl Adam strongly emphasizes that a conversation between the confessions will become fruitful only when the starting point is placed at the original dividing of the ways, namely, in Luther himself.[1] Occasionally we find him giving a positive interpretation to typical statements of the Reformation—something unthinkable before. This is the case also in Hans Urs von Balthasar's treatment of the Lutheran formula *simul iustus et peccator* at the end of his study on Barth (*Karl Barth: Darstellung und Deutung seiner Theologie*, 1951). The same thing can be found in Hans Küng's recent work comparing the theology of Karl Barth and Roman Catholic theology on the doctrine of justification (*Rechtfertigung: Die Lehre Karl Barths und eine Katholische Besinnung,* 1957). In an interesting study the well-known Jesuit, Erich Przywara, argues in behalf of several of the most important ideas of Evangelical Lutheran scholarship against Lortz's thesis concerning Luther's basic subjectivism (*Humanitas: Der Mensch gestern und Morgen,* 1952, p. 376 ff.).

At this point we can sum up two important things arising out of the development I have drawn. The first is a new and more positive attitude towards the Reformation and the reformers who are now interpreted as representing a valuable intention even for the church and theology of today. The second is the fact that by taking up the Reformation as an essential theological problem, and not simply setting it aside any longer, the Post-Tridentine theology, having been constricted by the negative attitude towards Protestantism, will itself appear as a problem—and this is true not least of the traditional view of Luther.

This idea has been underlined as firmly as possible by Adolf Herte, a Roman Catholic scholar, in a work just over 1000 pages entitled *Das katholische Lutherbild im Bann der Lutherkommentare des Cochläus* (The Catholic View of Luther under the Spell of Cochläus' Commentary on Luther), published as three volumes in 1943. With an enormous amount of bibliographical knowledge he shows how, with hardly any exceptions, Roman Catholic literature on Luther (monographs, church history texts, encyclopedia articles) in Europe even until Grisar has been dependent—in a way unparalleled in other historical writings—on Johannes Cochläus' hateful biography of Luther printed in 1549, *Commentarii de actis et scriptis Martini Lutheri* (Commentaries on the Acts and Writings of Martin Luther). In a straightforward manner Herte shows how Cochläus' ignoble accusations and stories about Luther's reasons for marriage and way of living have been uncritically used, directly and indirectly, as a main source for the description of the reformer's person and doctrine. Even in our own times they reappear in work after work in a way that, according to Herte, makes one blush with shame.

Cochläus' dominating influence is visible also in French literature, according to Herte's comprehensive study. A recent but influential example of this is the picture of Luther given for the first time in 1923 in the book called *Three Reformers*, by Jacques Maritain, one of the leading representatives of neo-Thomism. This book which dealt with Descartes and Rousseau as well as Luther was published again in 1947 with the text unaltered but enlarged with a number of interesting notes, in which the author carries on a discussion with German Luther scholars, predominantly Karl Holl. Possibly very few examples can be cited which are as filled by a deep disgust for the object of research as Maritain's presentation of Luther under the heading "The Elevation of the Ego." "Wrath, abuse, hatred and lie, love of beer and wine, obsession with indecency and obscenity . . . and always . . . with the good flavor of Christian liberty," are typical, according to Maritain, of this so-called reformer. In Luther's theology these things have their counterpart in an egocentricity without parallel, a metaphysical egoism where everything is circling around one's own self and where man saves himself by a convulsively enforced trust in Christ.

In 1950 there was published in Paris a work of the greatest importance in this connection, *Vraie et fausse réforme dans l'Église* (True and False Reform in the Church). The author, Yves M.-J. Congar, a Dominican known for his interest in ecumenical questions, is also one of the most influential theologians in recent European Catholicism. Behind this book of 650 pages there stands, says the author, twenty years of studying the Reformation and the theology of the reformers. If I may relate a personal experience in this connection: Some years ago I walked together with Father Congar in the cloister garden of a French monastery. Our conversation was about Luther's Christology—and the man at my side quoted by heart long passages from Luther's writings with which I, a theologian within the Lutheran tradition, was not acquainted! Father Congar's work mainly aims to define the conditions for a true reformation—considered essential for the church at all times—within the Roman Church itself. So he begins by discussing a number of reforms which were being proposed within the Roman Catholic Church in France after the war.

From the whole history of the church material is brought forth to illuminate the main question; but a large section deals with the division of the church in the sixteenth century and in that connection a thorough analysis is made of Luther's concept of the church. It is especially interesting that the sixteenth century Reformation is clearly referred to as something that has addressed and is still addressing the Roman Church with important questions—questions which have never been taken as seriously as they deserve by Roman theology. Just as with Lortz it is openly and clearly acknowledged that the Catholic Church shares the responsibility for the circumstances that produced the Lutheran Reformation. Congar also criticizes the theologians who defended Rome against Luther. He also gives his opinion that it is a task of decisive importance for today's theology to create a situation which, had it existed in the sixteenth century, would have prevented these unfortunate events. He also points to the unhappy consequences of the fact that the church in her apology has often accepted the opponent's false questions and then become negatively bound by them. As an example he mentions the discussion of the relation between church and Scripture. Then along with the heresy the legitimate part of the Reformation protest has been repudiated. He mentions such examples as when every form of lay preaching was discredited after the condemnation of the Waldenses, or when, because of Luther's exposition, Roman Catholic theologians for centuries ceased to work theologically with the idea of the priesthood of all believers.

Of great interest is the way in which Congar tries to work out systematically the conditions for a true reformation within the church. The church is a divine institution—and as such is infallible—but at the same time it consists of human beings—and as such it is subject to the possibility of making mistakes and errors of judgment, something which has been proved by history. Several times in this connection Congar speaks of the treatment which Galileo received. Thus the church is at the same time "saint and sinner," and both these aspects are real and concrete, conditions that are truly inside the church. The special problem of the Reformation arises from the fact that the church is involved in the changes of history where she is perpetually faced by two temptations, defined as that of the synagogue and of Pharisaism. The former danger occurs when the church refuses to accept the fact that she is put into a world of change where every new age asks new questions. The latter is the temptation to allow the ritual of the church and its other forms of expression to become an end in themselves instead of mere means. True reformation does not take place merely when abuses are abolished—this can be done simply enough through new and better ecclesiastical decrees—nor does it consist in the doctrinal revolution of Protestantism, but it takes place when, under the guidance of the church, we return to and enter deeply into the fountains of the tradition of the church. What is demanded is a doctrinal renewal which also answers today's questions by delving deeply into the innermost nature of Catholicism.

In every reformatory movement there is a twofold possibility: either it can become something good or, if it develops one-sidedly, it can become destructive, and thus for Congar control by the leaders of the church appears absolutely necessary. The author mentions four conditions that must be met to bring about a true reformation. 1) It must be carried through by love of the concretely existing church and stand in direct contact with actual life in the parishes. 2) It must have a firm intention of remaining within the communion of the church, however much it might be regarded with distrust at the beginning. 3) Because of this it must have patience and power to wait until the time is ripe. 4) Finally, the renewal must take place by a return to church tradition as a whole, and not by one-sidedly stressing one thought and playing it off against the others. According to Congar none of these conditions was met by Luther, and that is why his reformation in spite of everything was a false reformation. Congar's criticism of Luther can be said to be directed primarily at two things: first, Luther's one-sidedness, which is defined as a "unilateral Galatianism," *i.e.*, driving home one idea from the Letter to the Galatians. Congar maintains that Luther appears as a parallel of Marcion in the ancient church; Marcion also said he wanted to return the church to its original but did so by cutting off vital parts of tradition. The second criticism is against Luther's "spiritualistic" conception of the church which made him deny "the principle of the formal visibility of the church," its divinely established visible structure, manifested in the continuity of the office. At this point Lutheran scholars might raise considerable objection to interpreting Luther's view of the church as setting the "internal" and "invisible" over against the "external" and "visible" church. Luther's doctrine of the church seems to be one of the most difficult points for Roman Catholic theologians to understand. But it is useful to listen to Congar's criticism of the Protestant theologians who are often willing to speak of how the church must always be reformed but to whom such statements seem to be of only theoretical interest. The question is whether like the Pharisee in the temple we do not often settle down with what once happened in Luther's time, and then thank God that we are not like the Roman Church. A work such as Congar's invites us also to take the principle *ecclesia semper reformanda* seriously for ourselves.

Let us then turn to another French work which has the Reformation as its center of interest. It was published in 1954 and has the title *Du Protestantisme à l'Église* (*Spirit and Forms of Protestantism*, English translation). It was written by Louis Bouyer, at present a professor of church history at the Catholic Institute of Paris. The author himself, formerly a Protestant, has the ability, more than most Roman Catholic theologians, to understand the main thoughts of the Reformation as well as evangelical religious life from the inside. The main thesis of the book is somewhat startling at first, at least for a Roman Catholic reader. It maintains that Protestantism is Christian not to the extent that it departs from the Reformation but to the extent that it returns to what constituted its original intention. This thesis is confirmed and advanced further when in the first half of the book the author analyzes a number of the main thoughts of the Reformation. By summarizing the thoughts from Luther's chief reformatory treatises Bouyer tries to show how the foremost intention of the reformers was a fight for "grace alone" against all kinds of Pelagianizing synergism. But this is, according to the author, nothing else but what the Roman Church itself has maintained sharply, and this is demonstrated with the help of quotations from the Council of Orange in 529, Thomas

Aquinas and the Council of Trent. The same is also shown to be the case with the special Calvinist form of "grace alone," namely, the idea of the absolute sovereignty of God, *soli Deo gloria,* which is said to be equivalent to the motto of the Society of Jesus, *ad majorem Dei gloriam*—and here the author could have brought in Thomas Aquinas as well. In a later section a very positive description of the Lutheran concept of faith is given on the basis of Luther's explanation of the second article of the creed. Here the common misinterpretations found in other Roman Catholic theologians are absent. Even the Scripture principle of the Reformation is evaluated as a positive thesis directed not primarily against the Roman Church but against the "enthusiasts." Bouyer quotes St. Jerome's words that "ignorance of the Scriptures" is the same as "ignorance of Christ." He writes extensively about the high authority that his church accords to the Bible and hence can find nothing even on the Scripture principle that must necessarily separate Protestantism from Rome. In the next section Bouyer explains why the Reformation in spite of all this must nevertheless be rejected by the church. The reason is found to be in the negative definitions that Luther felt compelled to give in the last analysis. Out of the early Luther's positive concept of faith there came faith *alone;* the idea of God's sovereignty became associated with a negation of man's activity; and the principle of Scripture was turned into a negation of any authority possessed by the church. Bouyer does not seem to see that such limitations might in the given situation be necessary to rescue the positive things he had just described. In spite of his most unusual qualifications and his comparatively high appreciation, the author has not here been able to understand the deepest intentions of the reformers. According to Bouyer there is deep tragedy in the fact that what led to the church's rejection of the reformers did not derive from "the fundamentals of the Reformation" but resulted from the theological decline in the nominalism of the late Middle Ages —a thesis which I do not think is historically correct. The author comes to the conclusion that all that the Reformation aimed at in a positive manner may be found intact in the Roman Church of today.

What I have said is meant to give an impression of the

change that has begun and is now taking place in the way Roman Catholic theologians are viewing the Reformation and not least Luther himself. The way of simple negation which recognizes no problems has been followed by a more positive evaluation which has brought about a new study of historical sources as well as new ideas on the basic problems that have existed. Even though the approach of the German theologians to the problem was first expressed by a reconsideration of church history, it has led of necessity to the point that is clearly indicated in the title of Lortz's work: *Die Reformation als religiöses Anliegen heute* (The Reformation as a Religious Concern of Today). As a problem of the most immediate interest within the church it has come up for fundamental and systematic theological discussion in French Roman Catholic theology, and the seriousness with which this has been done gives Protestant theologians as well every reason to listen with attention.

All this means that we have a new situation for the theological conversation across the confessional borders. In the study of the history and principles of the Reformation we and the Roman Catholic theologians meet at the point where once the ways diverged. This does not mean that we can now glimpse a possibility of a theological consensus—far from it! The contrasts become even more pronounced, not least when the view of the office of the church comes into focus. The new things that happen will, however, mean the possibility—not even imagined before—of understanding each other's deepest intentions and thus reach a fruitful dialogue. Protestant theologians for their part have the duty to abandon unreservedly their inherited prejudices and misconceptions of the Roman Church and its theology. The new situation ought to be a challenge to Lutherans to take part in this conversation with the same seriousness as is being shown by some of our Roman Catholic brethren.

In this connection we can note a trend during the past few years, especially within German Roman Catholic theology, which is of special interest to Lutherans. For a long time Roman Catholic theologians in Germany as well as in France have directed their interest in Protestant theology to Karl Barth and contemporary Barthian theology. There exists today quite a library of books and articles about Barth, on the whole characterized by a truly positive desire to understand his theology from within. However, in recent years we have discerned a new direction in this interest in Protestant theology. The discovery has been made that there are other great theologians within the Protestant tradition besides Barth. This means that Lutheran theology has been discovered as a conversational partner in a way previously unheard of. Primarily the interest has been directed to Luther's own thinking.

Let us offer a few characteristic examples. In 1957 a research institute was founded in Paderborn, Germany, with a very good library, several resident scholars, etc. The only purpose of this institute is to study Protestant theology. (There are also other institutes of the same kind in several places in Europe.) This institute in Paderborn is publishing some interesting studies on the subject of Protestant theology. Among these I would point out two which are of special interest in the context of this article. The author is Albert Brandenburg, a leading scholar of the institute, who wrote a book in 1957 by the title *Hauptprobleme der evangelischen Theologie* (The Main Problems Within Evangelical Theology), which can be recommended as an excellent introduction to exactly what the title suggests, at least with respect to the European situation. Characteristically enough, Barth is here dealt with only on the first six pages, while the remainder of the book is entirely concerned with the basic thoughts of Luther's theology and its consequences for the present situation.

The same author published in 1960 an even larger work which in its way is epoch-making. It is entitled *Gericht und Evangelium* (Justice and Gospel) and is a precise and thorough study of the theology of the early Luther, as this was developed in his lectures on the Psalms during 1513–1515 as a "theology of the Word of God." This is a very noteworthy attempt to understand from within the main features of the beginnings of Luther's reformatory thought.

It is a rather thought-provoking fact that Luther research today is no longer a prerogative of Lutherans and not even of Protestants in a broader sense. Just as one of the best introductions to Luther's theology has been written by a Methodist, Philip S. Watson (*Let God Be God: An Interpretation of the*

Thoughts on the Second Vatican Council

Karl Barth

In this article the eminent and influential Swiss theologian Karl Barth addresses some sage and sober words to his fellow Protestants on the significance of developments within the Roman Catholic Church. Noting the signs of new life in that church, Dr. Barth asks how things would look if Rome, without ceasing to be Rome, were "one day simply to overtake us and place us in the shadows, so far as the renewing of the churches through the Word and Spirit of the Gospel is concerned." For Barth the import of the present ecumenical contacts between Catholics and non-Catholics lies primarily in the possibility of renewal of the whole church of Christ, and he counsels non-Catholic Christians to be sensitive to what the Holy Spirit is doing in and through the renewal of the Roman Church. Dr. Barth wrote this analysis for the July 1963 issue of the World Council of Churches' *Ecumenical Review*,* before the second session of the Second Vatican Council—which did indeed encounter some of the roadblocks Barth alludes to. But there is yet ground for hope that the progressive tendencies will prevail. Now retired from the Chair of Systematic Theology in Basel, Barth continues to work on what is regarded by many as the greatest theological effort of our time —his massive, multivolumed *Church Dogmatics.*

My friend Dr. W. A. Visser 't Hooft has requested that I express publicly some of the thoughts which I presented to him in a personal conversation. I had confessed to him that, in view of the remarks (so far as I knew of them) which he and his circle in Geneva had made regarding the Council, I could not find anything to contradict and yet could not be altogether satisfied. Even after reading the fine lecture by Lukas Vischer on "Community of the Separated

---

* 475 Riverside Drive, Room 439, New York 27, New York.

Churches?" (in the "Polis"-booklet *Zwischen zwei Konzilsses-sionen*, Evangelischer Verlag, Zürich), I am not completely reassured.

If I have read and understood correctly, the interest of the Geneva central office of non-Roman ecumenicism has up to the present centred on the question whether, to what extent and in what form the result of the Council might lead to closer attention and greater receptivity on the part of the Roman Church for the rest of Christianity, and on this basis to new and more frequent contact and conversations, to a dialogue between Rome and the rest of us. This is certainly a legitimate and important question, which Pope John XXIII himself has actually stimulated by his wish (carried out against certain circles of his Church) to invite "observers" from the ranks of the World Council and some of the larger non-Roman churches. At a special reception in the Vatican he ostentatiously placed himself in the midst of these observers. They were supplied with the confidential literary material which was otherwise available only to the actual participants in the Council. They were constantly addressed in St. Peter's Cathedral as the *dilectissimi observatores*. Behind the scenes and privately, individually and in groups, they were evidently greeted, consulted and requested to express their views on the themes that were treated. What innovations! Certainly there has been a very remarkable beginning here of contacts between the teaching office of the Roman Church and representatives of the other confessions which are not subordinated to it and nevertheless have the intention also of being "catholic," with the result that the question about the continuation of such contacts is sensible and definitely worthwhile. However, for two reasons it seems to me not quite right to observe and judge the event of the Council primarily (not to say exclusively) from this one aspect.

Is there not in this way an underestimation of the significance which this no doubt important question has in the Roman Church itself? Our own side has realized and often stressed the fact that the Council is an affair of this church itself. Perhaps, however, this fact has not been accepted definitely enough. The task of the Council is the Church's *own inner renewal*, to be carried out in view of its present Christian and non-Christian environment. Its ultimate goal (stressed sharply enough in the first announcements of the Pope) is the development of its own splendour, a development that is in a certain sense *kerygmatic*, contemporary, inviting the Christian and non-Christian environment to peace, even to union with the church itself. Obviously to achieve this goal the church must be interested in gaining a full and accurate picture of its *immediate* or *Christian* environment, and in giving this also a clear picture of itself. But *this* intention (although not one that had become so evident in its previous history) was the basis for founding this astonishing relationship with the other churches—concretely, in the special activity of Cardinal Bea and his co-workers. And the intention would still be *this* one should this relationship be continued, perhaps even deepened and strengthened after the Council itself. As far as we others are concerned, the Council was called not in order to negotiate with us but in order to get to know us better and explain to us the true essence of the Roman Church, and in this way to impress us (in the best sense of the word). And matters will remain the same in all the developments that follow the Council. Is this fact not overlooked if someone should think that the Roman Church has an *independent*, a *primary* interest in the initiation and cultivation of those contacts? Are we well advised, therefore, to direct our interest in the Council all too intensively or even exclusively to those conversational contacts which have newly arisen and may perhaps be expanded, or to concentrate the question about certain communications that have arisen out of these contacts in the single question whether Rome is or may become willing to learn this thing or the other from us? (Such accents have already been sounded.) This is not to overlook or deny the fact that Rome may inconspicuously have learned from us and will continue to do so. The Church (and also the non-Roman Church) has always done well to learn (and to learn more than a little) from its heretics and schismatics. But still less can we overlook the fact (if we do not wish to bypass altogether the thought of our best Roman negotiators) that the papal *and* the conciliar Rome is today concerned centrally and actually with the renovation of its own house, and that only for this reason, peripherally and contingently, is it concerned to hear and accept us as its discussion partners. (This very fact could also be positively significant and exemplary for us.) This is the first reservation which I wish to mention here: our concentration on the question of present and future contacts and communication between Rome and ourselves seems to me to lack a certain sober realism with respect to the "ecumenical" purpose (precisely in *Rome*'s sense) which guides Rome in its Council.

My second reservation extends further and deeper. The concentration on that question seems to me to be *too formal* to be altogether realistic. It was certainly saying a bit too much when an enthusiastic Roman correspondent of the *Süddeutsche Zeitung* spoke of a "truly temperamental blowing of the Holy Spirit" under whose auspices the first session of the Council took place. But we others, no doubt, are not only allowed but even required to realize that both the convocation and the previous course of the Council are symptomatic of a certain landslide that is taking place in the Roman Church, a *spiritual* movement actually taking place there with whose possibility no one had reckoned fifty years ago. This movement was what demanded something like a renovation and a second Vatican Council. It expresses itself in the previous events of the Council. My question is whether it is not more important and imperative for us of "another faith" to direct our attention and controversy to it, instead of being so formally concerned with future contacts.

What is involved here? May not the old book of the Gospels which during the opening of the Council was laid in the direct line of vision of the bishops (and observers!) in St. Peter's Cathedral have been more than just a necessary piece of liturgical and ornamental scenery? What that very remarkable man Angelo Roncalli as Pope John XXIII undertook in this matter, and in bringing the bishops together—what the tenor of the opening address of the Pope displayed—what the majority of the Council characteristically was motivated by in the previous course of its proceedings: was all this not the dynamics of the beginning of a reorganization—precisely around the Gospel? The Bible of the Old and New Testaments was obviously for a long time past read more industriously and fruitfully, in clerical (and not only in clerical) circles of the Roman Church, than we had noticed or properly judged. (This was clearly expressed in the discussion and preliminary decision concerning "Scripture and Tradition.") Were we staring all too fixedly, perhaps, at the problematic formulas of Trent or the spectacular sorrows of those Catholic theologians who were laboring at scientific exegesis? Had we not put enough trust in the leavening power of the Word of Scripture, which after all is strongly represented in the Roman book of mass and the breviary? Were we confused by all the strange elements that encountered us there? And, through this presence of the prophetic and apostolic Scriptures, has not Jesus Christ inevitably stepped anew into the centre of faith of the Roman Christians and the thought of the Roman theologians—just at the place where he seemed increasingly called in question by the discouraging development of the dogmas about Mary? And as a result, have not surprising interpretations been offered of the questions which interested the sixteenth century concerning the relationship between divine and human freedom or between faith and its works—interpretations which explain in a remarkable way or even surpass the Tridentine doctrine of justification and also the doctrine of reason and revelation presented in the first Vatican Council? Can it be overlooked, furthermore, that the preaching in the Roman congregations is not only more industrious but also much more serious than our previous ideas would allow, and that in this matter there are often considerable surprises to be experienced, for instance on the radio, in comparison with many Protestant presentations? Moreover, has not a movement begun (extending even to the architecture of the churches) in the direction of a more active participation of the congregation in the altar service, which takes place no longer by a distant wall but in its midst, giving it its character as a worship service? This is the fact (with regard to the active hearing of the Word of God) which has become clear in the discussions of the Council concerning reform of the liturgy. Does not this movement spur us to closer attention and reconsideration, astonished as we were by the hieratic remarkableness of this altar service and its interpretations that were previously presented and heard? Certainly there is no occasion for overestimating in any dimension the spiritual event which is tentatively announced by all this, and there is reason to be prepared for every possible sort of road-block and reversal. Everything is still very imperfect and very unclear to us, both in particulars and as a whole, and things may remain this way for a long time, perhaps to the Second Coming of Christ. There is no reason for anyone to dream that the Roman Catholics might become "evangelical" in *our* sense, whether tomorrow, the day after tomorrow or at any other time. The very fact that this movement began altogether in the *Roman* Catholic sphere, in the form of its theoretical and practical decrees, leading nonetheless to certain explosions in the present Council at the real or supposed grave of Peter, explosions which will not be so easy to do away with—this fact itself could give to the movement its greatest significance for us.

Of course, that Mariological dogma with its so disagreeable development is still in existence, with its uncanny relationship to the essence and function of the Church. The present Pope apparently does not intend to take further steps in its development. But there is also no question of even its partial revocation. At the beginning of everything, beclouding everything, stands the dogma summarized and proclaimed in the first Vatican Council concerning the prolongation of the office of Peter in each bearer of the papal crown and the infallibility of his judgement in matters of doctrine and life when he speaks *ex cathedra* (with or without the agreement of the other bishops or the rest of the church altogether). And round about his throne are those invisible principalities and powers which are called the "curia," holding forth inscrutably through their varied interplay of forces. As to those dogmas, however, it may be noted that there is a flexibility, highly developed in recent Roman Christianity and ecclesiasticism and especially in recent Roman theology, with regard to the stress or lack of stress laid on the different decisions that were made in earlier times. There is also a remarkable proficiency in interpreting these subsequently *in meliorem* or even *in optimam partem*, that is to say, as "evangelical" (within the limits of their special ecclesiastical character). Let us wait and see whether these attempts will succeed, whether those biggest road-blocks which have not yet been noticeably touched by the movement that manifested itself in the Council will be subsequently presented to us in a clear and understandable form, in which they would appear somewhat more harmless and less worthy of our wrath than they now appear to us, even though we might still be unable to pass them unhindered. Is it altogether insignificant that the one occasion upon which John XXIII made use of his singular authority during the previous course of the Council was the reception of St. Joseph into the canon of the mass—the biblical figure, therefore, whose special character in relation to the son of Mary can be found only in his constant and unambiguous role as a *witness*? What is the Church if this witness is her "protector," as he has been named for a long time past? Certainly she is then not the image of a gleaming Mother of God and Queen of Heaven but instead the image of that altogether human "guardian father" who is easily overlooked because his relationship to the chief character is precisely that of a *servant*. Naturally I do not even dream of maintaining that this is what the Pope *intended* to say with his unexpected emphasis on Joseph. I only wish to note that in this way he actually ("infallibly"?) *did* say something that points in this direction. Likewise the principalities and powers of the "curia" have in fact already proven not to be altogether dominant in the previous course of the Council. One member of this circle has reportedly already spoken of its "martyrdom"!

My point in all this is to suggest that we should direct our attention far more to what is beginning to appear as a movement of renewal *within* the Roman Church, to what in fact has partially already been set in motion, rather than to the possibilities of a loyal correspondence between us and its representatives. In the last analysis, Rome and the non-Roman churches are not static power groups, buttressed and delimited within themselves and devoted to the preservation of their possessions or the multiplication of their prestige and influence. Both are directed to the unification of all Christianity as their final end. Both live by the dynamics of the evangelical Word and Spirit which are totally constitutive for both. Both live to the extent that they are living communities of the living Jesus Christ. The question that confronts them, first and last, each in its own way and both in their coexistence, is not the cooperation of their different doctrines and institutions but this dynamic movement. They are summoned to give mutual attention to *this* movement. And the present situation could be determined by the fact that for a change we *non-Roman* Christians are in a special way the ones who are *questioned*. Certainly, we are not asked whether we could, should or would wish to become "Catholic," but we are asked whether, in view of the spiritual motion that is taking place there, something has been set in motion—or not set in motion!—on *our* side, in the rooms of *our* church. In view of the certainly imperfect movement over there, do we think, speak and act in a movement of *our own*, similar in all its imperfection—a movement that consists not only in the preservation of the oft-cited "heritage of the Reformation," not only in the cultivation of our own customs and traditions, not only (as though everything on our side were basically in good shape!) in all sorts of contemporary controversies, concerns, corrections and new beginnings, but in the experience and fructification of a shaking of the foundations? Do we have any idea (for instance in the so doughty churches of the United States, but no less in the churches this side of the Atlantic) what such a fundamental crisis would be and what it could entail? Was it such a crisis that brought together, for example, the conference of New Delhi (which in itself is certainly to be taken very seriously)? Is such a thing possible at all in eastern Orthodoxy? And do we in the European West actually exist as *ecclesiae semper reformandae*? Or are there not among us all too many offensive movements that have made no progress, for instance in the Evangelical Church in Germany and its spiritual paralysis that began such a short time after the brief awakening during the time of the church struggle, so that now the "progressive" elements—in contrast to the situation in St. Peter's!—form a minority with its back to the wall? Do we non-Roman theologians not lack too much that interesting and progressive flexibility which characterizes many of our Roman colleagues, interesting because it does not exclude but includes an ultimate responsibility and clear direction? Does there not exist among us an express enmity against all genuinely disturbing factors? And as a complement to this, is there not far too great a measure of conformism with respect to the powers that rule in the people, state and society? What can be said to the fact that in Denmark Grundtvig has become far and away more influential than Kierkegaard? Or what about the fact that American Christianity seems inwardly incapable of measuring up to the problem of integration which is so pressing there? Or what about the fact that the brave statement of the Dutch General Synod on the question of nuclear armament, instead of becoming the statement of all our churches, remains isolated as a gratifying exception? And what about the feeble evasion, on the part of the governing body of the Swiss Union of Churches, of the problem of the military chaplain who was disciplined precisely on account of his standpoint on this question? Or would anyone pretend to deduce examples to the contrary from the yearly gatherings of the churches (*Kirchentage*), the Evangelical Academies, the skirmishes about demythologizing, hermeneutics and that sort of thing? Are there not also non-Roman, even "Protestant" Ottavianis (small and large, confessional and liberal, episcopal and presbyterial-synodal, eternally optimistic or also eternally tragic)? And are not these the ones who everywhere to some extent determine the appearance of the non-Roman churches? But if this is the case, on what topic and in what language do we propose to continue those discussions which have been hoped for with the Roman Catholics?

I freely confess that I am secretly troubled by one problem, which I cannot admit is overcome by the counter-criticism (though this lies close to hand and is certainly possible) that the "spiritual event" over there which first led to the second Vatican Council has no solid basis. How would things look if Rome (without ceasing to be Rome) were one day simply to overtake us and place us in the shadows, so far as the renewing of the Church through the Word and Spirit of the Gospel is concerned? What if we should discover that the last are first and the first last, that the voice of the Good Shepherd should find a clearer echo over there than among us? I once asked Hans Küng whether he would repeat *viva voce* what he has presented in his book on justification, if one fine day he were to become the Roman Pope (which of course is not an excluded possibility). "Of course!" was his immediate and undaunted reply, to which I could only say that then I really stood in fear and trembling for Protestantism, in whose ranks the theses of his Catholic book had by no means gained common acceptance, and which would therefore have to submit to being set aright (in this admittedly extreme case) from the throne of Peter, and that in a matter of its own most intimate concern. Hans Küng's reply was: "And that will happen too!" Whether "that" will happen is a question we may put to one side. But it could very well be possible that we others might find more to learn from the Roman Church than Rome for its part would have to learn from us, as we still assume with undue self-satisfaction. (We would learn, of course, not from its special doctrine, liturgy and other institutions but from a new Spirit that revitalizes and sets these dead bones in motion.) Certainly, many proper and important things have already been said (fortunately some things that were also offensive for certain ears) at Amsterdam, Evanston and New Delhi, and not first in the Easter Encyclical of John XXIII, about human rights, the problems of race, minorities, refugees and colonialism, the task of the United Nations, atomic and general disarmament. But why is it that the voice of Rome made such a far greater impression than the voice of Geneva on the world (from the editor's desk of *Pravda* all the way to that of the *Basler Nationalzeitung*)? Was it only because of the obviously greater historical and political halo which Rome possesses? Is the reason not also the fact that in the encyclical the same things were not only talked about but also *proclaimed*, that Christianity and the world were not only taught but also *summoned* unreservedly and bindingly with an appeal to the highest authority, that they received not only advice and admonition but also *directives*, in short, that the encyclical had more the character of a *message* than our previous ecumenical proclamations, in spite of its extensive use of terms and concepts taken from natural law? I think that our side, lacking this degree of natural law, could actually speak in this manner much more clearly. But at the present I do not yet see that we have done so. And therefore I am afraid that with respect to the external world, precisely in this decisive present of ours, we might be left far behind by a papal church that is making dynamic recovery. Will we also have to witness Rome's achievement of a Christian standpoint on the East-West-conflict, one which is freer and more productive of world peace, *before* we achieve this? I do not wish to overestimate this encyclical and therefore I do not say that things have gone so far already. But I think that a thoroughgoing reconsideration is called for by the very fact that the *threat* of an exchange of positions and roles is becoming visible today all along the horizon, an exchange in whose light our criticisms, justified as they are, of Mary and the infallible teaching office would necessarily become uninteresting. And this is the question which I with all respect would like to see the executive body of the World Council of Churches more diligently concerned with. Might it not be a sound Christian rule to attribute a little more worth to others than to oneself and to be a bit more critical of oneself than of others? Must not the Council (or rather what can be perceived on the Roman side in the background of the Council) give us occasion to sweep away the dust before the door of our own church with a careful but nevertheless mighty broom?

I can also formulate the question another way: should our prayer for the growing visibility of the unity of the Church of Jesus Christ not become, for our part (regardless of what may be meant in the prayer of the other side), quite freed from the thought that the brethren who are separated from us might become "evangelical" in our sense and style, that they might sooner or later be granted an insight (treading further along the obviously good way they have begun) into the greater propriety and importance of our form of the Christian faith, the faith that is common to them and to us? Should not our prayer in this matter express the quite firm wish that, in view of what seems to be beginning to stir over there as spiritual renewal (independently of the question concerning the depth and future of that renewal), something new might occur *among us*—a new attentiveness to the Word of God *among us*, in relationship to *our* form of Christian faith or its many forms that are included in our ecumenical movement—a new outpouring of the Holy Spirit (to speak with J. Chr. Blumhardt) *among us*? What help would all the prayers about the unity of the Church be to us as long as their central meaning were not the entreaty *Veni, creator Spiritus*? And what help would this entreaty be to us if we were to pray with a side glance toward those others instead of with our gaze firmly fixed on *our* churches, on our life in the sphere of *our* church orders, on *our* teaching, theologizing, preaching and instructing in the sphere of *our* knowledge and church confessions, on the bitter misery of *our* whole existence as a Church?

Let us turn once again to the beginning of this essay. Of what use would any conversation with those others be to us, and how could they be conducted with a view to a this-worldly or at least other-worldly unity of the Church, if the presupposition on our side were something else than the altogether concrete entreaty for the Holy Spirit within *our* troubled church? Once again, what humiliations could befall us in such conversations if it should prove to be the case that the participants on the other side were in this matter more seriously engaged, that the *Veni creator Spiritus* were present with them in a more concrete directedness, and that they were praying not in view of our own misery but with their gaze on their *own* Roman Church problems? From the one standpoint as from the other, the way to unity of the Church can only be the way of her renewal. But renewal means repentance. And repentance means turning about: not the turning of those others, but one's *own* turning. Is not the problem posed for the World Council of Churches by the Roman Council one of repentance and so of renewal of *our* churches, of all the non-Roman churches assembled in the World Council? And is not the continuation of our conversations with the others a secondary problem dominated by that primary one? This is the question (directed not last of all also to our "observers") which seems to me to be the *burning* question with respect to the conclusion of the Council and, in fact, far beyond this.

A Note on Imagination and Thought about God

Thomas Gornall, S.J.

Thomas Gornall, S.J., is both audacious and modest: audacious, because he dares to think and write in the mode of the natural theology of St. Thomas Aquinas in a day when many thinkers—including many theologians—consider such a theology to be impossible; modest, because he is fully aware of the limits of metaphysics and of the hard questions which skeptical modern philosophy has addressed to natural theology since St. Thomas' time. And while Father Gornall draws on Thomist thought, he is far from being a die-hard medievalist—a fact evidenced by his opinion of the doctrine of divine Ideas; this doctrine, "so dear to the medievals," has, he says, "produced far more harm than good," has resulted "in a colossal waste of time expended upon pseudo-problems." In this essay Father Gornall has some good things to say about imagination, but at the same time he has some severe things to say about a "faulty imaginative approach" to metaphysics. Modest also is Father Gornall's use of words—modest in the sense of economic; there are no spare words at all in this tightly written little treatise. Father Gornall is author of the recently published *A Philosophy of God*, and his present post is Professor of Natural Theology and History of Ancient Philosophy at Heythrop, a Jesuit House of Studies near Oxford. His piece is taken from his house's quarterly review, *The Heythrop Journal,** April 1963.

THIS NOTE is prompted by the opinion that thought about God and the world can be greatly helped or hindered by the type of imaginative background which goes with it—which is in fact a shorthand metaphysics.

The presence of an imaginative background to our thinking

* Available through Fordham University Press, New York 58, New York.

about God and the world is a matter for neither question nor regret. Imagination is not thought, but we cannot think without imagination. The fact that in many subjects we advert very little to our imaginative clues or "phantasms" as they are technically called is a testimony to the underlying immateriality of our thought. But, being human, we cannot dispense with imagination altogether. There is need to examine this factor from time to time, to make sure it is being the help it was meant to be and not a hindrance; all the more since our picture-clues are often so unobtrusive. (It is not suggested that imagination is purely visual though in practice it seems to be predominantly so. Obscure somatic feeling-phantasms, especially dynamic ones, are of far more importance to our thinking than is often supposed, and their role seems to be a neglected field of psychological investigation.)

As the background of our thinking, as a compendium of metaphysics, the power of these imaginative clues is enormous. All thinking is governed not by the explicit foreground of thought but by the implicit background of thought. It is what we take for granted that makes the difference. Hence the importance of metaphysics for every man and not merely for the philosopher or theologian.

We would suggest that the imaginative picture of God and the world (1) should consist simply of God above and the world below, with a line drawn between them; (2) that we may not cross that line, in either direction, by univocal thought; and (3) that (apart from the doctrine of the Blessed Trinity) we should envisage God always finally as undifferentiated infinite Being.

There can be found in traditional Christian thinking an apparent polarity—reaching back through Augustine to his Platonic sources—between God known as absolute simplicity and differentiations in our thought about God on the basis of what we know of him as creator of the world. We mention this to indicate that we do not forget it, and that our intention is dialectical rather than dogmatic. And again, we have not failed to put to ourselves the question, What is meant by absolute simplicity?

To proceed, then, on this understanding. We believe that the three canons, so to call them, which we propose are contained in the great tradition of Christian philosophy; and that any exception to them would be a declension. Yet there has always been more or less endemic in philosophy and theology an imaginative picture of God which in practice tends to make philosophers and theologians think and write of God univocally.

The first of our canons reminds us of the transcendence of God, that is, of his infinity and incommensurability with everything finite including finite minds. (The transcendence of God in this sense does not, of course, exclude his immanence, his creative presence in the world.) The second reminds us that whether we think of God's action in the world or of the relation of the world to God, there is no finite link between God and the world. God's knowledge, will, power, is not somehow canalized in his knowing, willing, producing the world. Whenever we speak of God we speak of the one infinite, indivisible divine nature.

Our third principle is in a way the most important of all and is the most frequently overlooked. We speak of many attributes of God—knowledge, including that of finite things, will, power, freedom, wisdom, justice, mercy; of his eternity, immensity and ubiquity; of his conservation and concurrence. But always we have to remember in the end that God is absolute simplicity; that the human distinctions in our thoughts about God are not divine distinctions; and that even the certain fact that he knows finite things in full detail is no basis for placing distinctions in God or for drawing further conclusions about how he knows and causes the world. Always in the end we can safely think of God only as undifferentiated infinite Being.

In the light of the principles proposed we may examine briefly (1) the doctrine of divine Ideas; (2) the use of *signa rationis* or distinctions of reason in our thought about God; (3) one or two of the great controversies in theology.

First the doctrine of divine Ideas. Much remains to be written on this subject historically and metaphysically. Here we would briefly advance the view that if the doctrine merely intends to state the fact that God knows finite things, actual and possible, in full detail, there can be no ground for complaint. If, on the other hand, it is claimed that the doctrine gives us, beyond the fact, some insight into how God knows finite things, then the claim should not be allowed. In particular, to imply that we have on the one hand the divine essence and on the other the divine Ideas, and that we can explain the relation between the two and the multiplicity, would be to violate our second canon by attempting to explain God in terms of univocal finite thought. To claim to explain in this way would be to cross the line from finite to infinite and set to work to explain—as distinct from stating—what is found there, with the equipment of a finite mind; and that would be a mistake of method. In general we would say that the doctrine of divine Ideas, so dear to the medievals, has produced far more harm than good, and that the harm is historically quite serious; not so much in terms of positive error —though that is not altogether absent—as in terms of a whole disorientation of mind resulting in a colossal waste of time expended upon pseudo-problems. For if we are on divine territory in roaming the fields of the divine Ideas, it is hard to see how we are not so in roaming the fields of our ideas about God. But in fact we are not.

We would claim further that while it is often permissible to distinguish *signa rationis* or abstract stages in God's knowledge and will, and to say that God knows what we thus distinguish, such statements cannot be taken as indicating distinctions in God. They can indeed indicate certain truths about God, but we have no right to imagine we have insight into their verification at a divine level. There is no harm whatever in distinguishing Peter—or Peter's action—as actual and as possible; nor in distinguishing what Peter does, what he was destined to do, and what he could have been destined to do. There is no anthropomorphism in saying that God knows the abstractions we thus distinguish. For we are merely saying what is true: that Peter need not have existed, that his existence is freely chosen by God, and that Peter could have been otherwise destined than he is. The only anthropomorphism would consist in imagining that this finite, univocal map of human knowledge is also a univocal map of divine knowledge. All this knowledge is in God's infinite knowledge which is his infinite Being. How it is there we are in no position to say.

We would go further and claim that in philosophy there is no ground to distinguish in God intellect *natura prius* to will. All we can say is that God is intellect-will in absolute identity.[1] In this connexion a useful test is the popular distinction that the essence of God, not his will, is the foundation of possibles, whereas his free will is the foundation of actuals. The text-books do indeed generally mention that *fundamentaliter* his essence and will are identical. But that is to answer a question at the level of human economy while raising another at a deeper level and leaving us to answer it as best we can. The net result is to produce the impression that the level of human economy is the one at which we can think most significantly, which is the opposite of the truth.

To turn now briefly to one or two famous controversies. Every so-called problem which is formulated in terms of *reconciling* something in the world with something in God, or of reconciling two facts about God, one of which is conceived as involving a finite factor, is to violate our canons and is a pseudo-problem; and all controversy upon such questions is mere beating of the air. We venture to think that the great controversies *De Auxiliis* could never have taken place if they had not been formulated in terms which were radically misconceived.

In parenthesis the problem of showing that in God all pure perfections are one simple infinite perfection is in a different class. This is not a pseudo-problem and it has an intelligible answer. For all pure perfections are judged to be infinite and are imperfectly conceived as infinite, with the question of the plurality pending. The plurality drops away as soon as we realize that it is essentially conceptual and human; just as it drops away for the same reason in the parallel case of the transcendental notions of being, unity, truth and goodness.

But a "problem" such as that of reconciling God's immutability with his freedom *ad extra* is in a different category. For the problem owes its vitality to the suggestion that the freedom *ad extra*, in its exercise, must make a finite difference to God. By starting with that suggestion we have conveyed across the line a contingent finiteness and set to work to reconcile it with God's non-contingent infinity, as though God's freedom were not God; as though God were composed of infinite and finite, freedom and necessity. To reconcile anything truly and objectively finite with God's infinity is to postulate a univocal ground on which we reconcile; to seek a finite link or cog that will engage with the finite link or cog in our minds. It is to violate our own first principles and to stultify our theological thinking.

More positively, what can be said about one of the greatest of all the "problems," the relation between our free will and God's knowledge and causality? So long as the imaginative background of our thought corresponds to our metaphysics we shall quickly see how much we are able to say and how to say it, and that any attempt to say more is to manufacture a problem, not to find one.

God is infinite Being. All we are required to do is to imagine infinite Being above the line and finite being below. Then we affirm, without any preoccupation, all that is true of God, whether in the sphere of knowledge or of causality, and all that is true of man. To be concerned about reconciliation is not merely to contradict our first principles; it is to inhibit ourselves from thinking and saying boldly all that we need to say of God and man. God as infinite Being knows and causes all finite being. Does Peter act freely? Then God is the cause of his acting freely, for his acting freely is being. Does God know what any possible man would do? Yes, for what any possible man would do depends on what God would will to effect or will to allow in his regard. The possible man's actions, whether good are bad, are all intelligible in terms of being, and God is infinite Being.

On the other hand, in the actual world—or for that matter in a possible world—does Peter act freely? Then his free act is produced by himself; he is *dominus sui actus*. Does he fail in goodness in his action? Then his failure is entirely his own failure and is caused neither negatively nor positively by God.

God's Being transcends all the finite kinds of being, free and not free, perishable and permanent, past, present and future. Even in a sense—though in a different sense—it transcends good and evil; for God wills to effect good and wills to allow evil. What and why evil is we know in man. About God's will to allow evil all we know is that it is contained in his will of which the object is infinite good; and that his allowing is the cause of evil neither positively nor negatively.

In an act of human free will, then, all depends on God and all depends on man, but not univocally. Even to allow oneself willingly to *feel* the situation as a paradox, a hard saying, as something that needs reconciling, is to cease to think as a theologian; because it is to cease to remember that we do not explain God. There is indeed something that we do not see, namely God. But in general there is not anything that we do not know. What we know is that God's infinite Being is infinite intelligibility; and that if we saw that infinite intelligibility we should see it not as divided into essence and causality, not as compounded of finite and infinite, not as containing the multiplicity of the categories of being; but as infinite Being, infinite intelligibility.

To explain in this way is to explain in terms of being and without remainder. More than that cannot be expected of any metaphysics. We also believe that it is to clear away an oppressive fog in which we cannot see or breathe, and to allow the sun to shine serenely on theology.

The same faulty imaginative approach which we have been trying to track down and banish is responsible for the split that has existed from the beginning—the oscillation between a philosophy that reads as if we were in possession of a detailed guide-book to the divine mind and essence, and the revulsion from that position which leads other philosophers, or the same philosophers at other times, to say that the divine essence is totally unknown to us. In our opinion these two positions are equally false; neither can be sustained except by approaching the question with the assumption that our knowledge of God in this life can be univocal. Analogical knowledge of God, when once we have set aside the endless discussions about formulation, is something perfectly simple: that God is in truth infinite Being; that this infinite Being is intellect, will, wisdom, power, freedom, justice, mercy, in absolute identity and without the limitations of time or place or any multiplicity. And all these things are meaningful to us. To attempt to say more, to try to "make it clear," is to cross the line from finite to infinite with no support but the broken reed of human finiteness and univocity.

II

Problems for Theology

Can Faith Validate God-Talk?

Kai Nielsen

Linguistic analysis, a mode of thought which has dominated the philosophical scene for some time now, has proved fruitful in terms of providing new questions for the never-ending dialogue between philosophers and theologians. Kai Nielsen's "Can Faith Validate God-Talk?" is a salient instance of how contemporary philosophy can challenge the more traditional defenses of religious faith. One such defense is fideism—a defense which deliberately eschews reason and frankly proclaims that God is "an utter mystery and a thorough scandal to the intellect." Fideism, says Nielsen, has an obvious appeal for those who prefer to ignore "the ambiguities of metaphysics and the rarefied atmosphere of philosophical analysis." But fideism will not do as an apologetic stance, he argues, because it *presupposes* that its religious claims are not only true but factually intelligible. We cannot accept on faith what we do not understand; the logically prior problem of the *meaning* of religious utterances must be dealt with before the question of their truth can even be asked. Dr. Nielsen is Professor of Philosophy at New York University, New York City. His article, from the July 1963 issue of *Theology Today*,* is reprinted by permission.

To be a fideist is to believe that fundamental religious beliefs rest solely and completely on faith. Finite and sinful man cannot by the use of his unaided reason come to know God. Belief and unbelief are intellectually on a par, religious experience is unalterably ambiguous as to the reality of its object, and the existence of God can never be established by empirical investigation or philosophical demonstration. But the storms and stresses of our lives will drive us to faith. We must turn to God to overcome despair and the "threat of meaninglessness." Without God life can indeed be nothing more than a "tale told by an idiot." Faith will give

* P.O. Box 29, Princeton, New Jersey.

our lives an anchor, will enable us to overcome that sickness unto death that goes with a loss of God, but with or without faith, we will only see through a glass darkly, for God remains an utter mystery and a thorough scandal to the intellect. Intellectually speaking, a belief in God is absurd; taken as a hypothesis it is at best fanciful. The believer, the "knight of faith," can only trust that he is not "whistling in the dark," is not believing something that is thoroughly illusory, when he accepts the God revealed in the Scriptures as an ultimate reality. Here, the quest for certainty or even for a guide that will give us "reasonable probabilities" is a quixotic quest. The believer must simply take the leap of faith without any intellectual assurance at all that he is leaping in the right direction. But this total risk is well worth it for without God man's life is without meaning.

Fideism has an ancient and respected lineage. One finds it in Tertullian, Pascal, Hamann, and Kierkegaard. In our time it finds expression in one way or another in the theologies of Barth, Brunner, Nygren, and the Niebuhrs. It is even a dominant motif in the writings of such a perceptive linguistic philosopher as Alastair MacIntyre.[1] But in characterizing fideism as I have, I have not been concerned to set forth a view which necessarily fits the exact views of any of these men. Kierkegaard, it seems to me, presents the purest case of such an orientation, but while I do not wish to do battle with straw men or tilt with windmills, I am not concerned here with the history of a movement. In the defenses of religion given by the men mentioned above, such fideistic approaches are dominant though other claims are made as well. I want here to take the core concepts of fideism—concepts that are frequently appealed to in theological discussion—and subject them to examination without attempting to prove that any theologian of note holds exactly the view I have characterized as fideism.[2]

I

Such fideistic approaches to religion have an obvious appeal. Natural theology, which has somewhat extravagantly been called "the Sick Man of Europe," can now be bypassed;

the harassed man who is struggling to decide whether he can accept the claims of religion can ignore the ambiguities of metaphysics and the rarefied atmosphere of philosophical analysis. Fideism provides him with a rationale for rejecting such claims as little intellectual games that are irrelevant to his quest for God.

It is true that we do not and cannot know whether there is a God, whether there is an omniscient and just Being who looks after us, as a perfect father would, or whether Jesus is God. If we feel this scepticism and if deep in our hearts the claim that Jesus is God remains—along with the other central claims of the Christian faith—a "shocking but relevant possibility," fideism will attract us.[3] Given that our need to believe is strong enough, it may incite our assent. By an act of faith we accept the absurd claims of Christianity not as mere possibilities but as actualities that will direct our lives and give fiber to our deepest hopes.

Yet the fact remains that for many philosophers of an analytical persuasion, it is just this initial claim that such alleged beliefs are *intelligible possibilities* that serves as the greatest stumbling block to religious belief. Christian and, more generally, theistic talk is indeed a part of the languages of the West. (There is, of course, no special Christian language.) If we can speak English we can and do learn to speak of God. If we take religion as a kind of myth (albeit an important and moving myth), we will generally have no overwhelming difficulty in understanding religious talk in the way we understand and accept all myths. But while no Jew or Christian should deny that religious discourse has mythical elements, the Jewish and Christian tradition would insist that there is something more there, too. In some sense, divine existence is taken to be more than a human creation, a human ideal, no matter how worthy, projected onto the universe. But in trying to *say* what more is involved, all the trouble begins.

When the fideist says that this "more" is a possibility he will opt for with his whole heart and his whole mind, it is the very *meaning* of his claim that perplexes the contemporary philosophical analyst. How can we presuppose it and then act on it? If it is a possibility, what would it be like for it to be actualized? What would have to happen or not have to happen in order for "Jesus is God" or "There is a God" or "God governs the world" to be either true or false? While the nineteenth-century sceptic characteristically puzzled over whether there was sufficient evidence for "There is a God" to be true or even probable, the twentieth-century sceptic has come to be perplexed over the question of what it *means* even to affirm *or* deny the existence or love of God. This last question was seen to be logically prior to questions about the truth of religious beliefs.

Here's the rub for the fideist. Before we can intelligibly say, as an atheist, "There is no God," or as a believer, either fideist or non-fideist, "There is a God," or, as an agnostic, "We do not have sufficient evidence to either affirm or deny there is a God," we must know what such sentences *mean*. But do we? Do we have any idea what it would be like for any of these utterances to be used to make true or false statements? Many philosophers, rightly or wrongly, have concluded that we do not. If they are right, these theistic utterances are then *factually* meaningless utterances, though they indeed have some emotive, ceremonial, or pseudofactual (ideological) meaning.[4]

These philosophical contentions themselves have been subject to fierce controversy among philosophers and theologians, but from this discussion it has become apparent that the logical status of certain crucial theistic utterances is extremely controversial. Some find the whole mode of theistic discourse in its essential respects meaningless or chaotic and, as a result, disapprove of religion; others argue that one can never justifiably say of a whole mode of discourse, a form of life, that it is meaningless or chaotic, and they may go on to conclude, as does the Oxford philosopher, I. M. Crombie, that "seen as a whole religion makes rough sense, though it does not make limpidity."[5] But for all parties, the central philosophical puzzle is about the very *meaning* of religious talk. The puzzle here is not only about various analyses of religious discourse but over whether central aspects of first-order religious talk are themselves intelligible.

It is tempting to suppose that fideism shows how the man, seriously involved with religion, can put such abstruse and baffling concerns aside as the twaddle of philosophers. Those who accept religion on faith, those who operate within "the circle of faith," need not bother about what "God" means. They clearly realize that they cannot understand what many of the central theistic claims mean. But this is just as it should be. After all, religion is a mystery. But God, in his majesty and grace, infuses religious utterances with meaning, though to man they remain meaningless. The man of faith does not and cannot understand them; he simply accepts God's word, though these words (as well as the very word "God") remain meaningless to him.

It can be plausibly argued that this fideist defense cannot be correct, for such remarks are without sense.[6] If the believer doesn't understand the utterances *at all*, he cannot accept or reject them, for he literally would not understand *what* he is accepting or rejecting. If they are meaningful *at all*, they must be intelligible to at least some men. If we do not understand what "God" means or what it would be like for "There is a God" to be true or false, to say we accept God on faith is like saying we accept Irglig on faith or "There is an Irglig" on faith. Before we can make the leap, before we can accept a claim on faith or refuse to accept it on faith, we must at least have some minimal understanding of *what* it is we are accepting or rejecting. *At this level,* faith cannot be a way to understanding. Faith cannot insure the meaningfulness of religious utterances; quite to the contrary, faith presupposes that the discourse in question is itself meaningful (intelligible). If we lack evidence for x, we may take x on faith, but we cannot by an act of faith step from what we do not understand to what we do understand. If I do not know what is meant by x, I cannot intelligibly say that I have faith in x, that I place my trust in x, or that I accept x on authority. I may say: "I have faith that segregation will come to an end in the South in the next five years" or "I have faith in the farm policies of Secretary Freeman." Here I mean that I trust Secretary Freeman or trust that his policies will work out for the best and trust that segregation will come to an end within five years. I trust that these things will take place but I have no evidence that they will take place or even that they are likely to take place. Yet I trust that they will. In the latter case, I might do this simply because I trust Freeman. As the fideist takes the Bible or the church as his authority in matters of religion, so I simply accept Freeman's statements as authoritative on questions of farm policy. But in the two non-religious cases, I know what it would be like for the authoritative statements to be true or false. The *meaning* of the statements taken on faith is perfectly clear. To understand their meaning we do not and cannot invoke faith. Faith has no role at all to play here. I *must* understand the *meaning* of a proposition before I can accept or fail to accept it on faith or on authority.

If we could reasonably assume that religious utterances were meaningful (intelligible), then the fideist's claim would be perfectly understandable, though it might still fail to be convincing. But this is just what we cannot assume, for it is just this that is at issue. Fideism works only when we know what the religious claims in question *mean* and simply lack evidence for their *truth*. For traditional fideists the appropriate question is not "What do they mean?" or "Are they intelligible?" but, granting they are intelligible, why should we accept them when we cannot establish their truth or even establish that they are probable. The fideists are trying to show us why we should believe, even though we haven't one iota of evidence for our beliefs. It is this last question that Pascal, Kierkegaard, and Barth wrestle with, while (in effect) assuming that there is no puzzle about the *meaning* of religious utterances.[7] But it is just this logically prior question that disturbs contemporary philosophers when they think about religion, and to this question it would seem that fideism is no answer at all nor is it a way around the problem. We are, whether we like it or not, left with the crucial question: Are religious utterances intelligible, can we meaningfully assert or deny there is a God? This logically prior question remains a question of first importance in an examination and defense of religion. Apologetics cannot reasonably skirt it. To ask someone to understand by faith is nonsense, though if he already understands what his phonemic sequences mean, then it may well be (in some contexts at least) perfectly reasonable to ask him to accept the truth of what they are used to assert on faith— that is, understanding their meaning, we may be asked to accept on faith that what is asserted by their use is true. We still may not find it reasonable to opt for anything for which we lack evidence, but like William James or Søren Kierkegaard we may so believe though we lack evidence for our beliefs. We may, out of our despair and infinite hope, come to believe in the absurd, take it on faith that there is a God and that for God all things are possible, and at the same time be fully aware of the intellectual scandal involved in such a belief. Here we can legitimately talk of what a man can bring himself to do or not to do. But we must *presuppose*, in all such reasoning, that theistic utterances are (in the appropriate sense) meaningful.

A man deeply involved in religion may indeed *not* wish to engage in the philosopher's abstruse talk about talk or (more accurately) talk about the *uses* of talk. "Leave that to the philosophers" is his feeling; "I live by faith and all such philosophical chatter is entirely irrelevant to my faith. I will not cry out, like John Osborne, that 'We're alone in the universe, there's no God, . . . (and) somehow we've just got to make a go of it.' I will believe!"

The fideist can of course say this and he can say it from the anguish of his heart, but unless he is clear, genuinely clear, in his own mind that he understands what is meant by "God," then he is really, consciously or unconsciously, being evasive and obscurantist. Fideism does not seem to provide an "out" here, for as a matter of fact questions about the very intelligibility of religious discourse are hotly controversial. If we wish to be religious and still wish to be non-evasive about our religion, we must tackle these difficult philosophical questions of meaning; we cannot simply go the way of faith.

II

I wish now to consider if fideism can in some reasonable way overcome the challenge put to it in section one.

It might be argued, as J. N. Findlay has argued, that it is a mistake to link "understanding x" or "knowing the meaning of x" too closely with "the method of establishing x to be true or false."[8] Just such a close linkage is implicit in my preceding argument. I have, in effect, argued that to understand the meaning of x, where x is a sentence purportedly used to state a fact, we must know what conceivably *could* count for the truth or falsity of x. For x to have *factual* meaning, x must have truth conditions. If we do not know what these truth conditions are, x is meaningless to us, and that God might know what they are does not make x an intelligible bit of human discourse. It still remains a factually meaningless English expression.

Findlay claims this is a dogma that has created "gratuitous quandaries which have haunted thought in the past decades."[9] It would be nice to know why this is so, but Findlay does not tell us; however, he does assert what could be good news for the fideist, namely "that we may go quite a long ways towards validating an assertion whose meaning we do not understand *at all*."[10] (If we don't understand it *at all*, *what* is it that we are validating? How could we possibly have the slightest notion that it was *it* that we validated?) Findlay says that we do this "whenever we pin our faith to an assertion that we do not understand, but which has been made by some expert or reliable person."[11] This would fit our fideistic interpretation of the religious use of language very well.

Yet there are plenty of difficulties in Findlay's account. Findlay goes on to say that "true" has a standard use in which we "lend assent to assertions with whose precise content we are not for some reason conversant."[12] We can know something to be true when we know little or *nothing* of it. "Physicists," Findlay points out, "assert and make use of many sentences to which they have not given a satisfactory sense." But the cat is out of the bag with "a satisfactory sense" or "a precise content." In order for a sentence to serve as the vehicle for a *factual* assertion, we must be able to say what would count for the truth or falsity of this putative assertion. It must have *that* much meaning and this is not excluded in the physicist's case, even though the precise content or the full elaboration of his sentence may not be clear.

But this will not cover Findlay's *first situation* where we do not understand the meaning of the utterance *at all*, for there we cannot understand what it is to which we are to lend our assent. If we do not have *any idea at all* of what an utterance means, we literally cannot lend or fail to lend assent to it for, after all, how could we identify what it is we are lending our assent to? The physicist can say, "We don't understand *very well* what we mean by 'x' but when this happens (and he specifies some state of affairs) we would say 'x,' and if it does not occur we would not say 'x.'" If the believer can say something similar about "There is a God," then his utterance can be said to have a factual meaning, though we need not and ought not assert "There is a God" is identical in meaning with a sentence asserting that these test conditions obtain. If this is the case, then the religious utterance has an appropriate meaning. But where we do not understand the utterance *at all* we cannot even say what would make it true or false; and this being so, we can have no idea of what it would be like to validate it. If x is meaningless, x can be neither true nor false, validated nor invalidated, accepted nor rejected. A completely meaningless set of marks can never become the object of faith or of disbelief.

Findlay might argue that this is too harsh. It does not at all fit our linguistic practice. Consider again the analogy with physics. Many intelligent and reflective people understand little or nothing of physics. They don't understand what the physicist is talking about when he makes certain crucial statements that are a part of quantum mechanics. They don't understand his utterances at all. But they have seen our technological transformation—transformations beyond the dreams of the bold men of the Renaissance. And they have been *told* that there is a very important connection between some of these technological transformations and the (to them) mysterious statements that are a part of quantum theory. They see the fruits of science—how could they not see them?—and they trust the physicist; they trust that there is this intimate connection between his theories and these technological transformations, though they do not at all understand the physicist's statements when he states some of the key claims of quantum mechanics. They are meaningless gibberish to the non-physicist, but trusting the physicist (having faith in the physicist and in physics) they accept them humbly on faith (trust) though they do not understand their meaning. To them they remain empty formulae, but they have faith that these formulae do in reality mean something, that the physicist is asserting *something* (the layman knows not what) that is true. Such a layman has faith that such formulae are part of a coherent language game.

Why cannot the fideist, the knight of faith, do exactly the same thing? A language game of ancient lineage is being played here. The believer does not understand what is meant by certain crucial utterances that are a part of this language game, but by an act of faith, of trust in his religious authority, he accepts that what is being said is not without meaning—is part of a coherent language game. Such a fideist freely admits that such key religious utterances are gibberish to him, but he has faith that his religious authorities are saying *something* that is intelligible to them (but not to him), *something* that is important and true.

The first thing to be noted here is that by making such a claim the fideist has changed the conditions of the argument. He is no longer claiming that he has faith in meaningless propositions. His present argument in fact commits him to the claim that the propositions are meaningful. He is now only making the much less exciting claim that he can believe them even though they are meaningless to him and others like him. If the analogy with physics is close, there are certain religious figures—priests, theologians, some kind of holy men—who understand these key religious utterances. The fideist trusts them; they are his religious authorities, but, on the argument presently being made, the religious utterances are meaningful to the religious authorities in question, though they are not meaningful to the ordinary believer. Such a believer trusts the religious authority—*assuming,* as Danto so nicely puts it, that somebody knows what he is talking about.[13] The believer, as a fideist, may justifiably bypass the puzzling arguments about the very intelligibility of key theistic utterances but only on condition that his religious authority does not do so, for to argue as our fideist just has is to assume that his religious authority understands what the words and utterances mean. But philosophically significant fideists make no such claim. The purer and philosophically interesting and significant fideism that we are talking about claims that the religious authority, no matter how august, is in exactly the same boat as the plain believer. Such religious authorities have no key to the meaning of religious utterances. The propositions are not only meaningless to the uninitiate, they are meaningless to the theologian and holy man, too. These men too must accept such propositions purely on faith. They do not understand their meaning any more than the plain man does. They accept them simply on faith, as we all must, if we are to be genuinely religious. In this respect, the theologian or holy man is in a very different position from the physicist; and such religious men seem to be very much in the intellectual predicament described in section one. If this is so the plain man—attempting to adopt a fideistic approach to religion—cannot with justice turn to the theologian here. The analogy with science won't do.

Secondly, even forgetting the very crucial difficulty noted above, there is still trouble with the analogy, as my last remark in the above paragraph should have suggested. If a man knows nothing of physics, it is reasonable for him to accept what competent quantum physicists claim is so about quantum mechanics. The religiously perplexed layman may feel that the same thing holds for religion. There is no more point in everyone being his own theologian than everyone being his own physicist or doctor.[14] There are crucial differences in the cases—differences that destroy the point of the analogy. The theologian whom the believer relies on will claim (if he is a fideist) that he does not understand the key religious claims involved, since he, too, is a man and finite, sinful man cannot possibly understand such claims. Everyone (including the theologian) must accept such claims simply on faith without understanding their *meaning*. But once this admission is made, the analogy with physics has been destroyed and the points made in section one become apposite. How can anyone have faith, if no one can understand what it is we are to have faith in or what it is we are to accept solely on faith? When the theologians or holy men insist that they do not and cannot understand what they call their "articles of faith," how can we be expected to go on trusting them?

To this it may be replied, "Well, we just do. We mouth (utter) the words they tell us to mouth (utter), pray, go to communion, orient our life ethically in the way they tell us to, not understanding the superstructure they attach it to. (We utter the words in prayer, but they are words without meaning.) This gives our lives a meaning." Such a defense might continue in this manner: "There are a bunch of words that are part of our language. They can be used to make what some people would be willing to call statements. We do not understand them—no one does except God and appeal to him here would be viciously circular. Yet as the layman can accept something in physics that he does not understand at all, so we believers can accept something in religion that we do not understand at all. We trust that these key religious utterances are sometimes used to assert *something*, though we and no one else can say what they assert."

If the claim is made this weak, then even a Freudian or Marxian may claim that he can, in a sense, go along with it. Such utterances do typically assert something but, such a critic might aver, they can go the believer "one better" and say what that something is. Such God-sentences really refer to one's father, though the person who asserts them is actually confused about their reference. But the fideist will, of course, claim that when he says that these religious utterances assert something, though we do not understand them at all, he *means* that they assert some supernatural, spiritual, or transcendent something. But then he seems to be implicitly admitting he does understand them to a degree, and he is bringing in with "supernatural" and the like just the sort of word he claims is not understood at all and need not be understood. But it now seems that "supernatural," "spiritual," or "transcendent" must be understood if he is going to be able to claim, as he wants to, that his key religious utterances assert something that is distinct from what such a Freudian or Marxist materialist would be willing to assert. At this point the fideist may latch on to the first part of his argument alone. All he can justifiably say, he now concedes, is that believers mouth (utter) certain words (words that we humans do not understand) and act in a certain way. But this, he contends, is enough for belief.

If such a reply is made it seems to me that the fideist, if he is really willing to stick with this, cannot be dislodged by rational argument or shown, if he does nothing to adorn this position, that his position is senseless or unintelligible. It *may* be an irrational position, a position which no thoughtful man, once he had taken proper cognizance of the many thousands of conflicting religions and sects, would wish to embrace, but it is not an unintelligible position and I know of no purely logical or conceptual arguments that would defeat it.[15] But it is important to take note that if someone chooses to rest his argument here he cannot draw sustenance from the analogy with physics, for the physicist has no such need to appeal to faith or to do things in conjunction with accepting formulae whose meaning he does not *at all* understand. In the religious case we have nothing that is genuinely comparable to following the doctor's orders, though we do not understand the rationale of what the doctor would have us do, or accepting on trust that the physicist knows what he is talking about though we do not. With the fideist we have the claim that *no one* understands what he is doing, no one understands the meaning of the religious utterances in question, but we are to accept them all the same. But where this is so, it is not at all apparent that to believe under such circumstances is a reasonable thing to do and we are left with our original nagging problem —a problem posed most clearly by modern linguistic analysis: what would it be like to accept on faith or otherwise something as a factual proposition if we have *no idea* of what would confirm or disconfirm it, if we have *no idea* of under what circumstances we would be prepared to say it was true or false? The fideist claims that it is a *fact* that there is a God, that God created the world, that God loves us and the like. But if we have no idea of what it would be like for such statements to be either true or false, how can we meaningfully assert that they are statements of *fact*? And if we cannot meaningfully assert that statements asserting these claims are in reality statements of fact, how can we accept on faith that "There is a God," etc. are facts? Can fideism non-evasively and justifiably avoid this problem? I have just indicated one "out" that can be taken, but this "out" appears to be evasive. There is one more, ostensibly non-evasive move that the fideist might make. Let us now examine that.

In attempting to avoid the difficulties mentioned in section one, a fideist might state his position in the following way: " 'There is a God' is true" *means*, where Jesus is the religious authority, "Jesus asserted 'There is a God.' " (If Jesus is not the religious authority, then whoever or whatever is the religious authority should replace "Jesus" in the above-mentioned sentence.) Let us designate as (A) " 'There is a God' is true," and as (B) "Jesus asserted 'There is a God.' " A fideist might argue that (B) is verifiable (testable) in principle. And that Jesus uttered, or would have been prepared to utter, the Hebrew equivalent of "There is a God" is indeed verifiable in principle. (B) is not a mysterious utterance. Its truth-value is plain enough. The fideist then stipulates either that when he affirms (A) he means (B), or that when he affirms (A), (B) is at least an essential part of what he intends. But since (B) is intelligible (has a truth-value), then (A) is, to that degree, intelligible, too, and the fideist hasn't fallen into the analyst's trap after all. It is true that he does not understand what "There is a God" or "God loves us" *mean*. These utterances are meaningless to him, but he does know *what* it is he places his trust in—his faith is in something he does understand, namely, he understands that Jesus (or his religious authority) asserted that there is a God or that God loves us.

When we ask the fideist what he means when he says " 'There is a God' is true," he can reply that he at least means this: "Jesus asserted 'There is a God' and because Jesus asserted it, it is true." If we ask, "*What* did Jesus assert?" he will reply that Jesus asserted "There is a God" and that we finite, sinful creatures no more understand "There is a God" than we understand "There is an Irglig." However, we don't have to, for all we need to know is that if Jesus asserts something, we are to affirm that phonemic sequence. To the question, "What are you affirming?" we answer that we don't know; but whenever Jesus asserts something, we properly apply "true" to it. Since this is so, our statements expressive of our beliefs have truth-conditions and thus are intelligible, factual statements.

It is not true that they are compatible with anything and everything; we can say something about the conditions under which it would be appropriate to assert or deny them. Thus, though they are meaningless in one sense, they are meaningful in another, and a person can proclaim and adhere to them as his most basic commitments, the deepest articles of his faith. God Himself is unknowable—we don't even understand what "God" means—but Jesus is knowable and we take on faith his assertions about God to be true. In this way true faith may precede understanding.

This reply has at least one crucial defect. It claims Jesus asserted "p" where "p" is admittedly unintelligible to believer and non-believer alike, though supposedly intelligible to Jesus. But does it make sense to say "He asserted p" where "p" is unintelligible to us? We could say "He *uttered* p" or "He *wrote* p" but are we entitled to say he *asserted* p or *stated* p?[16] To assert something is to vouch for its truth. Now, how would it be possible for us to know that someone had asserted something except by seeing that he was willing to stick by it, give evidence for it if some moral considerations did not intervene, attempt to meet counter-claims and the like? In general, to know that he had *asserted* it, and not just *said* it, would be to know that he had behaved in certain distinctive ways. Consider this case. I say "The river is over its banks and we will have to move out to keep from being flooded." I say this but I make no effort to move out and I have no idea of how to take or direct you to a place where you could make observations of the river. To compound the confusion I keep on making the above utterance no matter what happens. Finally —after being pressed—I acknowledge that I didn't mean to claim that what I said was true but that I simply wanted to perplex you and to exercise my vocal chords. In such a situation you would *not* be entitled to say that I had asserted what I uttered but only that I had said it without meaning it. To assert something is to claim with honesty that it is true. Phonemic sequences or sentences cannot be true or false; only statements or assertions made through the use of sentences can be true or false. Before we can say that something is a *bona fide* assertion, as distinct from a sentence or a phonemic sequence, we must know what would count as evidence for the truth or falsity of what we are saying. But if we do not understand what p means we cannot understand what it would *mean* to say that p is true. Not understanding this, we cannot say what would count for the truth of p. Thus (B) ("Jesus *asserted* 'There is a God' ") is unintelligible. But now we have also lost our footing for saying (A) is intelligible. Thus, our fideist has not by such a move been able to maneuver around the difficulty with fideism developed in section one.

It is not an adequate rebuttal to reply that it is enough to say "Jesus said 'There is a God,' " for "said" will either in this context bear the meaning of "asserts" or it will simply mean "uttered the sentence-token 'There is a God.' " If it means the latter it is indeed intelligible and would be just as intelligible if Jesus had said "Bright is the equation grief regains." But where "said" doesn't and couldn't do the job of "asserts" or "states," it is *not* correct to say that what Jesus said is *true* or *false*, and if that is so, then it does not make sense to say we will assert or deny what Jesus asserted or denied, for Jesus did not, and in this instance could not, assert or deny anything. For the same reasons, it makes no sense to say that Jesus's utterance is true or false, for an utterance or a sentence can't be true or false but only a statement, assertion, or a judgment can be true or false. Since in this instance he can't be asserting (or for that matter stating or judging) anything, he of course cannot be asserting (stating, judging) anything true or false. On this reading, (B) can't be an assertion—true or false—and since (A) has what meaning it has in virtue of (B), (A) cannot be an assertion either, and thus cannot be an object of our faith.

III

It is now time to sum up. Contemporary perplexity over religion typically arises from the conviction or anxiety that key religious utterances are in some appropriate sense meaningless. Fideism, I have argued, is no way around this problem. If we human beings have no understanding at all of what would or could count as an appropriate object of a religious attitude, we cannot understand what we are to take as the object of our religious trust, reverence, or faith. Such a "faith" is so blind, so objectless, that it is no faith at all. The best face we can put on the attempt to develop a fideism compatible with the admission that our key religious utterances are meaningless—utterly beyond all human understanding—comes down to the claim that "to believe solely on faith" consists in *nothing more* than repeating certain words we do not and cannot understand and carrying or attempting to carry out certain principles of action that we trust will give a deep, though not clearly definable, point to our lives. So limited, fideism is an intelligible theological stance, even in a world in which believers and non-believers alike acknowledge that God-talk or the crucial bits of God-talk are unintelligible. But it is natural to demand more of religious belief; and where more is demanded, fideism cannot justify bypassing the contention that the claims of religion are in reality no claims at all because key religious words and utterances are without intelligible factual content. If such a sceptical claim is justified, religious claims are illusory and fideism is no adequate defense of religion.

If the fideist finally grants us that we cannot have faith in or place our trust in what is meaningless and then goes on to say "But, of course, 'There is a God,' 'God loves us,' 'God created the heavens and the earth,' and the like, all do have meaning, for after all they have a *use* in our 'mother-tongue,'" he has shifted the argument. I have only been concerned here to argue that we cannot (with the qualification already mentioned) intelligibly maintain that we can have faith in meaningless propositions. If God-talk is meaningless or unintelligible, then fideism crumbles along with the other defenses of religious belief. If phonemic sequences like those mentioned above are understood as meaningful (true or false) assertions, then we can indeed believe they are *true*, *de fide*. Fideism would then be an intelligible though *perhaps* an irrational apologetic position. It seems to me, however, that we do not know the truth-conditions associated with "There is a God" and the like. In fact, we do not even know if they have truth-conditions. If this is so, then there seem to be no grounds for claiming that such religious utterances are used in such a way that they can count as assertions which we may take or fail to take on faith.[17] But this is a large subject that deserves attention on another occasion.

NOTES

1. See particularly his "The Logical Status of Religious Belief" in *Metaphysical Beliefs*, ed. S. Toulmin *et al.* (London: 1957) and his *Difficulties in Christian Belief* (London: 1957).

2. That such a view is not the straw man of an eager, all-too-eager, philosophical analyst, but a powerful tradition within Christian theology, is amply shown by Richard Popkin in his "Theological and Religious Scepticism," *The Christian Scholar*, Vol. XXXIX (June 1956), pp. 150–158 and in his "Kierkegaard and Scepticism," *Algemeen Nederlands Tijdschrift Voor Wijsbegeerte En Psychologie*, Vol. 51 (No. 3), pp. 123–141.

3. Paul Holmer, "Philosophical Criticism and Christology," *The Journal of Religion*, Vol. XXXIV (April 1954), p. 90.

4. For an analysis that construes certain key religious utterances as ideological utterances, see my "On Speaking of God," *Theoria*, Vol. XXVIII, Part 2 (1962), pp. 110–137.

5. I. M. Crombie, "Theology and Falsification," *New Essays in Philosophical Theology*, ed. by A. G. N. Flew (New York: 1955), p. 130.

6. See Bernard Williams' brilliant essay, "Tertullian's Paradox," *New Essays in Philosophical Theology*, ed. by A. G. N. Flew (New York: 1955), pp. 208–211.

7. They do not see or do not face the semantical puzzle, "What cognitive meaning could such utterances have if we *can* have no grounds at all for saying they are true?"

8. J. N. Findlay, "Some Reflections on Meaning," *The Indian Journal of Philosophy*, Vol. I (August 1959), pp. 15–16.

9. *Ibid.*, p. 16.

10. *Ibid.*, p. 15 (italics mine).

11. *Ibid.*

12. *Ibid.*

13. Arthur C. Danto, "Faith, Language and Religious Experience: A Dialogue," in *Religious Experience and Truth*, ed. by Sidney Hook (New York: 1961), p. 146.

14. If the "plain man" has read much theology or has run onto Walter Kaufmann's "Theology," he might, or at least he should, feel differently about this, though perhaps if he had done this he would not really be a "plain man." See Walter Kaufmann, "Theology," in *Self, Religion and Metaphysics,* ed. by Gerald E. Myers (New York: 1961), pp. 83–109.

15. I shall return on another occasion to the very strong claim that fideism in particular and theistic religion in general are irrational and therefore ought to be abandoned.

16. Some of the relevant distinctions between "saying," "asserting," and "stating" are nicely drawn by Isabel Hungerland in her "Contextual Implication," *Inquiry*, Vol. 3 (Winter, 1960).

17. If arguments like those made by Ziff in his "About 'God'" are correct what I have said here would need modification. But it seems to me that Paul Edwards' arguments against Ziff's contentions are very strong if not decisive. See Paul Ziff, "About 'God,'" pp. 195–202, and Paul Edwards, "Some Notes on Anthropomorphic Theology," pp. 244–245, both in *Religious Experience and Truth*, ed. by Sidney Hook (New York: 1961).

Nirvana and Kingdom of God

Thomas J. J. Altizer

"The first axiom of an authentically contemporary theology is the acceptance of the death of God." This statement, startling by itself, may seem somewhat less so when put in context, for the God who is dead, says Thomas J. J. Altizer, is the God of the speculative philosophers—God as the rational idea which crowns a metaphysical system—and such a construct has nothing in common with the God of radically eschatological biblical faith. If the Christian is to live in our revolutionary world, he must, insists Dr. Altizer, give contemporary meaning to the liberating New Testament teaching of the Kingdom of God. But then Altizer moves on to what will to many seem a startling proposition indeed—that the Buddhist category of Nirvana may be employed "as a mode of entry into the original form of Christianity." Many readers will not want to go all the way with Altizer, but few will deny that he argues cogently and tellingly. Pertinent to Dr. Altizer's essay, which appeared first in the April 1963 *Journal of Religion,** is his 1961 book *Oriental Mysticism and Biblical Eschatology,* published by Westminster Press. Dr. Altizer, an Episcopal layman, is Associate Professor of Bible and Religion at Emory University, Atlanta, Georgia.

1

OUR TASK in this paper will be to inquire into the relationship between Nirvana and the Kingdom of God in the perspective of our contemporary religious situation. First it is necessary to define this situation, if only to make clear what this paper will regard as valid principles, methods, and goals of theological inquiry in our time. For this paper rests upon two crucial assumptions: (1) The foundations of Western civilization—and of Christendom itself—are collaps-

* University of Chicago Press, Chicago 37, Illinois.

ing about us, and the root ideas and values of this civilization no longer have validity or relevance to the authentically contemporary man. (2) Christianity as we know it historically has been integrally related to Western civilization, and therefore insofar as Christian theological categories are a product of Western civilization—regardless of the effect which Christianity itself has had upon this civilization—they have neither validity for nor relevance to the contemporary Christian. While seldom stated explicitly, these assumptions are obviously operative to one degree or another in much contemporary theology (for example, in Bultmannianism and even in the call of some Continental Catholic theologians for a post-Constantinian Christianity). These assumptions also cast light on the baffling fact that dogmatic theology proper has virtually died in recent years, for it would seem that it is no longer possible to express traditional theological categories (such as Creation, Incarnation, Logos, Trinity, etc.) in contemporary language, that is to say, in language which is meaningful in our historical situation.

It is easy to state these assumptions but extremely difficult to assess their full meaning and impact. However, there are two problem areas where it is possible for the astute critic to sense the gravity of the revolutionary crisis in which we must live. These are (1) the idea and the doctrine of God and (2) the radical disruption between the biblical categories of faith, as revealed in historical scholarship, and the traditional categories of Christian theology. The latter problem is recognized by all—except perhaps dogmatic theologians—while the former problem is seldom discussed. Significantly enough, and despite its name, at no point is modern theology weaker than in its doctrine of God—it could perhaps be said that the doctrine of God is the "Emperor's clothes" of modern theology, and it is a pity that no ironist has arisen to portray the nakedness of our theologians. The three most influential theologians of our time clearly illustrate this problem. Thus the Barth of the *Dogmatik* has constructed a magnificent trinitarian doctrine of God which is overwhelming in its sheer power and comprehensiveness; but it succeeds in its purpose only by isolating all theological meaning from man's historical life or his existence as man—nevertheless the *Dogmatik* performs the invaluable service of demonstrating the archaic nature of the orthodox theological tradition, for perhaps nowhere else may one encounter so many meaningless sentences. Tillich, on the other hand, has constructed a philosophical doctrine of God as the Unconditioned which is intended to have both existential relevance and religious reality; yet Tillich's Unconditioned eventually disappears into a mysterious Ground of Being, which is construed ambiguously either as a mystical Godhead (the God beyond God) or as absolute Immanence (or Dionysian in the Nietzschean sense, as brilliantly demonstrated by Jacob Taubes). Finally, Bultmann has attempted to collapse theology into anthropology, which, if nothing else, indicates that for the Bultmannian school the idea of God no longer has existential significance.

One is tempted to note that in the Western tradition the idea of God has always been philosophical rather than theological (with the possible exception of Augustinianism). Thus Western man has constructed an idea of God as a part of his project of understanding the world; the God of the philosophers is a rational idea, created both to make possible the philosophical project and to crown the systems of the philosophers: perhaps the last chapter in this history was written when Whitehead, who previously had shown no interest in the idea of God, seized upon the idea of God as a means of completing his metaphysical system. It is impossible for Western man to dissociate the idea of God from the idea of the *kosmos*, the idea of a rational order which is imbedded in the world. God and *kosmos* are polar expressions of one root idea: the rationality of the universe, or, rather, the very idea of the *uni*verse itself. Significantly, the dissolution of the idea of God in modern thought has been followed by an overwhelming sense of meaninglessness: with the eclipse of God, man has experienced himself as "thrown" into a mysterious void. But the idea of God was also imbedded with a pseudo-understanding of the world; the very assumption of a universal cosmic order represents a turning away from the concrete contingency of the world. Thus, when the world was most fully known—as in modern science—it was wholly detached from a transcendent ground. Accordingly, modern science spells the end of all teleology, and thus the advent of modern science—and of modern historicism—has brought about the death of the rational idea of God. All that which modern man genuinely knows—which is to say all that which he knows scientifically or historically—he knows only through the death of God, through the death of any absolute which could condition man's knowledge or experience of reality. The collapse of natural theology (which is to say of any sort of genuine philosophical theology) has long been remarked; but it is not often realized that the death of philosophical theology represents at bottom the death of the idea of God.

Nietzsche's proclamation of the death of God is at once the most accurate portrait of our religious condition and the most profound portrait of the situation of contemporary man. Surely it is not possible for any responsible person to think that we can any longer know or experience God in nature, in history, in the economic or political arenas, in the laboratory, or in anything which is genuinely modern, whether in thought or in experience. Wherever we turn in our experience, we experience the eclipse or the silence of God. To refuse to accept the death of God is to evade our actual condition, to turn our back on our historical situation. The most devastating attack upon Christianity from Marx and Nietzsche to Sartre and Camus is the charge that Christianity represents a flight from reality, a cowardly retreat—both in resentment and illusion—from the horror and chaos, the emptiness and vacuity, and even the actual problems, of man's naked existence in the world. The Christian is condemned for his evasion of suffering, for his refusal to accept the anguish of the human condition, for his inability to live in a revolutionary world, for his flight from the world itself. In our world, the "Christian" is both the sick man and the archaic man; too weak to bear existence in a seemingly meaningless world, he seeks solace in a vanquished world of the past to assuage the wounds to his tender sensibility. Consequently, the confession of the death of God is now the price which the Christian must pay for contemporaneity. And the absence of a genuine doctrine of God in the higher expressions of modern theology is mute testimony to its genuine contemporaneity. Indeed, the first axiom of an authentically contemporary theology is the acceptance of the death of God.

If the death of God has been thrust upon the Christian both by his immersion in modern thought and by his own immediate experience, it is Christian thought and scholarship which has revealed the chasm which lies between biblical faith and the Christian tradition. How startling it has been to encounter anew the God of the Bible, about whom Luther and Pascal once spoke with such confidence, and to realize that this God is truly the Wholly Other. Not only is the biblical God wholly other than everything which we know in the world, He—or should we say it? for we have lost that intimacy with God that alone makes possible the use of a personal pronoun in referring to deity—is now seen to be wholly other than the God of Christendom, including the God of Christian theology. Now we know that the biblical God—at least as known by the Christian—is the God of the End. For modern scholarship has conclusively demonstrated that the message of Jesus and of the primitive church (including Paul) was radically eschatological. The Christian God was originally known and proclaimed only through the announcement of the glad tidings of the coming of the Kingdom of God, whose coming would annihilate the world. In truth, the Christian believed that the Kingdom of God had broken into time with the resurrection of Christ, that the form (*schema*) of this world is passing away, and that life in Christ—which is to say life in the Kingdom—liberates the Christian from the values and reality of the world. The very power of the Gospel, including most particularly its ethical power, was created by the liberation which it brought the Christian from the world. Through being lifted out of the reality of the world, the Christian was able to reverse the values of the world, and thus to live in his new life the new reality of love (agape).

Thus the biblical foundations of the Christian faith were seen to be radically eschatological. Yet this eschatological form of faith rapidly disappeared from orthodox Christianity; or, rather, orthodox Christianity, as we first encounter it in the later writings of the New Testament and in the second-century Fathers, and then throughout the history of the main stream of Christianity, is quite simply non-eschatological. Furthermore, we can now see that the basic categories of orthodox theology only came into existence by means of a process of "spiritualizing"—which is to say of de-eschatologizing—all the fundamental categories of the original Christian proclamation. And it is obvious that it was the transplanting of Christianity from its Palestinian soil and its entrance Hellenistic world that occasioned the transformation of Christianity. Thus began the synthesis of Christ and civilization, leading thereby to the apparently inextricable association of Christianity with the civilizations that were descendants of the classical culture of the West.

Hence we face the dual dilemma of discovering that the forms and categories of our inherited Christian faith are both irrelevant to the actual world in which we must live and detached from a biblical ground. In very truth, the Christian God is dead. Now the Christian, too, must face that terrible abyss of the man in our time who is without faith; both must live in a new world, a revolutionary world which has destroyed all established meaning and values, and both must live in the world apart from any ultimate source of meaning or security. One of the most subtle problems which theology must now face is that of distinguishing the authentically contemporary Christian from the unbeliever who fully accepts and lives his actual condition and situation (in fact, there are some theologians who deny that such a distinction can be drawn). But perhaps the greater problem is that of attempting to apprehend the Christian meaning of the Kingdom of God in a situation in which God is dead; in other words, the problem of finding a genuinely contemporary meaning, a meaning which can be expressed in contemporary language, of that Reality which lies at the center of the Christian faith. Negatively, we are well prepared; for we are forbidden to make use of the traditional categories of the Christian faith, because they are both archaic and unbiblical. Yet, otherwise, we would seem to have no center or direction. All religious meaning has collapsed in our world; so long as we remain within our own world, our actual condition and historical situation, we can know only the death of God. Consequently, this paper has chosen the task of relating the Kingdom of God to Nirvana, for therein we can gain a new perspective, a perspective apart from the traditions of Western Christendom and apart from the radical immanence of the modern West. Thereby it may be possible to apprehend the Kingdom of God in a new light, and that light may prove to have a contemporary relevance.

II

Let us remember that the idea—or more properly the symbol—of the Kingdom of God is a product of the Jewish eschatological tradition (regardless of its presumed origin in Persian religion) and that here the Kingdom of God had never been associated with a rational understanding of either God or the world. On the contrary, here the Kingdom of God is identified with a New Creation whose coming must bring an end to the present order and structure of the world. To relate, in a positive or organic manner, the Kingdom of God to a presumed eternal order of the world is to dissolve the deepest religious foundations of the symbol of the Kingdom. While such was the path of the ancient patristic church—and later of Christendom at large—we can now see that this path leads to an obliteration of both the meaning and the power of the original Gospel. But here we may observe a decisive parallel with the Buddhist symbol of Nirvana. Throughout the Buddhist tradition, Nirvana is radically detached from all experience and understanding of the world. The Buddhist is forbidden even to speak of Nirvana, for language inevitably betrays the disordered and anguished state of man's life in the world (Samsara). True, Nirvana may be known, but known only in an interior mystical vision, a knowing which demands a dissolution of all thought and experience and which culminates inevitably in the dissolution of the self. Thus Nirvana tells us nothing about the meaning of the world or of human existence, except to identify it as the arena of pain, suffering, and death. When Nirvana is truly known, world and self disappear; for the realization of Nirvana can occur only through a radical transformation of everything which man knows as existence.

If we except the mystical form of the Buddhist quest for Nirvana, can we find anything in the symbol of Nirvana which decisively differs from the Christian symbol of the Kingdom of God? Without a qualm, the traditional Christian will say: everything! He will point to the nihilistic foundations of the symbol of Nirvana, its world-denying thrust, its dissolution of the human person and of human history, and its atheistic ground. And it is true that Buddhism stands wholly apart from the established categories of Christian theology. Yet which of these theological categories is consistent with an eschatological form of faith? Let us begin with the claim that the world-denying thrust of Buddhism sets Buddhism radically apart from the Christian faith. It is true that classical Christian theology created the idea of the Creation, an idea which represents a synthesis of the Greek idea of the *kosmos* and the Old Testament–priestly symbol of the Creation, and classical Christian theology has maintained both that the Creation is real and that the Creation is good. But insofar as the Creation is invested with the ontological idea of reality (which is to say reality in an ultimate sense) and the moral idea of good (which is to say intrinsically good, good according to its nature), then the idea of the Creation is not only inconsistent with, but represents an inversion of, eschatological faith. In the New Testament, *kosmos* means Old Aeon (as Bultmann has demonstrated), and, insofar as the Creation is identified with the world, it can only be known in eschatological faith as Old Creation—the arena of sin, darkness, and death. Now granting that the Buddhist understanding of the world as Samsara is radically inconsistent with the classical Christian idea of Creation, how does it radically differ from the eschatological symbol of Old Creation?

Again we must face the claim that the Buddhist denial of selfhood and the Buddhist quest for a selfless state are radically opposed to Christian anthropology. Here the problem is far more complex, and its complexity derives chiefly from the confused and contradictory state of the Christian doctrine of man. Nevertheless, certain observations can be made. The idea of the ultimate value and reality of the human person is a Western idea, having its roots in Greek thought and the Bible and its most powerful expressions in Augustinianism and in Renaissance and post-Renaissance Western thought and experience. But for Augustine, the human person can be known only through, and indeed only after, the experience of God; there is no basis whatsoever in Augustinianism for the idea of the autonomous value and reality of the person. This idea of the autonomous person has become the dominant Western idea, and it is clearly a product of Western secularization—which is to say that it is a post-Christian idea. Moreover, nothing could be further from eschatological faith than the idea of the autonomous person: for eschatological faith, the autonomous person is quite the sinner, the "old self," the Old Adam, and, as such, personhood in this sense must be seen as being wholly other than the new life in Jesus Christ. While we cannot say that there is no idea of a person whatsoever in eschatological faith, we can say that the New Being of the believer is so intimately related to Jesus Christ and the Kingdom of God that he has no autonomous value or reality. Insofar as the Christian lives as a believer, he lives in Jesus Christ and the Kingdom of God; he lives a life which is not only open to, but indeed is caught up in, transcendence. Here, authentic existence—which is to say real existence—is existence in the Kingdom of God, not existence in the world, the flesh, or the self. Thus Christian existence is transcendent existence and thereby is wholly other than the autonomous existence of the dominant Western tradition and the immanent existence of the dominant contemporary experience. Accordingly, it seems obvious that authentic Christian existence is closer to the selfless existence of Buddhism than to the autonomous existence of Western man and that everything which we know as existence in the world (*Dasein*) must be annihilated in authentic life in Jesus Christ.

The charge that Buddhism is opposed to the Christian idea of history is perhaps equally complex, yet it is far more open to resolution. For in recent years we have learned that the idea of the autonomous meaning and order of history is not only post- but is deeply anti-Christian. Through the work of Karl Löwith, we know that even Augustine did not believe that historical events as such were either inherently meaningful or religiously significant. And we know that philosophers of history from Hegel and Marx to Spengler and Croce have at bottom been theologians of history, and it is clear that their theologies are patently anti-Christian. More deeply, through Nietzsche, Dilthey, and Troeltsch, we know that the modern historical consciousness itself is grounded in the death of God, in the eclipse of all absolutes; no way has yet been found of drawing a decisive line between historical thinking and historicism. Dilthey concluded his life's work with the judgment that "the relativity of all human concepts is the last word of the historical vision of the world." In response to this situation, Bultmann has followed Kierkegaard in insisting that the true events of the Christian faith are not historical events proper (*Historie*) but rather existential events (*Geschichte*) which are not susceptible to historical investigation—this is the theological reason why Bultmann has so deeply resisted the new quest for the historical Jesus, and it is a sad commentary that his followers seem so oblivious of the deeper consequences of their "new" quest. Finally, it is also now clear that an eschatological faith—as opposed to a messianic faith—cannot look upon history as the arena of the "acts" of God; for eschatological faith, God is the God of the End, and His "action" must bring history to an end. Here there is no room for a pattern or direction in history, except insofar as history must inevitably fall more deeply into darkness. Only a Christianity which has been profoundly molded by the autonomous and secular values of modern Western man could grant history an ultimate reality and value. In the original and purer form of Christian faith, history has no value whatsoever; it is looked upon with indifference if not with outright rejection; thus it is difficult to see where lies the decisive difference between the Christian and the Buddhist attitude to history.

Yet perhaps the most damning Christian charge against Buddhism is that it is atheistic, not atheistic in the Western sense, of course, but atheistic in the sense that it allows no room either for an idea of God or for a transcendent Being. First let us inquire into the reasons why Buddhism is atheistic. The Buddha forbade all theoretical questions—and therefore all theoretical thinking—because of his conviction that such questioning distracts the mind of the religious seeker from the religious quest itself, from the actual practice of the way to Nirvana. To translate this principle into Christian terms, we might say that the entertainment of the idea of God distracts the Christian from the actual presence of God, or that thinking represents a turning away from the religious life itself, from life in the Kingdom of God. Nor is it without significance that eschatological faith has never—whether in Judaism, Christianity, or Islam—produced a theology. But if we were to accept a certain continuity between Buddhism and Christianity at this point, how else but negatively can we react to the Buddhist refusal of a transcendent reality of any kind? Note should be immediately taken, however, of the fact that a transcendent reality (and with it the religious reality which Rudolph Otto termed the "numinous") is foreign to the Buddhist *religious* experience: Buddhism is closed to the experience of a Beyond. Nirvana is not conceived as an ontological state; and, in part, this is because Nirvana is not "known." For Nirvana is manifest only in conjunction with a dissolution of all man's faculties, only through an abolition of consciousness which shatters the self, thereby bringing human existence to an end. Thus Nirvana cannot be known as a Beyond, first, because knowing itself disappears with the advent of Nirvana and, second, because with the presence of Nirvana there is present no other reality whatsoever with which Nirvana could be contrasted. Not only does the self disappear in Nirvana, but with it all experience of a here and a now, all awareness of Samsara. Therefore Buddhism is closed to a transcendent reality if only because it is so radically open to—and so deeply immersed in—the salvation reality of Nirvana.

Surely it is just at this point that the Christian must be most deeply challenged by his encounter with Buddhism. And it is here that the real meaning of Buddhist nihilism is manifest. The world is known to be void (empty, *Sunya*) of reality in the moment in which Nirvana appears: for with the appearance of Nirvana all knowing comes to an end, all "reality" disappears. This means that for the Buddhist "reality" only appears (ex-ists) through the absence of Nirvana. The very category of "existence" is a product of ignorance (*avidya*), is created by desire or craving (*tanha*), and is grounded in pain (*dukkha*). Hence Buddhist nihilism is the product of a purely religious apprehension of the world. When the world is most deeply experienced—which is to say when it is apprehended apart from all human "experience"—it manifests itself as being void of "reality," as being wholly other than that which man "knows" it to be, in short, as being the Nothing. Samsara is known as pain and suffering only when it is known by man, only when it is consciously experienced and wilfully grasped. Through the advent of Nirvana, Samsara as Samsara (as pain and suffering) disappears. Yet do we not find here an amazing coincidence with eschatological faith? For the appearance of the Kingdom of God brings an end to the reality of the world; the God of eschatological faith is the God of the End, and therefore the manifestation of his Kingdom occurs only through an annihilation of "reality," and he is known in faith only through an abolition of self, of existence (*Dasein*), and of sin.

III

Now it must not be thought that at all these points Buddhism is superior to Christianity, or purer than Christianity, or, for that matter, that Buddhism is any closer to the religious Reality than is Christianity. Need it be said that Buddhism appears purer to us because we are not Buddhists! We have not lived in the Buddhist tradition, have not been forced to bear the terrible imperfections of the human and historical expressions of Buddhism, and even today are not dependent upon the weak scattered fragments of a once vital faith. But we must bear Christianity in all these forms: indeed, it is impossible for us to see Christianity apart from them. Furthermore, the Christianity that we know is the product of almost two thousand years of secularization—for secularization began with Christianity's acceptance of the world, with Christianity's submission to the very reality of the world. Thus we can look at Christianity only through a glass darkly, and, for those who live in our time, and are thereby destined to live the death of God, there can be no assurance that what we see through our dark glass will be Christianity. For all of these reasons it is imperative that we gain a new perspective, a new vantage point, from which to look at Christianity. And Buddhism is ideally suited to play this role: it is rivaled only by Christianity as a higher expression of religion; it has no relation to the Near Eastern eschatological religious tradition; it has never been associated with Western civilization; and it is a genuinely universal religion.

If we are to employ Buddhism as a mode of entry into the original form of Christianity, then we must do so by means of comparison of the primal Buddhist and Christian categories of Nirvana and Kingdom of God. Unfortunately, the Christian tradition has succeeded in isolating the meaning and reality of God from the eschatological category of Kingdom of God. This it did under the impact of Greek theoretical thinking, and whether or not this impact was mediated through Philo as Wolfson maintains, it effectively merged the biblical-numinous apprehension of the holiness of God with a rational idea. This idea has a number of names (all of them unbiblical)—such as absolute, infinite, unconditioned, true Being, etc.; it is grounded in a rational apprehension of the world, and it can know God only as a God who is in essential continuity with the world, with "being." Thus the orthodox Christian tradition postulates God as Being qua being: and if we were to trans- late this rational theological idea into eschatological terms, we should discover that here God is known as Being qua Old Being, or Being qua Old Aeon, which is to say that classical Christian theology has only *known* God insofar as it knew a world turned away from God. Thus the God of theology is closed to the God of the Gospel, and theology itself has been closed to the eschatological meaning and reality of Christ and the Kingdom of God.

A major task of contemporary theology is that of recover- ing—or should we say creating—an eschatological vision of God, and it is just at this point that Buddhism has a deep relevance to our task. Buddhism has never attempted to relate Nirvana to a reality beyond or apart from it; indeed, it has never allowed itself to speak of true reality (as opposed to the reality of Samsara) as a reality apart from Nirvana. Therein it has recognized that the mere awareness of a genuine reality apart from Nirvana is both a distraction of the mind of the seeker from the salvation-reality of Nirvana and a threat to the very reality of Nirvana itself. It is this latter point that we Christians need to learn: mere awareness of a reality which stands apart from the Kingdom of God is only possible through a turning away from the power of the Kingdom. And to know God apart from his Kingdom is to know a God who is a God only of *this* world, and never the God proclaimed by Jesus Christ. It also follows that to the extent that we understand God rationally, that is, the extent to which we apprehend God by a thinking that arises out of our understanding of the world, we are doomed to dissolve the God of faith. Simply to think of God in this manner is to know him through categories which are a reflection of the world, to submit him to the reality of being; and against this enslavement of God to being the prophetic tradition has always violently rebelled (as witness especially the orthodox Muslim reaction to the advent of philosophy in Islam). And most significantly of all, to know a God whose very reality is in continuity with the reality of the world is to make impossible an ethical act that reverses the values and reality of the world, despite the fact that this reversal lies at the center of Jesus' message, and of the Christian life itself.

Therefore the time has come for the Christian theologian to bring an end to the *idea* of God, for the idea of God as we know it is inconsistent with eschatological faith and makes impossible the practice of the Christian life. Already we have seen that the life which we are now called upon to live, the existence into which we are "thrown," is a wholly immanent reality, a reality created by the collapse of the transcendent realm. We must live the death of God if we are to exist in our world, for the confession of the death of God is now the price of the Christian's contemporaneity. Yet not only does the confession of the death of God liberate us from an archaic retreat from our destiny, it also liberates us from a tradition that was closed to eschatological faith and grounded in a reversal of the message of the Gospel. By living the death of God, we can both accept our destiny and be open once more to the radical call of Jesus' Word. No longer can the idea of God bring us security in the world; no longer can the Christian know God as the Absolute who is the source of all meaning, order, and reality in the world. And no longer can the Christian know God as Being itself; for therein lies a retreat from the actuality of the world and an idolatrous identification of the God of faith with the presumed orders and structures of the world. Not only must the Christian be open to the death of God, he must live the death of God with all the passion and depth that Nietzsche demanded.

Now the time has come to face the final problem of this paper. Can the Christian live in the terrible void with which we are confronted, or must he turn away from this void in his quest for the Kingdom of God? Does faith isolate the Christian from the emptiness, the meaninglessness, and the sheer horror of our world? Is Christianity a retreat from reality, a flight from anguish, death, and pain? All of us must say no to this question, and say no because we know that the Christian is called to share Christ's Cross and Passion; but do we have a theological ground upon which to say no? Certainly no such ground is provided in the theological tradition, and we must note that Christian existentialists from Kierkegaard to Bultmann have spoken of the *leap* of faith which liberates the Christian from his existence in the world. At bottom, Christian existentialism is grounded in the Kierkegaardian fallacy that authentic human existence culminates in the passion of faith, an assumption that denies the authenticity of the terrible anguish of contemporary man. Yet again we must turn to our Buddhist perspective. However, if we look at Mahayana Buddhism, a baffling paradox is apparent which casts both light and darkness upon our problem. Here, the highest ideal of the Buddhist life is the path of the Bodhisattva, a path which entails the renunciation of salvation (Nirvana) and an identification with the suffering of all sentient beings (Samsara) until such time as these beings themselves pass into Nirvana. Yet at the same time, and deeply imbedded in the very way of the Bodhisattva, we find a mystical identification of Nirvana and Samsara, based upon a denial of the independent reality of either Nirvana or Samsara and culminating in a denial of the reality of either the Bodhisattva or the sufferer, either the Buddha or suffering itself. This identification is grounded in a mystical apprehension of the oneness of reality, an apprehension which makes void or empty (*Sunya*) the reality of Nirvana and Samsara alike. There is but one Reality: when known to consciousness, and manifest in history, it appears as Samsara; but through higher mystical intuition (*prajna*) and self-giving compassion (*karuna*), it appears as Nirvana.

It is difficult to resist the temptation to translate this Mahayana position into Christian terms. Forgoing all prudence, let us make the impossible attempt. There is but one Reality: when known to consciousness, and manifest in history, it appears as Old Aeon; but through faith and self-giving compassion (agape) it appears as Kingdom of God. Now obviously this translation does violence both to the eschatological form and to the religious meaning of Christianity. Nevertheless it may illustrate a Christian truth which has been obscured by Christian theology. Faith, for the Christian, is not a turning *away* from the world but rather a turning to God *in the midst* of the world; not a turning to a God who is Beyond, but rather a turning to the Kingdom of God which breaks into time in our midst. Thus the very idea of a *leap* of faith is foreign to the innermost religious life of Christianity: for it arises out of an evasion, a flight from, the anguish of the human condition; it represents a refusal of the presence of the Kingdom. Understandable as such a refusal is on the part of the Christian who must live in our world, this refusal nevertheless remains unchristian insofar as it must seek the Kingdom in a beyond. Yet if the Christian is to know the Kingdom as present in the world, he cannot know the world as "world." Insofar as the man of faith knows reality as "nature," "history," "world," or "being," he is closed to the presence of the Kingdom and turned away from the call of Christ; nor can he, while in such a condition, live the life that Jesus demanded. But insofar as the Christian knows reality as God's Kingdom, he knows the presence of Christ, and therein gives himself—spontaneously, immediately—in compassion to others. Here, the giving of one's self to others in an immediate response to a new condition, the dawning of the Kingdom of God. But the Kingdom does not dawn "above," it dawns "here"; it dawns in our midst. Therefore it does not take us *away* from the "here" and "now" as such, it tears the veil from our reality and draws all reality into itself. Through the advent of the Kingdom, the world appears in a new light, for now the world gives witness to its ultimate end, when the world will be transfigured by a New Creation, when God will be all in all.

True, the appearance of the Kingdom effects a reversal of the reality of the world; but, as in Mahayana Buddhism, reality, as known in sin, is reversed and not annulled or annihilated. To be sure, the reality of the world (Old Aeon) is annihilated insofar as that reality is created by sin, by a human existence which is turned away from God—that is, the world as "history," "nature," and "being" is brought to an end. Yet must we not insist that it is not *the* world, the creation, but rather *our* world—the world as manifest, as real, to fallen man—which is annihilated by the advent of the Kingdom? Granted that *our* world is the only world that we can know, the only reality that we as men can experience; yet in faith we know that this very world has come to an end, that its foundations have crumbled, that now it can only appear as Old Aeon. In faith we know that our world has come to an end because in faith we live in the Kingdom, and the Kingdom of God draws all reality into itself. Furthermore, our world is brought to an end only insofar as the Kingdom breaks into *its* midst: the Kingdom appears only in conjunction with a transfiguration of everything which we know as reality. For the Kingdom appears in *our* reality, it dawns in our midst; to the extent that the Kingdom appears "above" or "beyond" it has not yet dawned in us. Precisely because the coming of the Kingdom effects a reversal of the reality of the world, life in the Kingdom can take place only in the midst of the world. It is *this* very reality in its sheer actuality and immediateness which is being transfigured by the dawning of the Kingdom; God appears here and not in a beyond. Therefore the Christian must live *this* life, sharing all its fulness and emptiness, its joy and its horror, knowing that his destiny is to live *here* and *now*, allowing his life to be the metal which God's fire will transform into his Kingdom. And if we are to live *now*, we cannot escape the anguish of the human condition; if we are to live *here*, we cannot flee this condition by a leap of faith. It is our anguish that God's Kingdom will transfigure into joy: but the Kingdom will never dawn in us if we refuse our existence in the here and now. If our destiny is darkness, then we must believe that it is God's will that this darkness be transfigured into light.

Yet what of Dionysian existence? How is the Christian to judge the radical immanence of the contemporary sensibility, an immanence which demands a total immersion in the sheer actuality—the pure immediacy—of the here and now? Does Christian contemporaneity demand a merging of Christ and Dionysus (as Nietzsche in his madness foresaw)? Is there no real distinction between contemporaneity and faith? Let us but recall the words of the Mahayana: Nirvana is Samsara, and Samsara is Nirvana. Can the Christian, too, affirm that existence in *our* world is existence in the Kingdom of God? Certainly not; and yet, do we not believe that the Christian is bound to accept his destiny, regardless of what that destiny might be, and accept it through the power of the Kingdom of God, through his life in the Kingdom of God? Must the Christian pronounce an absolute "No" upon the autonomous existence of modern man, and thereby upon human creativity itself, upon man's existence in history? Is the Christian likewise called to condemn with a final "No" the radical immanence of the contemporary sensibility, thereby condemning the most profound engagements of man with the world, of man with time? Knowing that there can be no retreat to an earlier historical moment, are we forced to condemn human existence itself? How is faith to greet the Nothing which dawns upon the contemporary horizon? Wherever we turn in our destiny, we are confronted by the Nothing: for the death of God has been followed by the resurrection of the Nothing; the Nothing is now openly manifest in the deepest expressions of contemporary existence. Is the advent of the Nothing simply a divine judgment upon human autonomy, an inevitable consequence of a history—a *Dasein*, a movement of being—that has plunged itself into radical immanence?

This paper has moved beyond the limits of contemporary theological analysis for theological language is not yet prepared to meet such problems. Yet if we are here faced with mystery, it is a mystery which we must live, a challenge which our hearts, if not our minds, can by no means escape. Dare the Christian meet the Nothing which is now overwhelming

From the Church to the World

ON THE BONHOEFFER MONOGRAPH BY HANFRIED MULLER

J. M. Lochman

During the early part of his confinement preceding his execution by the Nazis in 1945, the German Protestant theologian Dietrich Bonhoeffer was able to keep in touch with relatives and friends through correspondence. In these letters, published posthumously, Bonhoeffer adumbrated a "religionless" Christianity which would shun inward-looking piety and upward-looking metaphysics and be marked by openness to the world and willingness to suffer on its behalf. These letters have exerted a remarkable influence not only on Western but on Eastern churchmen, some of the latter finding in Bonhoeffer's acceptance of the secular, "come of age" world a means of accommodation between Christian faith and Marxist socialism. Hanfried Müller, a professor at Humboldt University in East Berlin, has written a controversial book on Bonhoeffer which interprets him according to doctrinaire Marxist categories. Reviewing Müller's book here is another Iron Curtain theologian, J. M. Lochman of the Comenius Theological Faculty in Prague, Czechoslovakia. By and large Lochman seems to concur with Müller's view of Bonhoeffer. Yet he says that Müller's "dualistic evacuation of the positive effect of the Gospel from the realm of this world is a disruption of the biblical certainty concerning the indivisible rule of Jesus Christ over this world—here and now, despite the ambiguity of our earthly life, as Bonhoeffer confessed to the very end." Here Lochman appears to imply that Müller concedes too much to rule other than Christ's. Lochman's essay is from the Winter 1962 *Communio Viatorum,** published by the Ecumenical Institute of the Comenius Theological Faculty and the International Secretariat of the Christian Peace Conference.

DIETRICH BONHOEFFER was without doubt one of the most stimulating theological thinkers of the first half of

* Jungmannova 9, Prague 1, Czechoslovakia.

our century. Since he did not live to the age of forty, his work remained only a torso, an abbreviated offering—and this was especially true of the most important studies of his last years. Nevertheless, his work made such a violent stir in postwar German theology that the waves reached far into the theological life of our whole continent and today are affecting the thinking of theologians in the Anglo-Saxon countries as well. It is no wonder that there already exists quite an extensive Bonhoeffer literature, yet it was not until last year that a book was published in the German Democratic Republic which we can designate as the first integrated and systematic monograph on Bonhoeffer. It is *Von der Kirche zur Welt*[1] (From the Church to the World), the work of Hanfried Müller, an assistant professor at Humboldt University.

This dissertation (first drafted in 1956) is not a general monograph. As indicated by the subtitle, "Contribution to the relation of the Divine Word to *societas* in the theological development of Dietrich Bonhoeffer," Müller concentrates on one problem of Bonhoeffer's thinking—of course, the central and fundamental one. Nor is it a neutral and objectivist study: Müller consciously and admittedly gives a critical interpretation of Bonhoeffer's work, in a bold projection of Bonhoeffer's line to his own theological position. This is surely a risky act, as we shall show later. But on the other hand it lends a special vitality and excitement to the book: we see here a bit of militant theology, sharp and eloquent in the basic conception, and often very moving in its pregnant presentation of the thesis.

Müller summarizes the basic phases of Bonhoeffer's development in three stages. He determines the content of each in accord with the formulation of Bonhoeffer's closest friend, Eberhard Bethge: "Bonhoeffer of the 1920's said to the theologians: Your theme is the church! Bonhoeffer of the 1930's said to the church: Your theme is the world! And Bonhoeffer of the 1940's said to the world: Your theme, abandonment, is God's theme!" (pp. 33ff.) The fruit of the first period is the first two works by Bonhoeffer, *Sanctorum communio* (1930) and *Akt und Sein* (1936). These are very exacting and subtle analyses of the theological problems of the church. In the first-named the young theologian analyzed the structure of

human society in general and of the church in particular, trying to be just both to the theological foundations of the
church and to its empirical likeness, as shown by the fact that
he elaborated both the suggestions of the Barthian "dialectical
theology," then on the ascent, and the products of modern
sociology. In his *Akt und Sein* he then strove to apprehend
the final roots of the ecclesiological problems in connection
with the traditional polarity of both forms of classical theology, that is, the "actualistic" theology (based on the dynamics of Divine acts) and the "ontological" (developing
primarily the problems of the concept of being and its natural-
theological consequences). Both of these types of theology
(represented in the contemporary world of Bonhoeffer by the
Barthian current on the one hand, and on the other by Thomism) emphasize to the extreme the opposite poles of the fundamental ecclesiological dialectics, seen thus by Bonhoeffer:
In order that man may become a member of Christ's church,
he must believe—here being is anchored in the act; but at the
same time the contrary utterance is also true: Our faith has
its supporting basis in our existence in the church, for only
as a member of the church can man truly believe—here the
act is anchored in the being. In this way, therefore, is the
fruit of stubborn endeavors of the first stage of Bonhoeffer's
path an emphatic joining of all theology and existence to the
cardinal theme of the church.

Here, then, he begins the organic connection with the second stage of Bonhoeffer's work. Adhering to the church is not
a matter of theory—it is a matter of practice in a quite definite sense of the word: in the church's struggle against the
Nazi infiltration into the church. From the beginning, Bonhoeffer was a definite theologian of the decisive wing of the
"Confessional Church." Face to face with the temptation of
the German ecclesiastical situation, he did not hesitate to declare that whoever consciously distanced himself from the
Confessional Church was abandoning salvation. But at the
same time he struggled for an inner purity and humility in this
society. A reflection of this struggle was in his two subsequent
important works: *Nachfolge* (Cost of Discipleship, 1937) and
Gemeinsames Leben (Life Together, 1939). *Nachfolge*
was a passionate battle against the greatest temptation of the

German Church of that time, the declaration of a "cheap grace," that is, against a concept of justification by faith which makes of Christ's cross a paltry covering of our sin and weariness, which makes the justification of the sinner a justification of sin. Müller rightly considers this struggle by Bonhoeffer to be a renewal of the classical Reformation endeavor on a new front: "While the Reformation was a new revelation of the Gospel which had been buried under an incorrect use of the law, by nomism, the *Nachfolge* was a new revelation of the law which had been suppressed by an incorrect use of the Gospel, by libertinism" (p. 200). Bonhoeffer disclosed the pure dialectics of the Gospel and of the Law in the formulation, "Only he who believes is obedient—and only he who is obedient believes." At the same time, true obedience lies in following Jesus Christ—the obedience of the cross. The true church is only where this following is, that is the fundamental emphasis of this important work amidst the church struggle. Müller wholeheartedly recognized this emphasis, and thereby this work—with certain reservations towards its second part. But he just as sincerely raised problems in regard to the work which Bonhoeffer published almost simultaneously, *Gemeinsames Leben*. In this attempt to outline a thought-out order of things and cultivation of a common life (the book was written for the preachers' seminary of the Confessional Church) he saw a Catholicizing tendency, and the expression of a spirit of resignation over the development in the Confessional Church, even in a certain sense a direct escape from social responsibility to an ecclesiastical seclusion.

But that was only a detour. Soon began the third and decisive period of Bonhoeffer's life and work, governed by the question of the relationship between the Divine Word and society. As in the preceding stages, this was also a period of Bonhoeffer's literary creation (and this connection is one that Müller always applies emphatically) reflecting the new situation in the surroundings and in the personal life of the author. That is, it reflected the unleashing of war, and Bonhoeffer's definitive decision to oppose Nazism actively. The most important works that arose out of this are the posthumously published fragments of his *Ethics* and his letters from prison, published after the war in a collection entitled *Widerstand und Ergebung* (Letters and Papers from Prison, 1951). In many ways, these are enigmatic works, full of contradictions, and Müller analyzes in detail the heterogeneous motifs, for example those within the *Ethics* and then the differences between that and the letters from prison—and yet in them we find what is Bonhoeffer's most singular contribution and legacy. At the same time, in Müller's opinion, *Ethics* is an ambiguous work, not yet ripened and, in relation to the author's development, full of moments of retardation. Müller particularly objects to Bonhoeffer's inclination towards a Christian "theology of history" as it appears in his expositions of the Christianity of the European heritage (by which Bonhoeffer fought against fascist brutality, but, says Müller, this was in the name of the past rather than the future), as well as to the traditional, and in place explicitly conservative, content of his concept of God's mandates. But Müller finds Bonhoeffer's concept of "naturalness" excellent, in its moment of individuality as opposed to any religious determination. This is already a start towards that vision of reality which triumphs in the letters of the collection *Letters and Papers from Prison*.

Müller concentrates on this book with special attention. Face to face with the final sacrifice of his own life, Bonhoeffer's ideas matured rapidly and acquired a truly prophetic and testamentary nature. This is true even of the basic theological conception which is the basis for these expositions: Müller designates them as a dialectical joining of a consistent "theology of the Cross" with an immanent optimism in approach to the secular and social problems. Here we find the historical contribution made by Bonhoeffer: "It seems to me that this is the first time in the history of theology, that Reformation theology not only attests to the Christian's freedom in a desecularized church and in a declericalized world, but further than that, makes use of this freedom in a positive, optimistic, immanent way, instead of relinquishing the tasks of this world in conservatism or in resignation." (p. 356) Then this excellent theological foundation leads to no less excellent concrete theological discoveries and emphases. Among these, particularly worthy of attention are his brilliant expositions of a "mature world" and of a "non-religious interpretation." In the first conception, Bonhoeffer pays the debt, long outstanding, of Christian theology to the modern world: justifying theologically the assent to its immanent autonomy. In the second conception he then, in liberating fashion, opens the way to preaching the Gospel even to unreligious and antireligious men: to him who adheres to a non-religious view of the world, the Gospel can be preached without forcing him to change his atheistic approach to the world (here Müller sees a similarity to the situation of the early church: one could become a Christian who did not accept the Jewish custom of circumcision, and so can a modern man become a Christian without undergoing a philosophical "circumcision" of his modernity). Thus, in the non-religious interpretation it is truly not a question of the hermeneutical problem, of conveying the problem of "how we will expain this to a modern person," but instead an "act of the objective liberation of the world for Christ" ("How can Christ become Lord of the non-religious people, too?") and an "act of liberating Christians for a mature world." It is precisely in this perspective that Bonhoeffer made a providential contribution to the Christians of today's world—especially to the Christians of a developed socialist society. In the clear elaboration of these motifs is also the most intrinsic intention—and also the indubitable contribution—of Müller's penetrating interpretation.

Müller's book arouses intense sympathy and violent opposition. Perhaps this is commensurate with its theme: Bonhoeffer's work was never lukewarm and neither does Müller intend to be lukewarm. His book is consciously partisan in its program—in two senses of the word. First of all it is "immanently" partisan in its approach to the material, in the interpretation of Bonhoeffer's work. Müller regards this work from beginning to end in a quite definite point of view: in the perspective of Bonhoeffer's ideas on a mature world and on a non-religious interpretation. It is from this, according to his opinion, that there falls a light on Bonhoeffer's whole path—and therefore one must start here to judge and evaluate all its stages. This tendency makes it possible for Müller to form a striking and straightforward conception of Bonhoeffer's work, proved in many individual details, even where in the early works there are only hidden nuclei of the later development.

But at the same time there is hazard in this interpretation: it goes too far in compressing the tempestuous theological path and the rich variety of Bonhoeffer's work into one framework, it cuts off the branches too rapidly, when they stretch farther than this framework (let us compare Müller's impatient judgments on *Gemeinsames Leben*, although we can regard even this work positively if we place it in the truly broad development of the author, despite all its problematic qualities, as the "anchoring" of his expositions on the "mature world"). In a thinker so supremely "polyphonous" as Bonhoeffer was, both in regard to program and to facts, this approach means, in the final analysis, a definite impoverishment.

Müller's book is, however, partisan in another sense of the word, too: it means a definite "yea to the created, to what is in birth, to what is growing, blossoming and giving fruit." This is how Müller cites Bonhoeffer's words—and himself makes them more concrete: he takes the side of the mature world, and of its so far highest form, of socialism, and its ideology of Marxism. In his exposition of Bonhoeffer, and in elaborating his approach to the world, Müller even uses Marxist categories. He outlines the class profile of Bonhoeffer (he is a "bourgeois, who feels bound by the conservative tradition, up to the point where he has a free outlook on the new era, and here he is no longer a bourgeois," p. 7, cf. also p. 270); he rightly classifies Bonhoeffer consistently in a broader relationship of social events; he is profoundly convinced of the laws of these events in the sense of scientific socialism (pp. 336, 362, et al.); he bases himself in noetics on the theory of reflection, and in ontology on the fundamental materialistic theses opposed to idealism; he adheres even to an atheistic philosophy in his approach to this world. The presence of Marxist motifs in Müller's book meant that there were many critical remarks from the reviewers and readers, especially in western Germany, even a more or less open accusation of Marxist infiltration of his theological work. I do not intend to join in these views. Besides, they are unconvincing because they raise an alarm against this certain philosophy, while the ideological gleanings from idealistic philosophies, e.g. from existentialism, are passed over only too magnanimously. It is true that too close connections with any philosophy constitute a serious problem for theology—and this problem applies to Müller. But it also applies to everyone! And on the other hand: a proper use of philosophical categories—including Marxist—need not be a sign of selling out. On the contrary, it can be a sign of a Christian's freedom.

Müller's book instead evokes question marks in regard to its *theological* conception and tendency. Let us concentrate a little more on this aspect.

We cannot better characterize Müller's theological conception than by the formulation he used to greet the most individual contribution Bonhoeffer made to the history of theology: the joining of the theology of the Cross with immanent optimism. Indeed this dual emphasis also characterizes Müller's own position. Its theological fundament is an emphatic and consistent *theology of the Cross*. "Only under the Cross do we 'have' God in man abandoned by God" (p. 386). True, the Gospel brings other tidings, too: it also knows the tidings of the incarnation of God's love and of the resurrection of the Lord. But these dual tidings must not be considered as "parenthesis" to the tidings of the Cross. On the contrary: the tidings of the Cross determines the place for the other two. The Cross is not just one "locus" of theology, the Cross is the key to all other themes. From this the "theologia crucis" acquires fundamental significance in Müller's method: it is supreme and, in the final analysis, the sole principle of theological work and theological existence on this earth. Therefore he feels an explicit disinclination for the "theology of incarnation" or the "theology of resurrection," not only in the cases of their isolation from the tidings of the Cross (when they were truly in danger of oversimplification) but also when this theological triad—the Cross, incarnation, resurrection—was protected from any over-simplification by mutual theological balance: there is no such balance—only the Cross is the genuine principle. As long as we are on this earth we see only the Cross—we can only have faith in resurrection. The only present thing for us is, therefore, the Cross, only that do we have "in re," resurrection is given only "in spe" (p. 509). And it is also God's only presence on this earth. This is how Müller interprets the Gospel: God's presence in Jesus Christ was exclusively and totally a presence of suffering and the Cross, presence in infirmity. Sections like the pericope on the Mount of Transfiguration (Mark 8, 2-8) are called by Müller the "most religious passages" in the New Testament, and he thereby disqualifies them. In reality not even faith can see anything in this world but God's infirmity and suffering—the Cross. God's acts, God's rule over this world is imperceptible even for a believing person (p. 427). "God's descendence is a real abolition of God's transcendence" (p. 421).

And yet, the Cross, the sole reality of a Christian's life and the sole principle of legitimate theology—here lies the second emphasis of Müller's theological views—must not be raised to the only principle for explaining the world. This Müller asserts most vehemently, as opposed to the traditional temptation of Lutheran theology to derive from the theology of the Cross a philosophical pessimism in viewing the world and its history. Kierkegaard, for example, was guilty of this type of pessimism when, in the name of theology of the Cross, he went forth to battle against all worldly optimism. Müller fully shares Bonhoeffer's criticism of Kierkegaard in this respect. And even more emphatically he joins in *optimistic* evaluation of the mature world and its future, especially in view of the perspectives of a socialist society. The Cross of Jesus Christ is not an obstacle under a Christian's feet: a Christian's place is among the active builders of a new world.

One can scarcely imagine a more extreme, indeed a more paradoxical, theological position, than Müller's theological construction when thus established. An extreme theology of the Cross on one hand—a decisive social-political optimism on the other. In the paradox of this position is indeed—as Müller points out in regard to Bonhoeffer—a definite novelty in the history of theology. In the previous course of Protestant thinking, two developed lines opposed each other, or rather, stood side by side: an emphasis on the theology of the Cross usually led to a pessimistic and therefore conservative-restorational conclusion in the orientation of the world (especially in Lutheran circles), while on the contrary the theology of the Resurrection led to social-political optimism (especially in the left wing of the Reformation, or even in the Calvinist tradition). Both could be formed into a certain organic whole containing dogmatic roots and ethical conclusions. Müller attempts to make a new combination, one that is much more difficult because it is paradoxical. How is he able to hold it at all?

There is only one way in which he can justify it to a certain extent, and that is the path of a sharp *dualism*—a position which would radically separate the matter of faith and the matter of reason, the matter of the Gospel and the matter of politics, the matter of the church and the matter of the world, and place them in two spheres completely separated from each other—in the traditional terminology, in two realms. This is the path taken by Hanfried Müller. His theology continually advocates the dualistic motifs. This is especially significant in connection with his interpretation of Bonhoeffer's well-known categories of the "ultimate and penultimate." Bonhoeffer means by this differentiation the relation between the final reality of God's justification on the one hand and the penultimate realities of our earthly life. For Bonhoeffer they are in dialectical connection: the ultimate is never the same as the penultimate but neither are they sharply divided from each other—the penultimate has no value in itself (cf. *Ethics*, pp. 79 ff.). With Müller there is a perceptible shifting of emphasis: he underlines in a one-sided way the diastasis between the ultimate and the penultimate (cf. p. 380)—so that the ultimate becomes practically irrelevant. The declaration that it is solely the object of faith (correct in itself) eliminates it practically from our orientation in this world. And this tendency also appears in other connections. Apropos here is the repeated warning of Müller that the Gospel should not be directly applied to questions of ethics[2] or to questions of the ecclesiastical order.[3] A similar tendency is shown by his words on the question of the relationship between the law and the Gospel, when he opposes Karl Barth in defending the traditional alignment "law-Gospel," with the justification that, while the law affects us in the present, the Gospel is our future—that is, again: without direct relevance as a standard for us here and now. Thus Müller's conception gravitates toward a strict differentiation between the two realms (explicitly on p. 217, for example)—and thereby toward dualism.

This dualism, which is a further striking trait and peculiarity of Müller's conception, is in no way static. The relationship of the two realms should not be perceived as a timeless polarity of two constants, but as motion with a definite tendency. The direction is most eloquently characterized by the title itself: From the Church to the World. This title surely means in the first place a shift of theme in Bonhoeffer's theological evolution. But immediately thereafter it has also a more profound and fundamental meaning. It is a question of the basic orientation of Christian faith in a modern world—away from all ecclesiastical self-sufficiency and self-concentration toward society and the world. This movement begins with a thoroughgoing resistance against any patronizing attitude toward the world on the part of the church. Nothing goes so against the grain with Müller as an inclination toward clericalism. He consistently takes the side of the world against any theological tutelage. It is not just a question of expressions of ecclesiastical "imperialism," which, of course, he always tries to nip in the bud. He also opposes any form of ecclesiastical interference in the matters of this world—in practice and in theory as well. Thus Müller rejects every form of "theology of history"—he senses in this a threat to the autonomy of this world. Similarly any "Christian speciality" —even ethical—arouses his suspicion: it is a matter of our acting as Christians in the name of God the same as others do in the name of man. Thus, in the final count, there is no visible difference between Christians and heathens. And the church also should in the future relinquish every special ostentation. In his exposition of the "arcane discipline," Müller explains that in Bonhoeffer's demand it is not a question of creating some sort of "religious space" in the world, but quite the contrary, of overcoming this by "ending the public nature of Christian religiosity" (p. 400). The idea of "Christianizing the world" seems to him in this sense quite horrible: what is to come in the future is rather a profane existence of Christians in a modern world. Thus a theologian and the church should not make problematic the enclosed profanity of this world, but, on the contrary, should confirm it (cf. p. 544). A consistent theology of the Cross leads from the church to the world. I believe that in this consistent guarding of the au-

tonomy of the modern world against all disturbing interven-
tion by theology and the church we have laid before us the
basic tendency of Müller's theological endeavors. A thoroughgoing theology of the Cross truly leads, through the dualistic
evacuation of the Gospel from the immanent region of this
world, from the church to the world.

There are a whole series of points where we agree with
Hanfried Müller, and where we can learn from his penetrating book: from concrete questions of Bonhoeffer's interpretation to his endeavors for a positive orientation of the church
toward a socialist society. In this regard his book fills in a
considerable gap in research on Bonhoeffer, and, moreover, it
pays part of the heavy debt of evangelical theology to the
modern world in general and to socialist society in particular.
Here everything in the emphasis and tendency of Müller's
work is close to us. Where we differ is in the theological foundations, in his conception of the theology of the Cross, in his
dualism, his version of the movement "from the church to
the world." I believe that his concept of the theology of the
Cross is a definite narrowing of the biblical message—a conversion of the polyphony of the Gospel, including the teachings of Christ's incarnation and victory in an indivisible
chord, with all its consequences for our life here and now,
into an intolerable monotony, even though it be the monotony
of its central element. I am of the opinion that his dualistic
evacuation of the positive effect of the Gospel from the realm
of this world is a disruption of the biblical certainty concerning the indivisible rule of Jesus Christ over this world—here
and now, despite the ambiguity of our earthly life, as Bonhoeffer confessed to the very end. And I believe that an otherwise pleasing stress on a movement from the church to the
world, in the sense of overcoming all clericalism, in the end
erases the glory and reality of the new creation, the special
role of service of the "exceptional people"—even in this modern world. Our question is whether these theological accents
do not weaken the decisive intention which we fully share
with Dietrich Bonhoeffer and Hanfried Müller: an endeavor
toward a trustworthy testifying to the Gospel in a hopeful
inclination to our modern world.

NOTES

1. Koehler u. Amelang (Leipzig: 1961), p. 575.

2. He says that only in a double respect can the Gospel serve ethics: "It beckons man under the Cross and thus breaks up human ethics in that it calls from action to suffering; it calls man to maintain the previous order of this transitory world and thus directs man's attention to his profane action, as proper to this world—in such a way that a Christian is to do in the name of God what other people do in the name of man" (p. 514). It is obvious that this conception of ethics is in tension with the clear and positive imperatives which the Gospel and the Epistles to Christians continually present, in the call itself to positive following.

3. "The Gospel cannot lead to a positive ecclesiastical order" (p. 259). We understand the fear of a legalizing of the Gospel which is evident in this position; still, attempts to form in the light of the Gospel a positive Church order need not be legalistic, if there is no legalistic imitation, but a committed following. I am convinced that this corresponds to the intentions of the biblical imperative—and to the intentions of Bonhoeffer. Therefore Müller's abrupt rejection can scarcely be in the right.

III

Theology in Extension

The Worship of the Church and the Modern Man

E. S. Brown, Jr.

Interrelated with the ecumenical movement is the liturgical movement. In recent years committed Christians of various denominations have sought to achieve a renewal of the church's forms of worship that would be meaningful to modern man—a revivification that would build on the church's ritual traditions, but in ways that would transform them rather than merely parrot and preserve them in antiquarian fashion. "The church," insists E. S. Brown, Jr., "is concerned not only with the 'ins' but with the 'outs' and with that great segment of the populace that knows not whether it is 'in' or 'out.' " For this reason the problem of how to make the church's cultus relevant cannot be clear-cut, nor its solution easy. Dr. Brown, as director of the Commission on Worship of the Lutheran Church in America, is ably equipped to come to grips with this problem. His paper, reprinted from the March 1963 issue of *Studia Liturgica*, "An International Ecumenical Quarterly for Liturgical Research and Renewal" edited in Rotterdam in the Netherlands,* was originally read at a series of theological meetings sponsored by the Lutheran World Federation in Oxford, England, and Hesselberg and Berlin, Germany. Among Dr. Brown's other published writings are *Living the Liturgy* and *Symbols and Terms of the Church*.

Introduction

AT THE outset we must begin with certain definitions. To use the term "worship" is to focus immediately upon all that the church does within the sphere of its cultic activity. Popular usage has all but divorced this term from its more accurate designation as that total response to God of the grateful Christian. Yet the New Testament evidence is un-

* Circulation office: Postbus 2, Nieuwendam, Holland.

mistakeably clear. St. Paul's admonition to the Roman Christians (12:1) "that ye present your bodies a living sacrifice, holy, acceptable unto God, which is your reasonable service," is far more than a call to cultic performance.

This distinction is important because it demonstrates that the Christian's life cannot be compartmentalized. Whatever he does, be it the celebration of the liturgy or the loving service of his fellow men, all this, so long as it is done "to God," is properly labelled as worship. This is not to infer that man is thereby given a choice between two roads down which he may travel as he responds to God's grace. *Leiturgia* (or cultus) and *Diakonia* (or ethics) are not mutually exclusive. It is not a case of "either – or," but of "both – and." We shall say more of this later.

Having said this, that the force of the term "worship" is so broad as to be designative of all that man does in his response to God, we must now acknowledge that for the purpose of this essay we are here concerned with worship primarily as a cultic phenomenon.

Secondly, we must determine what we mean by "modern man." Since we are dealing with the church in its cultic manifestations, have we to do here only with the Christian "modern man," that specimen, now becoming so rapidly extinct in some areas of Christendom, who by his attendance at services participates, whether knowingly or unknowingly, in the cultic action? If this is what we mean by "modern man," then our course is fixed: to make of the liturgical action a vital, relevant, significant thing to one already committed. This is a task which is challenging, although not impossible.

But is this the end of our responsibility? What of the pagan "modern man" for whom the church has little if any meaning? Since his only contact, if any there be, with the church, is more likely than not with the public services of worship, is there not also a commensurate responsibility to so conduct our cultus that it will have relevance, even appeal, as he struggles to meet the problem of life?

It would seem, therefore, that when we speak of "modern man" we are faced with Tweedledum and Tweedledee, a set of twins in so many ways singularly alike, and in another diametrically opposite. Yet even the problem of making our worship significant to both the Christian "modern man" and the pagan "modern man" is not insurmountable, providing, of course, that we can distinguish our dealings with both, the one from the other. Even so, the distinction is an artificial one. The "modern man" with whom we have to deal is not so neatly pigeon-holed into the precisely defined categories determined above. All too often the church finds itself facing a *tertium quid*—"modern man" in what might be called an intermediate state who though baptized and maintaining a nominal relationship with the church by making an infrequent appearance at services (festival celebrations, weddings, funerals, etc.) feels little if any compunction to identify with the church's cultus the larger areas of life.

This type of "modern man" and his attitude to the church and its worship is described by Ignazio Silone:

> One fine Sunday some of us stopped going to Mass, not because Catholic dogma seemed to us, all of a sudden, false, but because the people who went began to bore us and we were drawn to the company of those who stayed away . . . what characterized our revolt was the choice of comrades . . . Without the slightest attempt at resistance, indeed with the well-known fervor of neophytes, one accepts the language, symbols, organization, discipline, tactics, program and doctrine of the party to which one's new comrades belong. It is hardly surprising that rarely should anything learned in the catechism and schoolbooks hinder one's docile acceptance of the new orthodoxy. Indeed, one does not even feel the need of refuting them, because all of that has become part of the world one has left behind. They are neither true nor false; they are 'bourgeois,' dead leaves. . . .[1]

Obviously, this description fits the man who has gone all the way, but what of the thousands who are neither hot nor cold? What of the drifters, the people for whom religious observances are not much more than quaint customs and folklore, practices, by the way, which are fast being displaced by customs rooted and grounded in completely secular culture? Ought we not be concerned for them also?

It would seem then that if we are to talk of the relationship of worship to the "modern man" we must be careful to guard against defining too narrowly what we mean by "modern man." Rather ought we to consider worship as it relates to *"modern men,"* i.e., all mankind, who because of many and varied stimuli stand in differing relationships to the Gospel.

In the light of the foregoing definitions we find that our basic inquiry in what follows must be directed to the following questions: What are the problems facing the church as it attempts to relate its cultus to the modern man, in whatever his relation to the Gospel, and what can the church do to overcome these problems? Even before the mind has opportunity to catalogue some of these problems, as well as to dwell upon attempted solutions now being experimented with in certain quarters of Christendom, another question insinuates itself into our thinking: do we change the liturgy to suit modern man, or is the church's task to fit modern man to liturgy?

Some will argue that this is the wrong way to begin. Not only should we *not* even attempt to answer these questions, but the very fact that the questions have been allowed to be asked betrays a lack of understanding on the part of the person raising such questions. Says one Old Testament scholar:

> What is the nature of the act of worship? It is now taken for granted that the purpose of the church is the worship of God, and the starting point for most discussions is that which is done in church on Sunday morning. This is good linguistic method, but poor theology, for the startling fact is that on that basis of biblical usage there is very little authority for calling a church ritual worship of God.[2]

Whether this view can be defended or not is an issue which will have to be considered elsewhere. Nor do I feel that the limits of this article allow for opening up the whole question of the nature of worship itself. Were we to allow this here we should have to rehearse the arguments of those who so minimize the cultic action of the church as to make it unnecessary to the church's existence in the world. (One can't help wondering, however, what these "anti-cultists" would put in its place. Is the Christian response only an act of intellectual and/or ethical discipline?) Rather I feel that we must begin where we are. We are here concerned with the cultic action itself, and for that reason I propose to concentrate primarily upon the liturgy.

The Human Party to the Dialogue of Worship

(A) THE STRUCTURE OF THE CHURCH'S WORSHIP PATTERNS

The word "liturgy," like the word "worship," has undergone a metamorphosis. Once used to designate the broader arena of the Christian's response, it came in time to be identified with any cultic pattern of worship. More accurately it signifies one particular rite, the classic combination of the *missa catechumenorum* and the *missa fidelium*. This is the central cultic act of Christian worship which in its unity provides for both the preaching of the sermon and the reception of Holy Communion. It is in this sense that I plan to use the word "liturgy" in what follows.

If we begin with the liturgy, and by association include also the offices (Matins, Vespers, the Litany, etc.) in our consideration of cultic patterns now in use in the church, we must ask another question: for whose use were and are these forms intended? Obviously the answer is clear, these orders of worship are to be employed by the initiated member of the *corpus Christi*. This is particularly true of the liturgy, as recall, for example, the traditional dismissal of the catechumens which preceded the "unveiling" of the "sacred mysteries."

Does this mean that the preaching of the Word, which is so much a part of worship in Protestant churches, has no relevance for the person who is not a member of the *koinonia*? Krister Stendahl reminds us that Acts 2:42

> . . . speaks about Teaching rather than Preaching. What we have come to call the *kerygma*, the announcement of the gospel as a creative power to salvation, is in the New Testament directed to the outside world. It is missionary preaching. Within the church this kerygma is referred to as the glorious Word by which salvation *was* offered to and accepted by the members of the church. They are now ad-

monished to live accordingly. Even the great Christological truths are not promulgated as a creative kerygma to the church; the church is reminded of the grace of God which *came* to them by the gospel and they are urged to draw the consequences thereof in their daily life. Hence the Word is the basis, the Magna Carta, the deed of adoption by which the Christian is what he is and is urged to become what he *really* is in Christ (Romans 6). This is the role of the Word in the Liturgy. It presupposes a clear distinction between the 'at home' of the church and its missionary activity where the two-edged sword of the preaching was handled and its judging and saving power manifested itself.[3]

Considering the kinds of sermons one hears from so many pulpits, one wonders if the preachers have learned to keep this distinction clearly in mind. Moreover, where this distinction is not made in the preaching what kind of an effect does it have upon the hearers? The same question arises out of any consideration of certain portions of the liturgical rite. What can the recitation of the creed or the singing of the *Gloria in Excelsis* mean for the non-initiate? And how can an act of confessing one's sins reach the heart of a person for whom the word "sin" is not so much an offense against God as, for example, a petty infraction of some now-outmoded moral code enforced in childhood by a puritanical parent? If we are able to determine nothing else from a scrutiny of our present liturgical forms, we are forced to conclude that they have little if any real significance for any but the faithful, practicing Christian.

(B) THE DISTINCTION BETWEEN THE CHRISTIAN MODERN MAN AND THE PAGAN OR AGNOSTIC MAN

If the church were concerned to make its cultus relevant only to the faithful Christian who was diligent in his devotional obedience, the problem would be singularly clear and the solution relatively easy. A program of education couched in the thought forms and vocabulary familiar to the already initiated member of the family and applied with vigor to young and old alike would solve the problem nicely. But, as we said earlier, the church is concerned not only with the "ins" but with the "outs" and with that great segment of the populace that knows not whether it is "in" or "out."

To determine who or what is responsible for this situation ought not detain us now, although honesty demands that we acknowledge that the burden of the responsibility rests upon the church itself. All too often in the past the church has flung wide its doors in a great crusade of missionary zeal, which regrettably has been characterized more by emotional enthusiasm than by any clearly defined strategy of what to do with the people when they do come in. Advertising campaigns urging people to "Come to Church Next Sunday" or "Get a Lift at Church" employ the techniques of the world of commerce and they do reap fruit. But the deeper results, sad to say, are plainly evident. It makes about as much sense to invite an outsider to attend the secret meeting of a Masonic assembly (even if he were allowed to enter) as it does to urge a person who had little understanding of the Gospel to participate in the liturgical action of the Christian fellowship. The visitor to the Masonic lodge wouldn't expect to understand what was happening. "After all," he reasons, "these people are 'peculiar,' and I cannot know what they're doing until I join them and submit to their discipline." Yet seldom if ever is the same logic applied to the church. How often does one hear that the church is a "peculiar" fellowship? Because what is done in the churches is not always immediately meaningful to the occasional visitor, it is the church, not the visitor, who is criticized.

We may take some comfort when we apply this situation to the modern pagan. We ought be less sanguine, however, when we consider that "modern man" who though reared in the church and frequenting its services from time to time is in reality indifferent to all that the church stands for. He is a member of the family, albeit an inactive one, and because he is indifferent in performance of his liturgy the church needs to inquire why he has reached this state. Here perhaps is the most complicated segment of our problem, and the one which we do well to keep uppermost in all that follows. Have we been guilty of assuming that because a man is baptized, been exposed to the customary pre-Confirmation instruction, and then been admitted to the Eucharist, that his life in the spirit will be derived by a sort of religious osmosis? Has the church kept abreast of man's intellectual explorations, spurred as it has been by scientific, economic and political developments, so as to relate the Gospel with a brilliant relevance to the world in which man lives? These and many more are the sort of questions that ought to concern us as we proceed.

Lest we be diverted from the main stream of our investigation however, let it be clearly understood that what follows has to do primarily with the meaning and practice of worship as this is employed by the Christian initiate. Only by indirection can we relate our problem to the "outsider." The church must make a clear distinction between evangelism and the "family conversation" of its liturgy.

Criticisms Levelled against the Church's Worship from Within

(A) COMMUNICATION

1. Language

One of the frequently heard criticisms of Christian worship is directed against its language. Among Protestants in the United States, the King James Version of the Bible (1611) continues to lead the field, this in spite of the best efforts of publishers, advertising techniques, and parish education specialists to substitute the Revised Standard Version (1952). Most of the Lutherans in America have a new liturgy which perpetuates the familiar Elizabethan English but congregations have the option of reading the appointed liturgical lessons from either the KJV or the RSV. Imagine the result. Shall we read, as we do in the Epistle for Cantate Sunday, "Wherefore lay apart all filthiness and superfluity of naughtiness" (KJV, Jas. 1:21), or shall we instead read, "Therefore put away all filthiness and rank growth of wickedness" (RSV)? Perhaps we ought to use the New English Bible, "Away then with all that is sordid, and the malice that hurries to excess . . ." or shall we go a step further and read the translation of J. B.

Phillips: "Have done, then, with impurity and every other evil . . ." The decisions may be easily made by a comparison of texts. After all the language of the liturgy ought to be relevant so that we do not repeat the error of Rome with its bilingual missals or of the Russian Church with its archaic Church Slavonic. But how far does one go? Even the most ardent devotee of relevance in liturgical speech has difficulty phrasing a prayer which uses the modern forms for the second person of the personal pronoun rather than the more familiar "thee" and "thou."

There is a deeper issue involved here. Certain words may be archaic. For them modern substitutes can be found. But what about those words which while still a part of the contemporary idiom have become so encrusted with "churchliness" that they have little significance in common speech? If the church knows what it means by, for example, the word "redemption" but society identifies this with coupons or "trading stamps" what good is the word to the church's parlance? Henry E. Horn tells of a certain college where freshmen are assigned readings from a pamphlet entitled *Evolution and Religion*, this to introduce them to the prevailing thoughts of modern man. Specifically listed are:

1. Space—Copernicus: *On the Revolution of the Heavenly Bodies*, 1543
2. Time—Lyell, *The Principles of Geology*, 1830–1832
3. Life—Darwin, *The Origin of Species*, 1859
4. Society—Marx, *Das Kapital*, 1867
5. Mind—Freud, *The Interpretation of Dreams*, 1900
6. Method—Einstein, *The Special Theory of Relativity*, 1905

Pastor Horn then continues:

If one can believe that these men actually changed the thought patterns in their various fields of endeavor, then the largest part of man's experience has changed—and all this happened *since the Reformation*. And this in a time when familiarity with the biblical language and typology was fading away. Today the most earnest seekers are again and again blocked and offended by the language of our worship. This offense is muddied by the fundamentalistic memory that most Americans have of the teachings of the church.

Though biblical studies and existential psychologies deepen the meanings of the old words in the church, these same words convey strange emotional pictures to the unenlightened, which bring up visions of a narrow literalism of long ago.[4]

Remembering that the church is a "peculiar" society with a "peculiar" conversation, yet which is constituted of persons who also live in the world, are we not in danger of presenting our people with a choice of being either a schizoid or an ostrich? The cross may be foolishness or a stumbling block to those who will not or cannot accept it, but must it be clothed in unintelligible speech and ideas?

2. Tradition

Along with the wealth of its insistence upon an active apostolate in both cultus and life, the liturgical movement has opened the door to a repristination of the rites, ceremonies and furnishings for worship from other ages of the church's history. In those segments of Protestantism which have experienced the ravages of rationalism and pietism this development has had a wholesome effect upon worship. In place of lengthy services filled with verbose prayers and exhortations, ponderous sermons, and little music save the singing of pietistic hymns, we now enjoy rites which restore to the people their rightful liturgy. The ordinary of the mass, derived mainly from the classic western rite and Luther's liturgical revisions together with the better church orders of the sixteenth century, forms the basis of customary Lutheran Sunday worship. Church buildings employ the best of the artist's crafts, clergy and choirs are now vested in traditional garb, and ceremonial practices have added a dimension to the cultus.

Yet all this has not been without criticism. Some have properly cautioned against a rigid liturgical order which allows no room for development.

> . . . What at one time was decisive in the history of the liturgy is not an indisputable necessity for the present-day congregation. The liturgical creativity of the spirit in the contemporary congregation dare not be disregarded. It is, therefore, always dangerous to enforce forms upon a con-

gregation which were produced in another era. A liturgical revival dare not take as its ultimate goal the mere renaissance of discarded liturgical forms.[5]

Vajta's point is well taken, but I take it to mean that he is not saying that some repristination, if it serves the upbuilding of the congregation, is not invalid. To listen to some modern "iconoclasts" is to draw another inference. Any effort to improve worship if it draws from the past, according to these critics, is nothing more than "antiquarianism" or "estheticism." To cite but a few examples of the criticism levelled among American Lutherans:

(1) the use of the surplice by American Lutheran clergymen is improper because it is an "Anglican importation,"

(2) sanctuary lamps . . . are to be avoided because of their association with the doctrine of transubstantiation, and

(3) the celebration of the Holy Communion in educational institutions is to be "discouraged" because this is "primarily the responsibility of the organized congregation."

(B) RELEVANCE

No one will dispute the fact that the church has a paramount responsibility to make its cultic action intelligible to its people. This should be true in every area of communication, be it the spoken or sung word, the actions of the participants, or the accoutrements of and the place of worship itself. In this last we would place vestments, furnishings, symbols, art forms and the like. Whether it be a painted Chi-Rho on the soffit of an arch, the colored stole, or the spoken word, all these ought to "speak" intelligibly to the initiated beholder.

But the church is not an *ad hoc* assembly, created especially for this gathering of the people at a particular time in a particular place. It enjoys a history, and so has a heritage. The marks of this heritage are a part of its life. Because at one time the church spoke Greek, the liturgy still prefers to label its opening litany the *Kyrie*. Latin terms still survive as brief, yet adequate, titles for many portions of liturgical expressions, not to mention theological explication. Vestments in use today are not greatly unlike those worn fifteen hundred years ago, and the same can be said for ceremonies, rites and furnishings.

To many of the critics of current cultic practice in the church, the so-called liturgical revival is little more than unabashed romanticism. Completely impervious to the urgent demands of an anxiety-infected society, the modern devotees of the Christian cultus, say their critics, are "playing church" while Rome burns. It is a lot easier, and much more pleasant, to debate the color and shape of chasubles than to be afire for social justice or political freedom, not to mention the infinitely greater concerns for faith and grace. Unfortunately, there is just enough truth in some of this criticism to make it valid. Says Ernest B. Koenker in his *Worship in Word and Sacrament*:

> Do the Gregorian chant, vestments, and candles actually contribute to the spiritual edification of the worshiper, or are they merely an aesthetic consideration? Liturgy may become something vaguely sentimental or a cult of the beautiful. Instead of worshiping God in the 'beauty of holiness' we worship him in the 'holiness of beauty.' Beauty then exercises a demonic spell over the worshiper that blocks any real encounter with God. Liturgical forms no longer act as bearers of the holy but are viewed as holy in themselves. So the possibility of entering a relationship with the holy, the source of man's life and righteousness, is prevented by an idolatrous attachment to symbols robbed of their transparency.[6]

Certainly no churchman would wish to so pervert the liturgy as to vitiate its effectiveness as a vehicle of the Gospel, but does the fault rest solely with the forms that the cultic action takes? Is the quest for relevance, so ardently espoused by the anti-liturgical "crepe-hangers," simply to be resolved by providing new cultic patterns in a language and an action that is easily understandable to all comers? If it is true, as the critics say, that the liturgy fails to have significant relevance to the "modern man," then is man's attitude conditioned by the forms of worship or by what those forms intend to convey? It would seem to me that the answers to these questions lie in the fact that no liturgical form will make sense to its user, be he an active or passive participant, unless he is knowledgeable about the meanings of the symbols used therein.

(C) CONGREGATIONAL PASSIVITY AND THE WEAKENING OF THE CHRISTIAN RESPONSE

1. In the cult

It is most unfortunate that in those churches which did so much in the Reformation to restore the role of the people to genuinely corporate worship, there is so little appreciation of the fact that the liturgy is "the people's work." Instead of recognizing that he, along with his fellow Christians, has a responsibility to fulfill our Lord's command to "Do this in remembrance of me," modern man instead looks upon worship as an activity of professionals. Thus he becomes a spectator at a "performance" presided over by clergy, choirs, acolytes and ushers, and because he looks upon himself as a spectator he soon feels that he has the right (some even look upon it as a responsibility) to judge the "performance" in much the same way as he criticizes a play or concert.

What is the reason for this attitude? Undoubtedly some of the liturgies in use in the churches at different times have contributed to what we call "spectatoritis." If the people were given little or nothing to do, while the minister appeared to do everything, then it was inevitable that this situation would develop. I wonder, however, if the reason does not lie far deeper. Can it be that the interpretation so often heard in Lutheran articles (which stresses so persistently the role of God in worship, almost to the exclusion of man's part in the dialogue) has encouraged congregational passivity in Lutheran churches? Does the Lutheran insistence upon the gift in worship tend to give the cultus, and particularly the liturgy, such an *it-centeredness* that man feels he need do nothing? If we criticize the pre-Reformation church for that liturgical corruption which made of the priest an intermediary whose duty it was to say mass *for* the people, have we not simply shifted the problem by requiring that the minister provide Holy Communion *for* the people? If the burden of our theology stresses so strongly the notion that the liturgy is God's gift to us, without providing commensurate opportunity for the place to be given to our response to that gift, then the rite is celebrated for no other reason than the distribution of the gift. I go to church, therefore, in order to get, not to carry on a dialogue. Says J. A. T. Robinson in his book *Liturgy Coming to Life*:

> The parson becomes a sort of garage proprietor whose job is to be open (weekly, monthly, daily, according to demand) for any of his customers who require to fill up. Who comes and how often depends, quite naturally, on what the individual thinks he needs and how much he feels he gets from it.[7]

But where then is the liturgy of not only the minister, but of all the faithful? If the Word, by its very nature, demands that man respond either in faith or in unbelief, what then in what we tend to call worship is man's response? And, how does man make his response if, as so often happens in our churches, he is nothing more than a spectator? The very word "liturgy" is a lie unless all the members of the body take an active part in the divine-human dialogue.

If this attitude of the modern churchman, as outlined above, characterizes the worship that is celebrated at the time of the assembling of the congregation (and what other occasion for assembling the entire congregation is observed with greater or even equal frequency), what shall be the result of man's devotional life in smaller assemblies (parish societies, auxiliaries, etc.) and in his individual prayer life? And how can he move from a passivity in the cultus to a genuinely Christian activity in society?

2. *In group and private devotional life*

The sub-divisions of the congregation have specific purposes and causes, yet all are alike in that each draws its spiritual sustenance from worship. Thus the patterns of group worship on this level are but an extension of the worship of the total congregation. Whether the forms of the officially accepted patterns decreed by the church (e.g., Matins, Vespers, the Litany, etc.) or specially prepared patterns including psalms, lessons, prayers and hymns, they should provide for group participation, be relevant to the exigencies of life and communicate clearly. Unfortunately, much of what passes for "devotions" in the meetings of parish groups is little more than a bow in the direction of propriety, something to be done before turning to "more important matters." Such an attitude betrays a lack of understanding of the meaning of the cultus. It encourages a notion held by many a church-goer who usually regards the liturgical rite as nothing more than a frame for the sermon. This attitude also fails to reckon with the existence of the *ecclesiola* and the *Ecclesia*. Though the gathering be but a few in number it is still the place where God and man meet to share in the dialogue intended to effect all of man's existence. And it is only as this dialogue is carried on with intelligence and enthusiasm that all that follows can really make sense.

What has been said for group devotions must be repeated and amplified for private devotions. In spite of the tendency to engage in such exercises in a perfunctory manner, it must be borne firmly in mind that no man prays or meditates as an individual. Always, although he performs his devotions "in his closet" he is part of the church at worship.

3. In society

The American Roman Catholic priest H. A. Reinhold says: "We all know of daily communicants who fail to be a witness in their circles and whose only mark of lived religion seems to be their daily Holy Communion and what it involves."[8] Deploring this sort of monad Christianity, Reinhold says that "it is like high-octane gas in a broken-down, one cylinder motor."[9]

Here we come face to face with the most alarming condemnation of the church's cultic activity. What if after all our scholarly and poetic effort to provide cultic patterns that are both beautiful and relevant, our determined programs to train the people in their "proper" conduct of the liturgy, our enthusiastic sponsorship of the best in music and art . . . what if after having done all these, our cultus has failed to influence life? The following indictment of Jewish worship by Abraham

Heschel applies with equal force to what can happen in the church.

> Services are conducted with dignity and precision. The rendition of the liturgy is smooth. Everything is present: decorum, voice, ceremony. But one thing is missing: Life. One knows in advance what will ensue. There will be no surprise, no adventure of the soul: There will be no sudden outburst of devotion. Nothing is going to happen to the soul. Nothing unpredictable must happen to the person who prays. He will attain no new perspective for the life he lives. Our motto is monotony. The first has gone out of our worship. It is cold, stiff, dead. True, things are happening: of course, not within prayer, but within the administration of the temple.[10]

I say this could also be an indictment of Christian worship, and it rises to accuse the church if what we do in the cultus does not expand into life.

Yet look at the liturgy. The first post-communion collect of the liturgy in the American Lutheran *Service Book and Hymnal* leaves no doubt about the purpose of our eucharistic celebration:

> We give thanks to Thee, Almighty God, that thou hast refreshed us with this thy salutary gift; and we beseech thee, of thy mercy to strengthen us through the same gift, *in faith toward thee and in fervent love toward one another* . . .

The dimension of the eucharistic response is both vertical and horizontal. Says J. A. T. Robinson, "The sharing of Bread, concluded now sacramentally, must be continued socially—and thence economically and politically,"[11] and again, "The Communion is social dynamite, if we really take seriously the pattern of community known at the altar."[12] Any cultic pattern of worship, whether in the congregation or by an individual, is a mummery unless the conversation and action begun before the altar is continued in every moment of man's existence.

Says the aged archbishop in Bruce Marshall's *Satan and Cardinal Campbell*: "Two things can save the world: prayer and thought. But the trouble is that the people who think, don't pray, and the people who pray, don't think." Just as all of the deep-seated cogitations of theological inquiry are little more than a playing with words and images unless they find their fruition in the active obedience to the Gospel in our dealings with men and with God, so the divorce between liturgy and life betrays an attitude which if not checked will make of the church little more than a harmless yet pathetic society of antique-lovers. Liturgy without ethics is sterile. Ethics without liturgy is pagan. Well indeed ought we consider the proposal of Gustaf Aulén, who says that Gustaf Wingren

> suggests that the connection of the Holy Communion with mutual, human fellowship would have found a more prominent place 'had not the deterioration of the idea of sacrifice through the sacrifice of the mass made Luther so excessively suspicious of any mention of sacrifice.' The combination of liturgical and social elements which is found in Anglican piety 'must be accepted as a Christian heritage which we Lutherans unfortunately have lost.'[13]

The Direction of Recovery

It would be absurd to suggest that the above-cited difficulties facing the church could be resolved simply by fashioning new and different liturgical rites. The most extreme departure from the traditional forms now in use in the churches (and this has been done as witness the several attempts to set the classic mass to jazz, and the translation of the ancient texts to the *koine* of the beatnik) holds little hope for intelligible and obedient participation in the cultus without a basic understanding of that which lies behind our cultic symbols.

How then shall we proceed? Luther's admonition to the clergy of Luebeck in 1530 is as appropriate today as it was then.

> . . . do not begin with innovations in rites . . . Put first and foremost what is fundamental in our teaching, the doctrine concerning justification, namely, that we are justified by another's righteousness, even Christ's, which is given to us in faith and which by God's grace is apprehended by those who are first terrified by the law and who, struck by the consciousness of their sins, sigh for redemption . . . Re-

form of impious rites will come of itself when what is fundamental in our teaching, being effectively presented, has taken root in pious hearts.[14]

No cultic pattern, no matter how clear its theological expression, is ever adequate to corporate worship, unless it be intended (which God forbid!) that the regular assemblies of the congregation are nothing more than instructional in purpose. Nor should it be expected that the beauty of poetic imagery and expression in the liturgy can engender a devotion which is not rooted in understanding. Education, therefore, is the primary requisite. But where does one commence the process?

It is patently absurd to expect people to participate in worship forms so reliant upon the biblical idiom, if those same people have next to no knowledge of the scriptures. How can the majestic strains of the opening lines of the *Gloria in Excelsis*, for example, convey the force of the Incarnation except there be knowledge of the Bethlehem-event? How does one understand the *Benedictus qui venit* who knows not Palm Sunday, or the *Agnus Dei* without Good Friday? It is impossible for the church to couch its cultic language without drawing upon the scriptures, and this, of course, implies that the people must know the Bible.

A necessary concomitant of Bible study is training in theology. It is one thing to familiarize people with the contents of the Bible; it is another to get them to so adapt the fruit of that study that they see clearly before them the path of their Christian obedience. I need not stress the point; its import is clear. Rather let me express a concern for what I have come to feel is all too often a failing in too many quarters. Theological investigations are necessary. They are not, however, an end in themselves. In spite of the fascination most of us share in the pursuit of knowledge, which we trust will unfold to our gaze more and more about the nature and work of God, we need to remember that gnosticism, under whatever outward trappings, is still a heresy. The Athanasian Creed should be our beacon: "And the Catholic faith is this: that *we worship* (*veneremur*) one God in Trinity, and Trinity in Unity."

What Gordon W. Ireson has to say about the Church of England is true throughout Christendom: "For the vast majority of people in this country *worship must be preceded by instruction, and instruction must be followed by training in worship.*"[15] But this instruction is more than training in liturgical technique, although that is a part, albeit a minor one, of it. Rather we have to do with what Louis Bouyer calls the liturgical principle, "and this liturgical principle is, that we must not try to provide an artificial congregation to take part in an antiquarian liturgy, but rather to prepare the actual congregation of the Church today to take part in the truly traditional rightly understood."[16]

Some will argue that this is unnecessary. After all, doesn't the sermon achieve this purpose? Why should the church, faced as it is with so desperate a situation, take time from its heavily-crowded schedule to teach people how to understand and perform cultic rite? But, we must ask also, what is the effect of this cultic set upon our people?

A. G. Hebert says:

> By the influence of the Church service the regular Church people are moulded; for the things which they do in church make a deeper impression than the teaching which reaches their minds. Often they have thought that they came to church chiefly to hear the sermon. This, however, they forgot; but there were responses and prayers, commandments, creeds and scriptures, which impressed themselves on their mind by constant repetition. All these things, the church building and the ritual and the ceremonies which take place in it, speak of the reality of God after a manner different in kind from the exhortations of the preacher.[17]

Liturgy is both impression and expression, the vehicle for a dialogue between man and God which may and can go both ways at the same time. With the lips the worshiper may sing but words, but if he has been enlightened by *training in worship* he is also receiving a deeper appreciation of the words and the actions he has been taught to use. One could make an extended exercise in devotion, for example, by dwelling upon but one short phrase of the *Gloria in Excelsis:* "Thou only art Holy." Or take the *Verba Domini* of the Eucharist. These familiar words, seen both in their historical situation and as a parallel to what the contemporary Christian does as a part of his liturgy, unfold the Christian obedience both as to cultus and to life:

Our Lord . . . *took* bread and . . . wine . . .

This is the Offertory which provides for the offering of our gifts as a symbol of ourselves. As we set apart the bread and the wine in the cultus, so we offer our lives in service to our fellow men.

. . . And when he had *given thanks* . . .

Here is the great *anamnesis* which, with its recollection of the night of betrayal, makes contemporary the events of Calvary and the first Easter.

. . . He *gave* . . . to his disciples

By the action of eating and drinking all who share in the family meal are strengthened to their continuing apostolate of obedience.

It will be seen that through instruction in the meaning of worship, encouragement to participate will come of itself. Just as a member of the cast of a dramatic production would never think of "cutting" the performance simply because he wants an evening off, so the initiated Christian will see his responsibility to be a part of the family's celebration of the living God in the performance of its liturgy.

Moreover he will come to recognize the value of symbols and signs. The scene in Bernard Shaw's *St. Joan* where only after a soldier has fashioned a crude cross from two twigs does the martyr gain courage to face the flames, is a forceful witness to the use of matter in worship. The ceremonies, the furnishings, the gestures and other accoutrements of the cultus may evoke sneering derision from the more sophisticated, but it must never be forgotten that in just such a use of matter can the faith of "one of these little ones" be strengthened. If the adornment of liturgical activity has been accompanied in recent times in the churches by a revival of pre-Reformation practices we need to inquire into the cause for this repristination. And before we would discard such adornment and make substitution of that which fails to speak to our people, we do well to pause and determine our motives.

What we have just said points, I hope, to the need for renewed attention to and activity in the meaning and practice of worship. We have not as yet determined who shall be the subject of this instruction. Ireson in his book *Church Worship and the Non-Churchgoer* suggests that we not invite outsiders to our liturgical worship. For those who are outside the church, he suggests the restoration of the catechumenate. This would be a period of training in worship, beginning with guided silence, instruction, bidding prayers, etc. Only after he has evidenced his understanding of the action of this "peculiar" people should the neophyte be admitted to the Christian assembly. Peter Hammond tells of a structure in India

> where the church is approached through a narthex containing a large tank, which stretches across its entire width. All unbaptized persons must remain to the west of this tank until they pass through doors placed to the east of the narthex, and opening directly into the room for the eucharistic assembly.[18]

Such experiments are evidence of the growing desire to restore to the *whole* people of God the fullness of their liturgical ministry—both inside and outside the church. It is not enough to expect that the layman will simply take a pious yet passive role in either cultus or life. The universal priesthood has far wider implication than cultic practices heretofore have allowed. And it is precisely as he exercises his cultic priesthood to the full that his liturgy is made to be felt in all of life.

Conclusion

But all this cannot come about unless things are stirred up in the churches. Fortunately, things are beginning to move. Peter Hammond, whose exciting new book, *Liturgy and Architecture,* has done much to encourage the discussions, says:

> It is fast becoming a commonplace to observe that western Christendom is in the throes of a new reformation. Not since the sixteenth century has there been such a calling into question of received traditions or such a ferment of experiment. The sources of Christian tradition are being examined afresh in the light of modern biblical and historical scholarship. Theology has begun to shake off the influence of scholasticism and is rediscovering its biblical, patristic

and liturgical roots. There is a new sense of the meaning of the Church as the people of God and the body of Christ. A deepened understanding of the eucharist, and of its social implications, has transformed the life of many a parish and has effected something of a revolution in the celebration of the liturgy itself.[19]

The compelling promulgation of its doctrines and the loving service of its patterns of ethics may restore to the church the greater sphere of influence it desires for the Gospel. Yet always there must be that other activity of Christian obedience which nurtures the believer in his intimate relation with God. Thinking, knowing and teaching, together with unselfish service of one's fellows, can only draw their inspiration at the wellsprings of corporate devotion. In no other area of its activity does the church touch the lives of men with quite the same potential for impulsion to love that it does in its worship. The investigations into the meaning and practice of the cultus, and the accompanying experiments born of imagination, portend a hopeful sign. If these will but bear fruit in parish churches throughout the world—among the family of God—the future looms bright for the Gospel.

NOTES

1. Silone, *This Is My Philosophy*, Ruskin House, p. 240. Quoted in "The Plea of A Parish Pastor," an essay by Henry E. Horn, *The Living Liturgy*, papers presented at a Conference on Worship by the Department of Worship, ULCA, Nov. 29–30, 1960.

2. George E. Mendenhall, "Biblical Faith and Cultic Evolution," *The Lutheran Quarterly*, Vol. V, No. 3, August 1953, p. 238.

3. Krister Stendahl, "Theology and Liturgy," *The Living Liturgy, op. cit.*, p. 13.

4. Henry E. Horn, *op. cit.*, p. 7.

5. Vilmos Vajta, "The Theological Basis and Nature of Liturgy," *The Lutheran World*, Vol. VI, No. 3, December 1959, p. 239f.

6. E. B. Koenker, *Worship in Word and Sacrament* (St. Louis: Concordia Publishing House, 1959), p. 73.

7. J. A. T. Robinson, *Liturgy Coming to Life* (London: A. R. Mowbray & Co., Ltd., 1960), p. 60.

8. H. A. Reinhold, The Dynamics of Liturgy (New York: Macmillan, 1960), p. 16.

9. *Ibid.*

10. Abraham Heschel, *Man's Search for God*, p. 49. Quoted in Henry E. Horn, *op. cit.*, p. 8.

11. Robinson, *op. cit.*, p. 26.

12. *Ibid.*, p. 37.

13. Gustaf Aulén, translated by E. H. Wahlstrom, *Eucharist and Sacrifice* (Philadelphia: Muhlenberg Press, 1958), p. 80.

14. WA, Br, V, 220, 221. Translated in *Letters of Spiritual Counsel*, edited by T. G. Tappert, the Library of Christian Classics, Vol. XVIII (Philadelphia: Westminster Press, 1955), p. 296f.

15. Gordon W. Ireson, *Church Worship and the Non-Churchgoer* (London: SPCK, 1945), p. 22.

16. Louis Bouyer, *Liturgical Piety* (Notre Dame, Indiana: Notre Dame Press, 1954), p. 15.

17. A. G. Hebert, *Liturgy and Society*, p. 39.

18. Peter Hammond, *Liturgy and Architecture* (London: Barrie & Rockliffe, 1960), p. 46.

19. *Ibid.*, p. 13.

Franz Kafka
and the God of Israel

Erwin R. Steinberg

Simple and clear in terms of syntax and style but elusive and opaque in terms of substance and import, the nightmarish fantasies and fables of the Austro-Czech writer Franz Kafka continue to attract and perplex literary critics. Numerous commentators have noted that a sense of guilt seems to be pervasive in Kafka's novels and stories; Erwin R. Steinberg, in analyzing Kafka's early story "The Judgment," traces that guilt explicitly to Kafka's ambivalent involvement in the Jewish cultural community of his native Prague and his equally ambivalent repudiation of the Judaic faith. We offer Dr. Steinberg's essay as an instance of the increasing cross-fertilization of the disciplines of theology and literary criticism. Dr. Steinberg is dean of Margaret Morrison Carnegie College, Carnegie Institute of Technology, Pittsburgh, Pennsylvania. His paper originally appeared in the Spring 1963 issue of *Judaism*, a quarterly journal published by the American Jewish Congress.* A related paper by Dr. Steinberg, "The Judgment in Kafka's 'The Judgment,' " appeared in the Spring 1963 issue of *Modern Fiction Studies*. Another of his Kafka studies, "A Kafka Primer," was published in the December 1962 issue of *College English*.

THE EXTENT to which Jewish intellectuals may continue to respond or react, often unwittingly, to the formal religious observance of Judaism from which they have in practice withdrawn, is a matter of acute interest. In this regard, Franz Kafka presents a valuable case study.

Kafka was an active member of the Jewish cultural community. Max Brod reports, for example, Kafka's interest in 1910 in a "Polish Jewish troupe of actors who acted folk drama in Yiddish, and sang in Yiddish."[1] Brod says that

---

* East 84th Street, New York 28, New York.

Franz, after the first time I took him [to see the troupe], entered into the atmosphere completely. It was the same intense and creatively fruitful dogged determination with which he himself did everything. (p. 110)

Kafka himself indicated in his diaries his strong interest in a similar group which appeared the following year. Indeed, most of the entries between October 5 and November 11, 1911, concern themselves with this "Yiddish troupe."[2]

There were times, indeed, when Kafka was so taken up with Jewish cultural matters that he must have had little time for anything else:

January 24 [1912]. Wednesday. For the following reasons have not written for so long: I was angry with my boss and cleared it up only by means of a good letter; was in the factory several times; read, and indeed greedily, Pines' *L'histoire de la Littérature Judéo-Allemande,* 500 pages, with such thoroughness, haste and joy as I have never yet shown in the case of similar books; now I am reading Fromer, *Organismus des Judentums;* finally I spent a lot of time with the Jewish actors, wrote letters for them, prevailed on the Zionist society to inquire of the Zionist societies of Bohemia whether they would like to have guest appearances of the troupe; I wrote the circular that was required and had it reproduced; saw *Sulamith* once more and Richter's *Herzele Mejiches* for the first time, was at the folksong evening of the Bar Kokhba Society, and day before yesterday saw *Graf von Gleichen* by Schmidtbonn. (I, p. 223)

Kafka was quite aware that his interest in all these matters derived from the fact that he was conscious of being a Jew:

November 1 [1911]. Today, eagerly and happily began to read the *History of the Jews* by Graetz. Because my desire for it had far outrun the reading, it was at first stranger to me than I thought, and I had to stop here and there . . . to allow my Jewishness to collect itself. (I, p. 125)

Although Kafka plunged early into the cultural aspects of Judaism, he seems, however, to have rejected religious Judaism. For example, he makes several deprecating remarks in his diary about the Kol Nidre service he had attended in 1911.

Three pious, apparently Eastern Jews. . . . Two are crying,
moved only by the holy day. One of them may only have
sore eyes, perhaps. . . .

The little boy without the slightest conception of it all and
without any possibility of understanding, who, with the
clamor in his ears, pushes himself among the thronging. . . .
(I, p. 72)

In other places he distinguishes for himself quite clearly the
difference between religious Judaism, which he feels to be
meaningless, and historic, cultural Judaism, to which he is
drawn:

Today when I heard the *moule's* [*sic*] assistant say the
grace after meals and those present, aside from the two
grandfathers, spent the time in dreams or boredom with a
complete lack of understanding of the prayer, I saw Western European Judaism before me in a transition whose end
is clearly unpredictable and about which those most closely
affected are not concerned, but, like all people truly in transition, bear what is imposed upon them. It is so indisputable
that these religious forms which have reached their final
end have merely a historical character, even as they are
practiced today, that only a short time was needed this very
morning to interest the people present in the obsolete custom of circumcision and its half-sung prayers by describing
it to them as something out of history. (I, pp. 190–191)

January 6 [1912]. Yesterday *Vizekönig* by Feimann. My
receptivity to the Jewishness in these plays deserts me because they are too monotonous and degenerate into a wail-
ing that prides itself on isolated, violent outbreaks. When I
saw the first plays it was possible for me to think that I had
come upon a Judaism on which the beginnings of my own
rested, a Judaism that was developing in my direction and
so would enlighten and carry me farther along in my own
clumsy Judaism, instead, it moves farther away from me
the more I hear it. The people remain, of course, and I hold
fast to them. (I, p. 215)

Max Brod records Kafka's reaction when he took him to
"the house of a miracle-working rabbi, a refugee from
Galicia":

Franz, whom I took with me to a 'Third Meal' at the close of the Sabbath, with its whispering and Hasidic chants, remained, I must admit, very cool. He was undoubtedly moved by the age-old sounds of an ancient folk life, but on the way home he said, 'If you look at it properly, it was just as if we had been among a tribe of African savages. Sheerest superstition.'[3]

The entry in Kafka's diary recording that visit suggests his lack of response but contains no comment like the one Brod reports (II, pp. 128–129).

Even later, some time after March 1920, Kafka told Gustav Janouch: "I am bound to my family and my race. They outlive the individual";[4] and

> God can only be comprehended personally. Each man has his own life and his own God. His protector and judge. Priest and rituals are only crutches for the crippled life of the soul. (p. 93)

In the first statement, Kafka accepts his cultural Judaism, but, by not including it, rejects his religious Judaism. And in the second he not only rejects the God of Israel in favor of "his own God" but rejects also the ritual and synagogue worship that for so long have been considered to be at the core of the Jewish religion.

There is evidence, however, that Kafka was from time to time uneasy over his rejection of his religion. An entry in his diary two days after the one recording his visit to the miracle-working rabbi from Galicia contains the following sentences: "The Polish Jews going to Kol Nidre. The little boy with prayer shawls under both arms, running along at his father's side. Suicidal not to go to temple" (II, p. 130). Two years later the following entry appears: "I would put myself in death's hands, though. Remnant of a faith. Return to a father. Great Day of Atonement" (II, p. 187). An entry made several years later reads:

> January 23 [1922]. A feeling of fretfulness again. From what did it arise? From certain thoughts which are quickly forgotten but leave my fretfulness unforgettably behind. Sooner than the thoughts themselves I could list the places

in which they occurred to me; one, for example, on the little path that passes the Altneu Synagogue. (II, pp. 208–209)[5]

When one turns to Kafka's fiction, however, one can discern nothing overtly Jewish about it. It is true that critics have observed a reference to a Jewish problem here and there in Kafka's writings; and Max Brod claims that Kafka's Jewishness is central to all his works.[6] But Kafka cannot in any sense be considered "a Jewish writer," in the obvious way that Sholem Aleichem and Peretz, for example, are Jewish writers. He is not concerned with "Jewish" characters; nor does he seem to deal, on the literal level, with typically Jewish problems.

There is considerable evidence, however, that at the root of at least one of Kafka's short stories—one of his most powerful —lie strong guilt feelings which resulted from his rejection of religious Judaism. That story is "The Judgment," which, Kafka noted in his diaries, "I wrote at one sitting during the night of [September] 22nd–23rd [1912], from ten o'clock at night to six o'clock in the morning" (I, pp. 275–276).

"The Judgment" starts off quite disarmingly. Georg Bende-mann, a successful young merchant, is sitting in his room after having written to a friend who had gone off to Russia on a business venture. In this letter, after much hesitation, Georg has informed his friend that he was engaged to be married. After pocketing the letter, Georg goes into "his father's room, which he had not entered for months."[7] Upon seeing his father he comments to himself: "My father is still a giant of a man" (p. 9). When Georg begins to talk about his friend in Russia, the father starts to act peculiarly. Then he says to his son:

Georg. . . . listen to me! You've come to me about this business, to talk it over with me. No doubt that does you honor. But it's nothing, it's worse than nothing, if you don't tell me the whole truth. (p. 10)

And he questions whether Georg really has a friend in St. Petersburg. Georg tries to change the subject, but his father won't let him. In apparent guilt at having neglected the old man, Georg undresses him for bed and makes "a quick, firm decision" that after his marriage he will "take him into his own future establishment" (p. 13).

When Georg, in answer to a question from his father, assures him, "Don't worry, you're well covered up," a startling change occurs in the old man:

'No!' cried his father, cutting short the answer. [He] threw the blankets off with a strength that sent them all flying in a moment and sprang erect in bed. Only one hand lightly touched the ceiling to steady him.

'You wanted to cover me up, I know, my young sprig, but I'm far from being covered up yet. And even if this is the last strength I have, it's enough for you, too much for you.' (pp. 13–14)

The father goes on to say that he knows the friend in St. Petersburg well, has in fact been in correspondence with him; and he and Georg become embroiled in an argument. Finally the father cuts short the bickering by announcing in a loud voice:

So now you know what else there was in the world beside yourself, till now you've known only about yourself! An innocent child, yes, that you were, truly, but still more truly have you been a devilish human being!—And therefore take note: I sentence you now to death by drowning! (pp. 17–18)

Georg flees from the room, rushes down the stairs, out into the street, "across the roadway, driven toward the water." He swings over the protecting railing, hangs for a moment, calls, "Dear parents, I have always loved you, all the same," and lets himself drop (p. 18).

The two most curious facts about the story are, first, that the father not only sentences Georg to death but that he specifies *by drowning*; and, second, that Georg carries out the sentence on himself. The mystery disappears, however, when one returns to the date on which the story was written: ". . . at one sitting during the night of [September] 22nd–23rd [1912]." For in 1912 Yom Kippur commenced at sundown of September 21 and concluded at sundown of September 22. Evidently Kafka had his evening meal, and then sat down at his desk and wrote the story "from ten o'clock at night to six o'clock in the morning." In the Yom Kippur service we read:

> On New Year's Day the decree is inscribed and on the Day of Atonement it is sealed, how many shall pass away and how many shall be born; *who shall live and who shall die;* who shall attain the measure of man's days and who shall not attain it; *who shall perish* by fire and who *by water*; who by sword, and who by beast; who by hunger and who by thirst; who by earthquake and who by plague; who by strangling and who by stoning; who shall have rest and who shall go wandering; who shall be tranquil and who shall be disturbed; who shall be at ease and who shall be afflicted; who shall become poor and who shall wax rich; who shall be brought low and who shall be exalted.[8]

Whether Kafka was conscious of it or not, the motivation behind his writing of "The Judgment" would seem to have been an attempt to expiate his own guilt toward "the God of Abraham, the God of Isaac, and the God of Jacob."

The quoted passages in the summary of the story now take on specific meaning. Georg's failure to enter his father's room "for months" may well reflect Kafka's own lack of interest in the synagogue. (His failure to attend services is attested to by several of the quotations from the diaries given above.) The father's warning to his son that Georg is not telling him "the whole truth" could refer to the fact that Kafka did not confess his sins to God openly and freely in the manner prescribed during the High Holy Days: "Our Father, our King, we have sinned before Thee. . . . Our Father, our King, forgive and pardon our iniquities. . . ." (p. 476); "grant atonement for all our transgressions. . . . For the sin which we have committed before Thee under compulsion or of our own will, and for the sin which we have committed before Thee by hardening our hearts; . . . *For all these, O God of forgiveness, forgive us, pardon us, grant us atonement*" (pp. 421–422; the italics are in the original).

Georg's decision to take his father "into his own future establishment" after his marriage could reflect Kafka's indecision about whether to bring God into his own "future establishment," for he was at this time engaged to marry F.B., a

German Jewess. Or, again, it could be a reaction to his failure even to consider such an idea. The "covering up the father" parallels Kafka's attempt to "bury" God. And the father's sudden resurgence of power (and Georg's earlier noticing that his father "is still a giant of a man") suggests that, in Kafka's mind at least, God will not allow Himself to be buried.[9] Thus, Georg's guilty reactions throughout the story also take on heightened meaning.

Written immediately after the conclusion of Yom Kippur, the sentence to death by drowning echoes very closely the portion of the Yom Kippur service which describes God's inscriptions in the Book of Life: "who shall live and who shall die; . . . who shall perish by water. . . ." And Georg's acceptance of the validity of the sentence and his carrying it out probably indicate Kafka's own sense of guilt toward God. His avowal that "I have always loved you all the same" would seem to indicate either repentance or an underlying acceptance of God despite the conscious denial.

The diaries do not indicate whether Kafka attended Yom Kippur services that year. The fact that there are no entries for September 21 and 22 may suggest that he did. If he did, the argument for this particular interpretation of "The Judgment" is clearly a strong one. Even if he did not, however, the case is not really weakened—and may even be strengthened. The diaries show that Kafka attended the Kol Nidre service the year before (I, p. 72). And as a member of the Jewish community of Prague thoroughly immersed in cultural Judaism he could not have failed to know of the occurrence of Yom Kippur nor of the day's solemn significance. In fact, failure to attend services could very well have triggered the whole story: "He . . . went out of his room . . . into his father's room, *which he had not entered for months.*"

The fact that later references in the diaries to "The Judgment" do not recognize the relation between the story and Yom Kippur may only indicate that Kafka himself was probably not aware of it (I, p. 278). If his guilt feelings were as strong as the story seems to imply, it is understandable that he could not consciously recognize the "meaning" of the story. Nor is this analysis of the story necessarily in conflict with one which insists that the story reflects Kafka's inde-

cision about marrying F.B.[10] The two analyses actually re-
inforce each other. Note, for example, the analysis of the
passage about Georg's "quick, firm decision to take [his fa-
ther] into his own establishment" after his marriage.

Certainly Kafka was overwrought at this particular time in
his life. In a letter written to Max Brod soon after the com-
position of "The Judgment," Kafka says that he had contem-
plated suicide because of his dejection at having to spend
valuable time and energy that could be used for writing in
working at his father's factory.[11] The reason that Kafka gave
for his unhappiness may further indicate his ignorance of the
meaning behind "The Judgment." It may, in fact, be a worthwhile addition to our analysis of the story. For in the story
the father accuses Georg of having taken his business away
from him, and Georg's attempt to "cover up" the father could
reflect Kafka's anger at his father's insistence that he work at
the factory. Kafka's frustration at this waste of time is a per-
sistent theme throughout the diaries. The convergence of three
major problems in Kafka's life (the decision of whether or
not to marry; anger at the fact that his father insisted that he
had to work at the factory; and guilt about his rejection of
God, brought to a crisis by Yom Kippur) may indeed account
for the explosive way in which the story was written and for
its savagery.

Whatever the relative importance of the problems of his
impending marriage and having to work at his father's factory, it seems clear, however, that Kafka's continued denial
of his God and the occurrence of Yom Kippur are basic to
the meaning of "The Judgment," and that despite the relatively few overt signs that Kafka felt guilty about that denial,
his actual guilt feelings were strong enough to explode into a
short story. Either because he did not recite the Yom Kippur
petitions for forgiveness as a result of failure to attend services, or because the prayers simply were not effective for him,
they did not relieve his anxiety. One might even argue that
the literary explosion was more effective. It may have released
the tension enough not only to prevent Kafka's possible suicide but also to allow him to work efficiently as well.[12] (Kafka
himself considered "writing as a form of prayer."[13]) "The
Judgment" is Kafka's first important work. And the two

months following its writing were among the most productive of his life.[14]

Thus Kafka, who in many ways typifies "the modern Jewish intellectual," may have thought he had rejected the religion of his fathers without suffering any apparent after-effects. But in fact he enjoyed no such escape. Critics have pointed out that in many of his later works Kafka was concerned with man's relationship to God. And there is now, we trust, sufficient evidence that he was concerned specifically with his relationship to the God of Israel.

This is not to suggest that all modern "Jewish intellectuals" who attempt to reject God will suffer similarly from overwhelming feelings of guilt. For if Kafka's life typifies the lives of many who came after him, it also displays a unique character of its own. The appearance in Kafka, however, of strong religious guilt feelings below the surface when so few show above the surface may suggest a fresh examination of the works of other Jewish writers who also rejected religious Judaism to discover whether they manifest similar reactions.

NOTES

1. Max Brod, *Franz Kafka* (New York: Schocken Books, 1947), p. 110.

2. *The Diaries of Franz Kafka,* ed. Max Brod, trans. Martin Greenberg and Hannah Arendt (New York: Schocken Books, 1948), Vol. I, pp. 275–276.

3. *Franz Kafka,* p. 153.

4. Gustav Janouch, *Conversation with Kafka* (New York: Frederick A. Praeger, 1953), p. 61.

5. Brod records in *Franz Kafka* that Dora Dymant told him less than a month before Kafka's death that, in seeking her hand in marriage, Kafka "had sent her pious father a letter in which he had explained that although he was not a practicing Jew in her father's sense, he was nevertheless a repentant one, seeking conversion; and therefore might perhaps hope to be accepted into the family of such a pious man" (p. 208). Since Brod makes no further comment, it is difficult to tell whether Kafka actually intended to return to the practice of Judaism.

6. *Franz Kafka,* throughout, but especially Chapter VI: "Religious Development."

7. *Selected Stories of Franz Kafka,* trans. Willa and Edwin Muir (New York: Modern Library, 1952), p. 8.

8. Rabbi Morris Silverman, *High Holiday Prayer Book* (Hartford, Conn.: Prayer Book Press, 1939), p. 357. The italics are mine.—E.R.S.

9. Ironically for Kafka, there is a passage in the Yom Kippur service that warns: "Fear not, O Jacob; return ye backsliders; return, O Israel. Behold, the Guardian of Israel slumbereth not nor sleepeth. . . ." (p. 298). In "The Judgment" Georg tries to put his father to sleep.

10. See, for example, Kate Flores, "The Judgment," in *Franz Kafka Today,* ed. Angel Flores and Homer Swander (Madison: University of Wisconsin Press, 1958), pp. 5–24.

11. *Franz Kafka,* pp. 91–93. Brod was so concerned that he communicated his fears to Kafka's mother.

12. According to Brod, not long before (on June 6, 1912), Kafka complained in his diary: "The tremendous world I have in my head! But how can I release it and release myself without tearing myself apart?" (*Franz Kafka,* p. 90). This passage, however, appears in the diaries on June 21, 1913, a year later.

13. *Franz Kafka,* p. 78.

14. "Thus between the end of September and the end of November 1912 . . . three of Kafka's chief works came into being, or at least, as far as the novel is concerned, had reached the decisive stage" (*Franz Kafka,* p. 128).

A Fuller Definition of Civil Rights

James Sellers

What happens *after* desegregation? Viewing the civil rights struggle in the context of the on-going life of the community, James Sellers argues that bare justice is not enough, that "allowing" the Negro to buy his cup of coffee in the bus station cannot be the main goal. "This goal is to endow that cup of coffee with the sacramental value it has in all normal situations of American life, the value of fellowship." And achievement of this goal will require the use of a strategy currently in disfavor; while struggle and protest are not to be abandoned as elements of community change, in the area of race relations social action addressed to groups must be supplemented by a more intensely personal approach if bare justice is to be converted into the forms of authentic community. Dr. Sellers is Associate Professor of Christian Ethics and Theology at Vanderbilt University Divinity School. Born in Mississippi, Dr. Sellers was educated in Georgia, Florida and Tennessee, and was a Florida newspaper publisher and editor before entering the field of theological education. His article originally appeared in the Summer 1963 issue of the Abingdon Press quarterly publication *Religion in Life*;* several of the article's paragraphs and episodes are adapted from his book *The South and Christian Ethics*, published in the fall of 1962 by Association Press. Dr. Sellers is also author of *When Trouble Comes: A Christian View of Evil, Sin, and Suffering* and *The Outsider and the Word of God: A Study in Christian Communication.*

IN FLORIDA, the Grand Dragon of the Southern Knights of the Ku Klux Klan turned in his resignation, explaining, "I see no way to stop racial integration in the schools and it looks to me like the best thing to do is accept it. . . . I cannot agree to go outside the law to maintain segregation. I cannot agree to such things as bombing and burning

* 201 Eighth Avenue S., Nashville 3, Tennessee.

schools." But Bill Hendrix was not yet done. Though he was for law and order, "I still say I am for segregation." He made it clear that he was merely moving back to a new line of defense. For now, he said, he would continue his fight against integration through the church.

One lesson we can draw from this statement is that of realism. Even a Grand Dragon of the Klan knows segregation in public places is done for. Only the "woolly-minded," Ralph McGill commented, should miss the point now, after what Bill Hendrix said.

But another lesson is to be drawn, too. And this is that the center of the struggle for "civil rights" is changing and a new phase of it is beginning. As segregation dies civically, it takes on new life behind the scenes, in places where men gather voluntarily. Most conspicuous of these places, perhaps, is the church.

The time has come for us to reflect on the future of our efforts toward racial justice. I think we should consider five revisions in our outlook: (1) a sharper sense of the *full* meaning of civil rights; (2) a clearer confrontation of the segregationist with the *theological* character of his beliefs; (3) efforts by the nonviolent movement to become more *theologically* mature; (4) a more definite sense of the *time* and *place* dimensions of civil rights; (5) more stress on *"interpersonal penetration"* as goal.

The Full Meaning of Civil Rights

At many a bus station in the South today a Negro has no difficulty in buying a cup of coffee. If we limit our observation to empirical facts, there is little to complain about in such terminals. If we include something a little more intangible in our sights, however, if we go beyond the question of "rights" to the question of "community," we find much left to be desired. What about the look of contempt in the eyes of the waitress as she hands our man his cup of coffee? Is not the quality of the justice done him bled off a bit, downgraded by the barrier of estrangement? And what of the local coffee-drinkers who, be it granted, lift not a hand to bar our man from his traveler's coffee? They too look at him in the same way; he could not have sat with them for coffee. What is involved in the freedom to purchase a cup of coffee, anyway? Has it not been *truncated* in this case; left as a physical freedom, and not extended beyond, into that zone of sacramental meaning that the cup of coffee has in other circumstances in America—the zone of fellowship?

Attached to the 1961 report of the U.S. Commission on Civil Rights is a statement by one of its members, Theodore M. Hesburgh. "Federal action alone," he says here, "will never completely solve the problem of civil rights. Federal action is essential, but not adequate, to the ultimate solution." He goes on to point out that the problem is human and theological as well as political, that civil rights in themselves stand only for some larger reality, one that Hesburgh himself defines in the Judaeo-Christian tradition of love of neighbor.

This suggests there is a fuller way to look at the idea of civil rights, a way that seeks literally to integrate a man and his rights lastingly into the fabric of a community, and therefore a way that leads naturally into that fuller meaning of fellowship which lies beyond. I am aware that this means broadening the definition of civil rights. We have to go beyond the narrowest meaning of civil rights as "limitations on adverse governmental action." We even have to go beyond the more positive meaning of civil rights as "freedoms of action and thought" in various categories of social-political existence: insist on these freedoms but relate them positively to the communities in which they are to be enjoyed.

The Theological Attack on the Segregationist

A Columbia, Tennessee, man asserts in a letter to the *Nashville Banner* that desegregation of the public schools is not the proper concern of Christians. In fact, he argues, "Segregation is not a religious issue and never was. God is the author of segregation. He is a God of segregation." This may seem a contradictory set of assertions. How can segregation be both nonreligious and yet ordained of God? The author's meaning, I think, is this: Segregation is religious, all right, but it is not a religious *issue*. An issue is something you can argue about. Segregation, on the other hand, is so God-ordained, and therefore religious, that it is not in question. It must be accepted as a dogma rather than an issue, in the same way that the Virgin Birth or the infallibility of Scripture, for some, are nondiscussible dogmas.

Opponents of segregation have doubtless supported this brand of dogmatics without realizing it. When old-fashioned social gospelers, for example, insist in doctrinaire fashion that segregation is primarily a device of economic exploitation, they are agreeing with the white supremacist to the effect that segregation is not first of all a theological issue. The same thing happens when ministers broach the segregation issue to their congregations as exclusively a problem of civics: "Christians may disagree about segregation or integration, but every Christian must uphold law and order." There is a place for this argument, for often the minister can do more by encouraging definite, limited action—such as civic-minded school desegregation—than he can by preaching neo-abolitionism. Yet the question is not exhausted at the civil level; the question, finally, is the way men treat other men before God.

Each of the conventional interpretations of segregation—the economic, the civic, the sexual, and so on—has its place in understanding and pursuing the problem. But none of them really goes to the inner core of meaning that segregation has in the South. The white supremacist is often quite ready to insist that it's all a matter of economics, or sex, or local civic custom. The one area he dreads and resists discussing is the *religious status* of his convictions. William Peters reports the comment of the president of the Virginia organization that everywhere else goes by the name of citizens' councils: "The worst obstacle we face in the fight to preserve segregated schools in the South is the white preacher."[1] To discuss the problem as other than a religious issue is to be blind to the forces that the white supremacists themselves fear most of all.

Segregation is a theological system of belief that would protect its devotees from all that looms on their horizon as "the powers of death and destruction." It is a way of handling the menace of one's own impulses and the perils of the strange, modern world as well. It is, in fact, an unrepentant kingdom, offering the same comfortable, false piety to the white Southerner today that the institution of slavery did a hundred years ago. It is temptation, the invitation for the Southerner to build himself a proud world. A hundred years ago, perhaps this self-made world was an economic world, since the slave was to work the soil and the Southerner was to enjoy his domain, accountable to none. Today, the Southerner (and the Northerner, too, in his way) uses the Negro to build himself not an economic domain but a bastion of a more rarefied kind: the domain of superior status, a kind of edifice of self-worship.

If the majority of Southerners continue to affirm this kind of world, it is because they suffer from a lack of courageous and imaginative theological leadership that will offer them a better world. In any case, we do not go to the heart of the white man's world of segregationism simply by demanding justice alone (though we must indeed demand *at least* justice); hence we are required, in our struggle for civil rights, to become better theologians.

Theological Maturity in the Nonviolent Movement

There is nothing immature about the eight sit-in demonstrators who, as I write this, have just been sentenced to ninety-day workhouse terms for attempting to eat in a Nashville restaurant. These brave youngsters are more mature, by far, than the hosts vainly attempting to perpetuate an unjust, segregated society. It is because I regard the nonviolent movement as the South's best hope that I venture to suggest the need of more theological maturity in it—which can only strengthen and make more effective the personal maturity that is already present.

The segregationist classically insists on doing the Negro benevolences and favors, bestowing "friendship" on him in lieu of his rights. The Mississippi planter will not let his Negro tenants starve, though he doesn't want them to vote. The Georgia businessman will give generously to buy football uniforms for the Negro high school, but he isn't willing to have Negroes in the other high school. And so on.

One of the ironies in the struggle for civil rights is that the "new Negroes" of the nonviolent movement often commit the same error, formally speaking, as the segregationists. For they have their own form of the ethical dictum that "love" leads the way and "justice" follows after. This is seen in the insistence of the nonviolent demonstrators that they are going to "love" the white man as a way of getting "justice." The error here is both semantic and theological. Proponents of nonviolence assume that not using physical violence is a suitable referent of the verb "to love." What they do not readily concede, I think, is that the choice of weapons, violent or nonviolent, may have little to do with the inner state of the user of the weapon. He may or may not love his opponent. Clarity would be served by the frank recognition that boycott, civil disobedience, and nonco-operation are expressions of the *necessary conflict* that may have to come in the South now, if the Negro is to win his rights. These devices of conflict do, to be sure, amount to steps on the way to reconciliation, but no good is served by labeling these steps themselves "loving" acts, as the force of nonviolence lies not in any superhuman ability to love its enemies, but rather in its peculiar ability to channel discontent, dislike, anger, impatience, into quiet and effective outlets that really do move us toward justice.

A more seasoned understanding of the ethical bounds that surround every "right" would also stand the nonviolent movement in good stead. Every just demand has its limit, as is well recognized in law. The freedom to organize has its limit in the law of conspiracy, the freedom of speech in the law of libel, the freedom of protest in the eventual demand for freedom of movement by others in the public streets.

I mention one instructive case. On March 2, 1961, shortly after the noon hour in Columbia, South Carolina, two hundred Negro students left a meeting at Zion Baptist Church. They walked in small groups to the Statehouse. Their purpose was to protest segregation laws and customs while the general assembly was in session. They paraded forty-five minutes without interruption or interference from the police. Meanwhile, onlookers gathered, blocking both vehicles and pedestrians. Finally there were 550 people (including the paraders) crowding the intersection, one of the state's busiest. At this point police consulted the parade leader, informed him of the traffic problem, gave him fifteen minutes to disperse his followers. According to South Carolina Supreme Court records, "The leader of the group refused to instruct or advise them to disperse but instead began a fervent speech to the group and in response they began to sing, shout, clap their hands and stamp their feet, refusing to disperse."[2]

One can both support the nonviolent movement (as I do) and concede that Southern officials have often unfairly misused their police power (as I also do) without agreeing that a given demonstration is *ipso facto* entitled to continue forever, free of the limitations of finite existence. It is time, in short, for the nonviolent movement to think more carefully about the theological and ethical criteria that should govern its acts and expressions.

The Time and Place Dimensions

There is no question about the right time to press for civil rights—that is *now*; or the right place—that is *wherever* these rights have been withheld, especially in the South.

What do I mean, then, by the "time dimension" of civil rights? Chiefly, I should say, their duration. We should think of civil rights, not abstractly, but as meant to possess a lifetime, as having continuation, as including staying power, as living across time within the community, as "being there," to use the existentialist's catchword—as *prevailing*.

Civil rights cannot be part of a community unless they share the community's life and hence the community's time. For when civil rights are brought in as timeless abstractions, you often end up with truncated rights: the objective right to purchase a cup of coffee in the bus station, but not the lasting rapport that in natural circumstances goes with the right to stroll into a place and order coffee.

Taking part in a community's time means seeing its past for what it is; working to change the present; and not confusing the present with the future. "If you don't know what happened behind you," says James Baldwin, "you've no idea of what is happening around you."[3] Let us admit this argument has been turned against civil rights by some Southerners who argue: "Look at our past; we're not ready for changes yet." But we must insist to the white Southerner that he look at his own past and see it for what it is: a past of false security built at the expense of a minority. As James Baldwin also remarked, the Southerner is ordinarily forbidden by his fellows to do any serious excavation of his own dark past; it's time we insisted that he did.

Seeing our pasts will help us change the present. It will serve notice on those who have lagged too long in making changes. But it will also give healthy warning to those too unheedful of the truth that civil rights have to be incarnated into a community *across time* to be real. I do not ordinarily illustrate my ideas by turning to John Dewey, but Dewey's early remarks on the relation of a new good to an old evil, and the place struggle occupies in the community, are much to the point.

The bad man, Dewey argues, is the one who is satisfied with existing arrangements and lives off his old inclinations, "irrespective of the sufficiency of those inclinations in view of the changed . . . environment."[4] Goodness, on the other hand, is not at an absolute remove from badness. The right new action is always related in some way to the insufficient old arrangement; "good action is always based upon action [at least supposed] good once, but bad if persisted in. . . . This good, of course, does not involve the annihilation of the . . . present bad—but its subordination; its use in the new function." Evil is that in the community "which goodness has to *overcome*—has to make an element of itself." Christianity teaches us, Dewey goes on to say, that the individual, by identifying himself with other men, even bad ones, "might be freed from slavery" to past evil, his own and that of others; and that "by recognizing and taking for his own the evil in the world, instead of engaging in an isolated struggle to become good by himself, he might make the evil a factor in his own right action."[5]

The struggle for civil rights, I take it, should be seen as a good related to the bad in the community in just some such way as this. We are not seeking civil rights in isolation, for they are worthless in total disrelation to the community. Therefore we are not fighting a holy war of extirpation against segregationists. Rather, we are waging at the community level what might be called a justified war, to change the evils of old inclinations and arrangements into the good of a new order; the end that shapes our means is always the bringing of the new good—"civil rights"—into some *lasting* propinquity to the life of the community.

Similarly, what do we mean by the "place" dimension of civil rights? Simply this: We can't solve the civil rights problem spacelessly—i.e., without reference to particular places— nor even by the old frontier device of seeking new space, moving out. We can't set aside a black state as the Black Muslims want us to do. The sensitive white Southerner may heal his conscience by leaving, but the problem remains. We can't even expect the solution to come when the Negro goes North voluntarily, for in doing so he as often as not compounds and spreads the problem by worsening the dire situations of crowded life in the slums of large cities.

It is an error, of course, to locate the boundaries of the civil rights problem entirely within the South. Nevertheless, I would subscribe to the pragmatic argument that the worsening situation of Negro life in Northern cities can itself be most effectively treated as a function of the Negro's unresolved place in the South. To maintain that Negroes are moving to the cities and hence that our investigations must be largely shifted there would be to miss the point. The Negroes are leaving the South because life is intolerable there; more will continue to leave in the degree that we leave the deep human problems of the South unattended to. Thus the percentage of Negroes in Chicago grew from less than 10 per cent in 1940 to nearly 25 per cent in 1960. But the proportion could climb, according to estimates I have seen, to 40 per cent in 1970. Manifestly, the most basic attack on this problem and the deprivation of civil rights—e.g., in housing—that goes with it will have to be made in the South.[6]

In the struggle for civil rights, then, we need an acute sense of the "human terrain" where the problem arises. We need much more insight into the variations in human communities which give rise to a different form of the problem in each. Thus, the nonviolent forces had to learn the hard way that the successful 1955–1956 boycott in Montgomery, Alabama, leading to integrated city bus service, could by no means be readily duplicated in Albany, Georgia, where similar methods produced a stalemate in 1962. Strategies for protest and reform need to be devised with the way of life of particular communities in mind, and indeed with the differentiated shapes taken by prejudice and repression of the Negro in mind; some rights are assured in one place and wholly frustrated in another apparently just like it, while entirely different rights are withheld in the first place and enjoyed by all citizens in the second.

If this stress on time and place suggests there is little strength in demanding everything, everywhere, all at once, it also means forcing attention to injustice at the right time and on the very scene. It allows no arguments like "Give us more time," "We have no problems here," "Let the discontented ones leave." It makes clear, better than abstract definitions of civil rights, that the problems must be faced *now* and in *particular locations*—that the quest for human rights can no more be relegated to the lumber room of idealist clichés.

The Dimension of Interpersonal Penetration

In recent months I have talked to officials of some more or less determinedly segregated Southern cities. Here is what I often observed: If you happen to be talking to one of them as a friend, in close personal conversation, he will admit that much of what the Negroes seek is just. He may, as in the cases of several I have talked to, concede privately that he is not really a die-hard, metaphysical segregationist. "Personally," one told me, "I would like to see some changes made in this town; it's the old guard around here who resist."

Now take the Southerner who talks this way and put him in a group—say the city commission or, for that matter, the men's Bible class on Sunday morning. This individual sense of morality quickly evaporates and a group code appears. He now espouses the old, familiar, unrealistic, obsolete segregationist ideology. The more official the group he joins, the more this reversal is likely. What we have here is a form of the problem of "moral man and immoral society," to use the title of Reinhold Niebuhr's notable book. Men will uphold and sanctify injustices when they operate as groups, injustices they often will not countenance as individuals.

Contemporary social ethicists, recognizing this state of affairs, have tended to attack it by proposing vigorous social action addressed to groups. If men in groups are most prone to injustice, the thinking goes, we had better shape our strategy to move men in their groups. To insist upon an individualistic approach to morality when the evils are wrought by groups is to fall into naïve illusion.

This is peerless reasoning. Yet I wonder if it is not now time to amend it a bit in the field of race relations. Even after we reduce public injustices to a minimum, and community sachems "allow" the Negro to buy his cup of coffee in the bus station, the main goal is yet to be reached. This goal is to endow that cup of coffee with the sacramental value it has in all normal situations of American life, the value of fellowship. That is what is left over after the bare question of public morality has been resolved. Why should we not adopt a more intensely personal approach to race relations, not to replace the attack on group-fostered injustice but to supplement it? If men are most vulnerable to conscience when they are isolated as persons, and least so when they can take shelter under the umbrella of group thinking, why should we not attempt to deal with them as individuals to a larger extent than contemporary social ethics has thought proper? Instead of concentrating almost solely upon the propensity of men in the aggregate to compound and perpetuate evil, why not spend more time putting them under the searchlight of personal moral scrutiny?

The nonviolent movement, by and large, has dealt with the most influential people in Southern communities in an official, quasi-official, or group-oriented fashion. This is seen in the form negotiations usually take: the nuncios from one group meet and treat with the nuncios of the other group. The real friends of the nonviolent movement among the whites, its truest partners on a personal basis, have all too often been the rolling stones, the transients, guitar players, poets, collegians, and others not anchored deeply in the framework of community life. Whatever interpersonal communication there already is here, of course, is all to the good. I am suggesting, however, that if the goal of civil rights is to be integration, which means becoming a part of a political whole, becoming a part of a community, we ought to seek more deliberately to engage in interracial, interpersonal communication with the rank and file, the influential, and the permanent members of the community. Political results are too often the outcome of arrangements between "friends" for us to overlook this avenue.

Now this does not mean, as I have already said, that we should go around talking about how much we "love" the segregationists. We have seen how struggle and protest have to be elements of community change. But there is an inter-mediate quality between the bare justice of the City of Earth, won by conflict, and the completed love of the City of God, in which we do not live yet; this is simply the openness and casual acceptance that is possible among men in this mixed city of earth and heaven where we all live. Such openness is a movement toward fellowship among centered selves who cannot yet give up their selfhood if their object is communica-tion and interpersonal encounter.

James Baldwin senses the state of affairs, I think. "Nobody knows my name," he tells us. This is true in a poignant way of the American Negro; it is also true of every American. We do not yet know ourselves or each other. But this is not to say that we cannot move toward knowing ourselves and each other. For we must. "In order to learn your name," Baldwin told an interviewer, "you are going to have to learn mine."[7]

The struggle for justice to the Negro, even in its barest form, has not yet been won. Thus litigation, lawmaking and changing, nonviolent protest, and other forms of pressure are still needed. But it is folly not to see that the crucial center of the struggle for civil rights is subtly shifting. Enough justice has been won to permit us to begin thinking now, with part of our capacities, of ways to convert bare justice into the forms of authentic fellowship. Unless we go on to this fuller meaning of civil rights we will have paid a fearful price in America for the wrong goal.

NOTES

1. Peters, *The Southern Temper* (New York: Doubleday and Co., 1959), p. 102.

2. State v. James Edwards, Jr., *et. al.*, 123 S.E. 2nd 247: *Race Relations Law Reporter*, VII (Spring 1962), p. 107.

3. "Black Man in America," *WFMT Perspective*, X (December 1961), p. 38. James Baldwin is interviewed by Studs Terkel.

4. Dewey, *Outlines of a Critical Theory of Ethics* (New York: Hillary House, 1957), pp. 214–215. This volume is a reprint of the 1891 edition.

5. *Ibid.*, pp. 223–225. It is fashionable to remark on Dewey's early "Hegelianism" as exemplified here, but the picture of change-through-struggle Dewey provides seems much truer to what actually goes on in community reform, as I see it, than the stark antinomies offered by, let us say, American disciples of Kierkegaard who have become interested in the racial conflict.

6. It is true that a partial solution for the South may lie in some kind of out-migration from those former plantation areas where the Negro population is still densely concentrated. In any case, crash programs to ameliorate conditions in Northern slums, however necessary, do not get at the underlying problem.

7. "Black Man in America," p. 39.

IV

A Direction for the Future

Christianity and the Supernatural

Eugene R. Fairweather

All too often in contemporary theological discussions, contends Eugene R. Fairweather, attitudes are expressed which, if carried to their logical conclusion, would issue in one of two extremes: a purely this-worldly or a radically other-worldly philosophy. These extremes are a distorted reflection of the fact that Christian faith does have a two-sidedness about it— a two-sidedness which some churchmen, mistaking it for dualism, try to resolve "by an exclusive emphasis on one or the other of the severed elements of complete Christianity," on either the natural or the supernatural, the immanent or the transcendent. Such emphasis compromises the integrity of the Christian gospel and erects a barrier to authentic and effective communication of that gospel. Hence "no theological task is more important than the clarification of the true relation of man to the supernatural." Dr. Fairweather essays that task and makes a strong case for the view that faith and reason, grace and nature, God and man are not in necessary contradiction. Detailing the fallacies and inadequacies of both naturalism and antinaturalism, Dr. Fairweather's essay moves far toward an ontology of the supernatural—and in so doing takes some sightings on what may prove to be the territory ahead for tomorrow's theology. Dr. Fairweather, Associate Professor of Dogmatic Theology and Ethics in Trinity College, Toronto, is also editor of the *Canadian Journal of Theology*.* His article originally appeared as a two-part series in the issues of that quarterly journal for January and April of 1963.

The Meaning of the Supernatural

AT THE beginning of his provocative book, *Man's Need and God's Action*, Reuel Howe records a casual conversation with a typical secularized modern. His interlocutor lists a variety of this-worldly goods which he already possesses, and ends with the light-hearted prediction: "If we'll

* University of Toronto Press, Toronto, Ontario, Canada.

only use our heads and play it right, we'll soon have a way of life that will make religion and church unnecessary."[1] We can hardly help realizing that this is an accurate enough expression of a view held, at least tacitly, by a very large part of the population of the Western world. Millions of those to whom the Gospel must be addressed quite frankly doubt that the Church has any real meaning for their lives as human persons. That means that, if we are to communicate at all with the secularized masses, we must give serious consideration to the relation between their scale of values and the promise and demand of the Christian faith.

The trouble is that within the Christian community itself there are ominous signs of a widespread inability to deal with this problem in adequately Christian terms. It is painfully obvious that many Christians tend to assume the standards of secular society, so that for them the Church fulfils its vocation by searching out the "felt needs" of modern man and then outbidding other agencies in meeting such needs. Starting from the reasonable assumption that men and women want peace of mind, domestic happiness, social success, economic prosperity, and international order, they present the Christian ethic as the surest way of securing these goals, or perhaps, where the memory of traditional theology is greener, they offer the grace of Christ as the strongest force making for human welfare. In sharp contrast to all this, in circles where man's transcendent destiny is more clearly recognized, we often hear an exposition of the Gospel which detaches man's ultimate concern with a right relation to God from the pressing realities of everyday existence. While this kind of thinking may preserve the Christian witness to the supernatural and eternal, it does so at the expense of any effective reference to the natural and temporal circumstances under which man's eternal salvation must be worked out.

Perhaps it would be misleading to suggest that either of these tendencies had been systematized by responsible Christian thinkers as a pure theological position. Nonetheless, in contemporary theological discussion, attitudes are often expressed which, if they were logically developed, would necessarily issue in a purely this-worldly or in a radically other-worldly philosophy. To use the jargon popular among theological educators, some theologians seem to aim at "relevance" to life, superficially interpreted, at the expense of Christianity, while others manage to defend the Christian faith only at the risk of real "irrelevance" to man's temporal existence.

This dilemma is not simply a matter of human perversity—of a brash materialism, perhaps, countered by an escapist spiritualism. The essential structure of the Christian faith has a real two-sidedness about it, which may at first lead the unwary into dualism and then encourage the attempt to resolve the dualism by an exclusive emphasis on one or other of the severed elements of complete Christianity. Indeed, I think that such a dissolution is inevitable once we lose our awareness of that ordered relation of the human and the divine, the immanent and the transcendent, which the Gospel assumes. For the integrity of the Gospel, then, no theological task is more important than the clarification of the true relation of man to the supernatural. As Hendrik Kraemer put it more than twenty years ago, in an influential assessment of the task of the Church in the modern world: "The Christian Church in the West and in the East, despite the difference in background and history, is virtually confronted with the same fundamental problem: the relation to the world and all its spheres of life, and the same danger lest it solve it in the wrong way."[2] And as the same writer has observed more recently, this amounts to raising the ultimate question of the relation of created nature to God and his grace. "Instead of the term: Church–World, one can use the term more hallowed in the history of theology, that is to say: the realm of Grace—the realm of Nature."[3] In other words, the practical problem of the mission of the Church drives us to face the theological problem of the transcendent being and the manward action of God.

The terms of the question can be diversely stated from different viewpoints, so that we may speak of the creaturely and the divine, the secular and the sacred, the historical and the eschatological, or the natural and the supernatural, but all these dualities point to the same primary truths. On the one hand, man's life is the product of creaturely processes and it has to be lived out in this world of space and time. On the other hand, the ultimate foundation and the final destiny of that same life lie in a supratemporal relation to the reality which transcends all creaturely existence. If we accept the easy solution, as we readily do, and minimize either aspect of this two-sidedness of human life as seen by Christian faith, that faith is in imminent danger of losing a good deal more than half its meaning.

It is the uniqueness of this particular duality that makes it so hard to understand and express. We bring to the apprehension of the ultimate duality a mind formed by our experience of the manifold dualities of our temporal life, in which again and again an "either–or" decision is forced upon us, because to choose between temporal goods is necessarily to exclude as well as to affirm. For that reason, it is fatally easy for us to reduce the divine–human relation to an ordinary duality, and to fail to see that it is a relation "in depth"—an ordering of means and immediate ends with reference to their ultimate end—rather than a simple juxtaposition of two similar realities. Consequently, we produce at best a simple "two-storey" picture of nature and the supernatural, and then, having assumed that we can occupy only one storey at a time, we find ourselves driven to choose between a secularist rejection of the supernatural storey and a pietistic suppression of the natural storey of our misconstrued Christianity. We urgently need, then, to move beyond such initial misconstructions to a more fully Christian vision of the two levels of reality.

The problem of nature and the supernatural forces itself on our notice in the very form of Christian faith as expressed in the Creed. For the Creed witnesses to our faith in the eternal, living, and true God, Father, Son, and Holy Spirit—in God who creates man in the world to fulfil his purpose—in God who takes our manhood in the Incarnation—in God who through the Church sanctifies human life for eternity. But to say all this is to say that the supernatural creates nature for its own supernatural purpose, or, more fully, that God, who infinitely transcends every actual or possible creature, creates finite beings to participate in his life, and acts through them and in them to bring them to that destiny. To profess our faith in the triune God, in his creative love, in his redemptive acts, and in his grace in his Church, is in effect to acknowledge that the intrinsic structure of Christian theology must be described and defined in terms of the relation of nature to the supernatural.

Admittedly, the actual term "supernatural" has a rather complex history and its proper theological definition is a complex problem. In particular, it is essential to keep from being misled by the apparent analogy with such expressions as "superman" into thinking that the "supernatural" means the "natural, only more so." Whatever the verbal difficulties, however, the idea itself is an inescapable requirement of Christian faith. It is true that the wide-spread use of the word in Western theology dates only from the work of St. Thomas Aquinas.[4] But Aquinas seems to have derived the term from such influential transmitters of Eastern Christian thought as John Scotus Erigena and Burgundio of Pisa, who in their respective translations of the Pseudo-Dionysius and St. John of Damascus had used the adverbial form, *supernaturaliter*, to render the Greek *hyperphuōs*. Moreover, while it is the "Areopagite" and the Damascene who gave theological currency to this particular Greek term,[5] from an early period the concept of that which is "above nature" had been seized upon by Christian theologians as an appropriate means of stating the core of the Gospel. So, for example, Origen tells how God "raises man above human nature (*hyper tēn anthro-pinēn physin*) and makes him change into a better and divine nature." In a similar vein, St. John Chrysostom speaks of men as having received, by grace, "health, beauty, honour, glory and dignities far exceeding our nature." In the West, perhaps the most concise expression of the idea is to be found in the Leonine prayer: "Grant us to be partakers of his divinity, who deigned to become partaker of our humanity."[6] In these and a multitude of patristic texts, the essential point is just this, that God, who is essentially "supernatural," perfect with a perfection beyond creaturely comprehension, nevertheless elevates human creatures to a true participation in the divine life—an indwelling of God in man and man in God.

The same idea finds an eloquent modern expression in some sentences of the great German theologian, Matthias Joseph Scheeben:

If the lower nature is raised in all these respects to the level of a higher nature, and especially if this elevation modifies the lower nature so deeply and affects its inmost being and essence so powerfully that the limits of possibility are reached; if God, purest light and mightiest fire, wishes thoroughly to permeate His creature with His energy, to flood it with brightness and warmth, to transform it into His own splendor, to make the creature like to the Father of spirits and impart to it the fullness of His own divine life; if, I say, the entire being of the soul is altered in its deepest recesses and in all its ramifications to the very last, not by annihilation but by exaltation and transfiguration, then we can affirm that a new, higher nature has come to the lower nature, because it has been granted a participation in the essence of Him to Whom the higher nature properly belongs.[7]

That something like this is the ultimate meaning of the Christian Gospel seems to me to be beyond question. It is not just that the credal confession of God's purpose, from creation through the Incarnation and the work of grace to eternal life, makes real and full sense only in the light of this eternally intended coinherence of the divine and the human. The New Testament itself seems to support such an interpretation of the Gospel, when we reflect on its familiar phrases: "partakers of the divine nature"; "God shall be all in all"; "I am glorified in them"; "God gave us eternal life, and this life is in his Son"; "It is no longer I who live, but Christ who lives in me"; "changed into his likeness from one degree of glory to another."[8] The problem, then, is not so much to defend the reality of man's supernatural life in God as to state the relation of human nature to the supernatural in such a way as to affirm and clarify the full reality of that relation and not, in effect, to obscure or negate it.

On this level, the crucial task is to disentangle the authentically supernatural from the pseudo-supernatural in both its antinatural and its naturalistic forms. By antinaturalism, I mean a doctrine in which the supernatural or divine is falsely identified with some supposed principle to which the entire natural order stands in no real and positive relation but which is thought of rather as being in the sharpest opposition to the natural. By naturalism, I mean the identification of the divine with the natural order as a whole or its reduction to some element of that order which, as such, cannot stand in a unique relation to the whole of nature. In either case the distinctive meaning of the supernatural as the transcendent fulfilment of nature in its completeness, at once really and uniquely related to creatures, is obscured, and as long as we remain in the sphere of the pseudo-supernatural we are ostensibly left with a choice between the simple assertion of the antinatural and the idolatry of the natural. My fundamental concern in this study is to make it plain that this is a false dilemma.

"Every theology of grace," writes a contemporary theologian, "must safeguard at the same time the *primacy of God*, who alone justifies and sanctifies man, and the *realism of regeneration*."[9] I shall begin with the second point, as in many respects the more urgent one in the face of contemporary theological transcendentalism. I am convinced that much modern naturalism stems from the repeated assertions of the "primacy of God" by an antinaturalism which has failed to show that there is anything real to assert, and that bruised and battered naturalism would be ready enough to admit the transcendent if it could only see that it *is* real. At any rate, the first aspect of the genuine supernatural which we are to consider is its reality as ground and end of nature.

What I am getting at is that the relation of nature to the supernatural must be presented in "ontological" terms if it is to be genuinely intelligible. This means that Christian thought must resist the temptation to glorify God and his grace by asserting what is technically called the "equivocity" of being, which in this context means the utter and total unlikeness of the creature to the Creator. Once the latter position is taken up, any real divine purpose in creation and redemption becomes unintelligible, since the relation of nature and the supernatural is simply a matter of the divine will and decision, without any consideration of creative wisdom or of a created order which can be fulfilled in a real relation to the divine nature. On this showing, man's relation to God can be nothing more than a blind submission of the human will to the inscrutable divine will. As an inevitable result, the whole complex structure of man's nature and man's world ceases to have any theological meaning.

It is to this kind of theology, of course, that interpretations of the divine-human relation in terms of simple interpersonal relationships belong. Whether we find the heart of the Gospel in the complex of divine Word, responsive faith, and justifying forgiveness, in a personal "relationship" grounded in God's "acceptance" of man, or in an "I–Thou" relation deliberately and exclusively contrasted with a real relation of beings to Being, we are at least implicitly reducing the real richness alike of man's creaturely nature and of God's infinite love and grace to a simple dialectic of decisions, rooted in sheer will apart from any ontological foundation. But this is to deprive the supernatural of any intelligible significance for human nature and to strip the natural of any real supernatural orientation. Uniquely important as personality is in the Christian scheme of things, its importance must be evaluated in an ontological frame of reference, and will must not be left as the sole principle of cohesion between nature and the supernatural.

If, however, we assert a real ontological relation as one aspect of the Christian doctrine of the supernatural, we must immediately affirm the unique and analogical character of this relation, and so avoid what A. E. Taylor called "the old and deadly error" of supposing that the "equivocal" and the "univocal" are exhaustive alternatives.[10] If it is true that a non-ontological doctrine detaches the supernatural from the natural, it is also true that an ontology which posits the univocity of being—that is, the doctrine of being as simply a *summum genus*, realized in all particular beings—loses the supernatural in the natural and, by so doing, turns its back on the eternal mystery of the true God only to find itself left with an incredible imitation. If, on the assumption of equivocity, the creature can have no real supernatural significance, for a univocal ontology there is no real supernatural significance for any creature to have. For the former, the Christian mystery of divine action is at least a magnificent manifestation of the divine will; for the latter, however, it can hardly be more than a "mythological" puzzle, to be translated, as soon as our philosophical equipment is equal to the task, into the conceptual terms of a naturalistic metaphysic. It is to this final philosophical *débâcle* of a non-analogical theism that

Sidney Hook points, when he rather ambiguously compliments Reinhold Niebuhr for "his canny refusal to give his theology a systematic character or to defend an ontological religion," and attributes this refusal to Niebuhr's awareness that "such theologies cannot survive the probe of reason."[11] Leaving Niebuhr to defend himself as he sees fit and passing over the interesting question of how we can be sure that pure reason, after alighting tentatively in such places as Athens, Alexandria, Paris, Oxford, and Berlin, has finally folded its wings in Washington Square, we should recognize what Hook is really getting at. He is saying (and quite rightly) that on the presuppositions of a univocal ontology *there can be no God*. We can have the sheer Will of equivocity, the divine Being of analogy, or nothing—save perhaps an idol which a whisper of rational criticism will shatter.

Even this is not quite the end of our critique of non-analogical theology. I have already argued that antinaturalistic doctrines of the divine will deprive the supernatural of any meaning for human nature, but I should add that in the end the strange dialectic of antinaturalism leads to the total disappearance of the supernatural and transcendent. The theology of sheer will is ultimately incapable of maintaining the transcendent reality of God, because its very concept of divine will, if an analogical interpretation of the divine–human relation is excluded, must be either surreptitiously univocal or totally contentless. In either case it can have no transcendent content, which means that at last we have disclosed the naturalistic skeleton which lurks in the antinaturalistic cupboard. I suggest that what in fact happens in the formation of an antinaturalistic theology is that some concept derived from our natural experience—such as the notion of "personal will" —is posited over against nature as a description of the transcendent. The contradiction inherent in this procedure is obvious enough; a concept which arises out of our knowledge of creatures is used without question to point to the "wholly other" Creator. Once we recognize this, however, the dilemma of the antinaturalist is perfectly plain. He must either fall back into naturalism or decline to speak of the transcendent at all. But the latter alternative is itself only another road to *de facto* naturalism, since to affirm a "God" without expressible content is to leave naturalism in complete possession of the mind. At the beginning, perhaps, the theological voluntarist's assertion of "personal will" may seem plausible to the Christian believer, because he spontaneously reads into it the traditional ontological associations of the term "God." But when the rejection of analogy and univocity strips away all these vestiges of ontology, we are left with a transcendent self-assertion minus a self. Those readers of Lewis Carroll who have had some difficulty in grasping the notion of the grin that remained after the gradual disappearance of its ontological basis in the "Cheshire cat" will possibly be the first to recognize the nature of this theological version of their old problem, but a little reflection will make the lesson plain to all. In the end, the antinaturalistic alternative to naturalism is illusory, since it begins with the projection of a natural entity over against nature—hence the inevitability of antinaturalism at this stage, expressed in the affirmation of will against will —and ends with a retreat into naturalism or an advance into nihilism, which means in effect that nature is allowed to choose between being sacrificed to an idol and being immolated before an illusion.

In view of all this, it is not surprising that the implicit or explicit decision of most thinkers in the tradition of historic Christianity has been to speak in terms of analogy, as the only valid formula for the relationship between nature and the supernatural.

> Because it is so fundamental to the Christian experience and religious consciousness, analogy is normative in distinguishing Christian philosophy from its secular competitors, be they rationalist or irrationalist in spirit. The philosophers of analogy emphasize that this mode of understanding is intrinsic to Christian thought. . . . Analogy is of particular value in the exposition of theism because it presupposes both sides of the experience of the divine presence, immanence and transcendence. . . . It is the acknowledgement that the relation of man to God must be interpreted from a perspective which allows for both likeness and difference, immanence and transcendence. Analogy joins both in a dynamic unity.[12]

Historical Notes on Christian Supernaturalism

The historical interaction of supernaturalism, antinaturalism and naturalism—i.e., of analogy, equivocity, and univocity, respectively, in the correlation of divine and creaturely being —is much too complex a tale to be summarized here with any pretence of adequacy. Nonetheless, it will be necessary to point out certain highlights in the story, both as a partial clue to the understanding of some of the most tenaciously held positions in contemporary theology and as an indication of the predominance of authentic supernaturalism in the great tradition of Christian and Catholic thought. The biblical teaching itself will serve as a starting-point.

The Scriptures, which provide the primary text for all Christian theology, are neither in intention nor in fact a source-book of ancient ontology. In any case, we can hardly suppose that we are committed to the incidental philosophical ideas of the biblical writers, any more than to their scientific notions. At the same time—and this is what is really important for the Christian philosopher and theologian—certain metaphysical ideas appear to be natural expressions of biblical faith, reflecting as they do that understanding of the divine-human relation which is implicit in God's historical self-revelation. On this level, it can be cogently argued that Christian doctrine itself, in its primordial expression, points directly to realism and to transcendence—that is to say, to the essential marks of an analogical ontology. For instance, the Bible, for all its emphasis on the sovereign freedom of the divine purpose in history, speaks of order, of inherent and unassailable law, of a "righteousness" which defines the divine character, of a divine "image" in which God's purpose for man is initially expressed, and all this leads us to look for intelligibility and moral coherence in the revelation of God's nature and purpose. As for the other aspect of an analogical doctrine, the Bible speaks of the "holiness" of God, of his eternal transcendence, of his initiative in divine-human relations—all in terms which make impossible any simple mutuality in man's relations with God. When we put all this together, it seems to point to analogy, rather than sheer voluntarism or univocal naturalism, as the structure of our understanding of divine revelation.

When we turn to the first post-biblical exponents of the Christian tradition, the Greek Fathers, we find the same attitude expressed against the background of a different intellectual history. In the first place, we have an insistence on the coherence of God's purpose in creation and salvation, a lively awareness of the intelligibility of the divine nature and action, and an affirmation of the real possibility of man's perfection in a vital union with God. In particular, as Jules Gross points out in his careful study of the Greek Fathers, one of their dominant concerns is the expansion of the Pauline "Christ-mysticism" and the Johannine doctrine of "eternal life" into a full-blown theology of man's participation in the divine nature as the end of God's action in creation and salvation;[13] such a doctrine, however, assumes a coherence between human nature and its divine destiny. At the same time, we have an emphasis on the gulf between creature and Creator, expressed both in repeated assertions of the divine mystery—for instance, against Arian attempts to interpret the doctrine of the Trinity univocally—and in the doctrine of God's "divinizing" action—that is to say, of the elevation of man's being by the divine indwelling—as the necessary ground of personal communion with God. It is not, I think, sufficiently recognized that the latter doctrine, however realistic its idea of sanctified man's communion with God may be, expresses an awareness of divine transcendence, deliberately formulated in opposition to those neo-Platonic ideas of the divine in human nature which are the real Eastern equivalent of Western Pelagianism.[14] Once more, transcendence united to realism defines an essentially analogical viewpoint.

Perhaps all this is best illustrated by reference to the fundamental concern of the Greek Fathers with the Christological problem, from the early struggles with Docetism to the Council of Chalcedon and beyond. The Christological dogma, elaborated as it was to safeguard the fundamental Christian truth of man's eternal salvation through the real yet unconfused union of the genuinely human with the truly divine in the mystery of the Incarnation, provides the perfect, concrete expression of the two correlative aspects of an analogical realism. On the one hand, it insists on the essential diversity of the divine and the human, while on the other hand it points to the possibility of their fruitful union through the loving condescension of the transcendent God. In other words, the doctrine of the two natures, each irreducible to the other, speaks of the ontological contrast between Creator and creature, but at the same time the doctrine of the unity of person reflects the unshakable conviction that the creaturely nature, made in God's image, is capable of the most intimate communion with the divine. At the very heart of their theological teaching, then, we find the Greek Fathers working from what we have seen to be the fundamental principles of biblical faith —the unapproachable holiness of the transcendent God and the gracious approach of that same God to his creatures, made for fulfilment in his love.

When we come to the Latin Fathers, we shall perhaps expect, in view of their more extensive interest in legal and moral questions, to find signs of a naturalistic idea of communion with God through the observance of a moral code, in place of a proper ontology of the supernatural. It is true enough that they are more obviously concerned with the concrete conditions of the moral life of conformity to the divine law than with the analysis of the relation of manhood, as such, to the supernatural, and that as a result they tend, in interpreting God's dealings with man, to present us with expressions of the moral duality of sin and *healing* grace rather than the ontological duality of nature and *supernatural* grace. Moreover, the greatest of the Latin Fathers displays a tendency to guarantee the transcendence of grace, given man's fallen state, by asserting the sheer freedom of God's will in predestination, instead of emphasizing the ontological gap between Creator and creature, and in this way provides an opening for some of the interesting variations of later theology on the theme of divine voluntarism.[15] Nonetheless, when he looks beyond the Fall to the grace of Adam and the angels, or talks about the grace of *caritas* as the condition of the beatitude for which man's created nature longs, and above all when he states the meaning of our sonship to God in Christ, the ontological structure of Augustine's real doctrine comes to light. It is unmistakably plain, for instance, when he comments on a striking passage from the Psalter:

> Consider whom he addresses in the same psalm: 'I have said, Ye are gods, and ye are all the sons of the most Highest. But ye shall die like men, and fall like one of the princes' [Psalm 81 (82): 6f.]. It is manifest, therefore, that he called men gods who were deified by his grace, not born of his substance. For he justifies who is just through himself, not by another, and he deifies who is God in himself, not by participation in another. Now he who justifies, also deifies, because in justifying he makes sons of God. For 'he gave them power to become sons of God' [John 1:12]. If we have been made sons of God, we have also been made gods, but this takes place by the grace of adoption, not by natural generation.[16]

If, then, Augustine tends to be preoccupied with the analysis of the truly virtuous life, so that the concept of grace as *adiutorium*, or divinely bestowed power of action, predominates in his thinking, his insistence on such grace as the indispensable condition of true righteousness is rooted in a realistic interpretation of human goodness as determined by certain ontological conditions. Thus, while it is in less spectacularly influential theologians, like St. Ambrose and St. Leo, that we find the most explicit reflections of the Greek patristic ontology, it is undeniable that the same correlation of realism and transcendence underlies the wider developments of Latin patristic thought.

Nevertheless, Latin theology first achieves a systematic statement of an analogical ontology only after a delay of eight centuries. It is in the thirteenth century, when the tradition dominated by Augustine is enriched by fresh contact with the Greek Fathers and stimulated by the challenge of the Aristotelian renaissance, that we find this new and clear awareness of the ontological structure of Christian doctrine. When it comes, however, it marks a definitive advance in theological understanding. As Christopher Dawson puts it, in assessing the work of St. Bonaventure and St. Thomas Aquinas:

> While preserving the broad lines of the Augustinian doctrine, they laid a much greater emphasis on the ontological

character of the supernatural order. While Augustine conceives grace primarily as an act of divine power that moves the human will, Thomas considers it, above all, under its essential aspect of the new spiritual principle which transforms and renews human nature by the communication of the Divine Life: in other words, the state of deification of which the Greek Fathers habitually speak. . . . This combination of the Augustinian tradition with the characteristic doctrine of the Greek Fathers is perhaps the greatest theological achievement of the scholastic period, though it is usually little noticed in comparison with their philosophical synthesis.[17]

One might perhaps suggest that there is a closer connexion between their metaphysical thinking and their "emphasis on the ontological character of the supernatural order" than Dawson seems to realize. But the most important implication of his statement is the traditional character of the fundamental theological ideas of the greatest thirteenth-century thinkers, whose great achievement lay in giving articulate expression to the main stream of Christian thought, not in bringing off a doctrinal revolution. The revolution was to come in the following century.

The "anti-ontological deviation"[18] of the fourteenth century was the result of the union of an exaggerated "Augustinianism" with a new strain of philosophical "nominalism." Thanks to this deviation from the main line of Christian thought, arbitrary will came to the fore as the true definition of God and the sole principle of coherence in reality. Whereas older theologies had tended to think of God's power as ordered by the law of his nature, the new theology developed a doctrine of his absolute power (*potentia absoluta*) as above intelligibility and order, which meant that the order of his *potentia ordinata* was conceived simply as a matter of divine choice, itself bound at most by the law of non-contradiction.[19] As a result, all kinds of theological hypotheses appeared, in which the actual finality of God's action in nature and history was ignored for the sake of speculation about possible alternatives to any given element in the Christian mystery, and the latter was turned into a mere sequence of arbitrary divine decisions.

Having obscured the ontological relation of creatures to the Creator, the new theology proceeded to destroy the essential dependence of nature on grace and the intrinsic orientation of grace to glory by speculating about a possible communion of man with God apart from grace and a possible dissociation of the present state of grace from the future state of glory. In such an ostentatiously incoherent theology, grace becomes an ornament casually bestowed by a divine fiat, rather than the supernatural fulfilment of a nature purposefully created by divine wisdom. The one significant reality that remains is God's will, whose typical act with respect to man becomes "acceptation" rather than "new creation."[20]

All this theological demolition, ostensibly undertaken in the interests of the sovereign Lord of biblical faith, led (as "biblical theology" often does) to an ambiguous result, in so far as the Christian God took on a striking resemblance to the divine ideal assumed by Ovid's heroines when they insisted that the mark of "true gods" was that they "could do anything."[21] It is true that as long as Ockham's voluntarism was fortified by copious infusions of St. Augustine, some semblance of the authentic supernatural remained, but the principle of voluntarism makes the relations of creature and Creator inherently unstable. Ockham's critics, then, were quite right in suspecting Pelagian tendencies in his doctrine, for once the analogy of being is broken down, even in the supposed interests of transcendent liberty, the transition from an initial antinaturalism to naturalism is only too easy. As I have already hinted, one might well argue that, once the supernatural is reduced to self-assertive will, the question of whether there is anything "there" at all refuses to be suppressed. But even on the level of less radical questioning, once the supernatural reality of God and his grace is replaced by an omnipotent will and its groundless decision, we can legitimately ask if we may properly conceive of that will as granting salvation by way of covenanted reward for the observance fo a legal morality. The human will then becomes, in a sense, determinative, since it is permitted to earn salvation by its own natural activity. But if it is conceded, even hypothetically, that man's works can have saving efficacy, the barrier against Pelagian naturalism is broken down, and the end product is a notion of the divine-human relation as a simple interplay of wills—univocally con-

NOTES

1. Reuel L. Howe, *Man's Need and God's Action* (Greenwich, Conn.: Seabury Press, 1953), p. 3.

2. Hendrik Kraemer, *The Christian Message in a Non-Christian World* (London: Edinburgh House Press, 1938), p. 30.

3. Hendrik Kraemer, *Religion and the Christian Faith* (London: Lutterworth Press, 1956), p. 32.

4. Cf. A. Deneffe, "Geschichte des Wortes 'supernaturalis,'" *Zeitschrift für katholische Theologie*, 46 (1922), p. 349.

5. Cf. Pseudo-Dionysius, *Ep. 4 ad Caium* (*PG*, 3, 1072); John Damascene, *De fide orthodoxa*, 4, 13 (*PG*, 94, 1145).

6. Origen, *C. Cels.*, 5, 23 (*PG*, 11, 1217); John Chrysostom, *In Ep. ad Rom.*, 10, 2 (*PG*, 60, 477); *Missale Romanum*, prayers at the Offertory.

7. M. J. Scheeben, *Nature and Grace* (St. Louis: Herder, 1954), pp. 30f.

8. 2 Pet. 1:4; 1 Cor. 15:28; John 17:10; 1 John 5:11; Gal. 2:20; 2 Cor. 3:18.

9. Charles Moeller, "Théologie de la grâce et Oecuménisme," *Irénikon*, 28 (1955), 22.

10. A. E. Taylor, *The Faith of a Moralist* (2 vols., London: Macmillan, 1937), Vol. I, p. 51.

11. *The New York Times Book Review*, 29 January, 1956, p. 22.

12. Niels C. Nielsen, Jr., "Analogy in Christian Philosophy," *Anglican Theol. Rev.*, 35 (1953), p. 182.

13. Cf. Jules Gross, *La divinisation du chrétien d'après les Péres grecs* (Paris: Gabalda, 1938), *passim*.

14. Cf. C. Moeller and G. Philips, *The Theology of Grace and the Oecumenical Movement* (London: Mowbray, 1961), pp. 6f.

15. Cf. Augustine, *De dono perseverantiae*, 16 (*PL*, 45, 1002); *De civ. dei*, XXI, 12 (*CSEL*, 40/2, 541); H. Rondet, s.j., *Gratia Christi* (Paris: Beauchesne, 1948), chs. vi–viii.

16. Augustine, *Enarr. in Ps.* 49, 2 (*PL*, 36, 565).

17. C. Dawson, *Medieval Essays* (London: Sheed & Ward, 1953), pp. 101f.

18. E. Cailliet, *The Christian Approach to Culture* (Nashville: Abingdon-Cokesbury, 1953), pp. 131–141, speaks less justifiably of the "ontological deviation" in early Christian theology.

19. Cf. H. de Lubac, s.j., *Surnaturel* (Paris: Aubier, 1946), pp. 266f.

20. Cf. P. Vignaux, *Justification et prédestination au XIVe siècle* (Paris: Leroux, 1934); W. Detloff, o.f.m., *Die Lehre von der Acceptatio divina bei Johannes Duns Scotus* (Werl i. W.: Dietrich-Coelde-Verlag, 1954).

21. Cf. Ovid, *Metamorphoses,* IV, 272f.:
   pars fieri potuisse negant, pars omnia veros
   posse deos memorant. . . .

22. The theology of "historical nature" is well represented by the Dominican Cajetan, optimistic naturalism by Baius, and "synergism" by the Jesuit Molina.

23. Cf. J. Maritain, *True Humanism* (London: Bles, 1938), ch. I.

24. Cf. F. X. Jansen, *Baius et le Baianisme* (Louvain: Museum Lessianum, 1927), p. 86; M. Thurian, "L'anthropologie réformée," *Irénikon,* 25 (1952), 24f.

25. Louis Bail, quoted by F. X. Jansen, *Baius,* p. 87.

26. The assertion may seem to many to be unfair and misleading, in view of the fact that the Reformers, at any rate, clearly intended to affirm the real "newness of life" of believers in Christ. Nonetheless, as the argument in the text indicates, Reformation theology seems unable to make room for a true renewal of human nature.

27. L. Bouyer, *Du Protestantisme à l'Église* (Paris: Les Éditions du Cerf, 1954), p. 164.

28. Cf. *Westminster Confession of Faith,* chaps. VI–VII.

29. Cf. H. Shelton Smith, *Changing Conceptions of Original Sin: A Study in American Theology since 1750* (New York: Scribner, 1955); L. Bouyer, *Du Protestantisme à l'Église,* p. 184.

30. *Ibid.,* p. 163.

31. Cf. K. Barth, *From Rousseau to Ritschl* (London: S.C.M. Press, 1959), chap. IX.